The Color
of Politics

The Color of Politics

Racism in the American Political Arena Today

CHRIS DANIELSON

Racism in American Institutions
Brian D. Behnken, Series Editor

 PRAEGER

AN IMPRINT OF ABC-CLIO, LLC
Santa Barbara, California • Denver, Colorado • Oxford, England

Library of Congress Cataloging-in-Publication Data

Danielson, Christopher.
   The color of politics : racism in the American political arena today / Chris Danielson.
      pages cm. — (Racism in American institutions)
   Includes bibliographical references and index.
      ISBN 978–1–4408–0275–1 (alk. paper) — ISBN 978–1–4408–0276–8 (ebook)
1. Racism—Political aspects—United States. 2. United States—Race relations—Political aspects. 3. African Americans—Politics and government. 4. United States—Politics and government. I. Title.
E185.615.D365   2013
323.1196'073—dc23   2012043953

ISBN: 978–1–4408–0275–1
EISBN: 978–1–4408–0276–8

17 16 15 14 13   1 2 3 4 5

This book is also available on the World Wide Web as an eBook.
Visit www.abc-clio.com for details.

Praeger
An Imprint of ABC-CLIO, LLC

ABC-CLIO, LLC
130 Cremona Drive, P.O. Box 1911
Santa Barbara, California 93116-1911

This book is printed on acid-free paper (∞)

Manufactured in the United States of America

Dedicated to Nancy, my mother

Contents

Series Foreword

It is with great pleasure that I write this foreword for the inaugural book in Praeger Publisher's new series, Racism in American Institutions (RAI). The RAI series examines the ways in which racism has become a part of the fabric of many American institutions. For example, while the United States may have done away with overtly racist policies such as Jim Crow segregation and disfranchisement laws, racism still affects many of the United States' established institutions from public schools to corporate offices. Schools may not be legally segregated, and yet many districts are not integrated. Prisons are another example, when one considers the racist policies within the legal and penal systems that account for so many people of color behind bars. This open-ended series of one-volume works examines the problem of racism in established U.S. institutions. Each book traces the prevalence of racism within that institution throughout the history of the United States and explores the problem in that institution today, looking at ways in which the institution has attempted to rectify racism, but also the ways in which it has not.

The first book in the RAI series is Chris Danielson's *The Color of Politics: Race and Racism in the American Political Arena Today*, an expertly argued history of racism in the American political sphere. Danielson is perfectly suited for this subject. An associate professor of history at Montana Tech, he has written about race and politics for a decade. Most recently, his monograph *After Freedom Summer: How Race Realigned Politics in Mississippi, 1965–1986* (Gainesville: University Press of Florida, 2012), explored the rightward shift of politics in Mississippi since the Voting Rights Act of 1965. Danielson ably examines not only racism within the party politics of the Magnolia State, he also explored African American political mobilizations and the presence of black Republicans in the Mississippi Republican Party.

In *The Color of Politics*, Danielson shifts his focus to examine how race and racism have been used as potent weapons by politicians for generations. He begins with prominent examples that hearken back to the overt racism of the 1950s and 1960s. Danielson then moves to the origins of the more hidden, or covert, types of racism that first developed in the late 1960s and early 1970s. He shows how events as diverse as Richard Nixon's "southern strategy," the Willie Horton ad campaign, and the federal government's response to Hurricane Katrina all fit the common pattern of institutionalized political racism. Danielson ends with the Tea Party movement and demonstrates how racism underpins many of the Tea Party's actions and claims about the United States. *The Color of Politics* wisely pays attention to racism on both sides of the political aisle, and includes Latinos, Asian Americans, and other underrepresented groups as recipients of American political racism.

Danielson concludes *The Color of Politics* on a cautious note, stating that "in elections from federal to local, the problem of institutionalized racism will play a major part in America's unfinished transition to a full democratic society." This suggests that racism in American politics is hardly a thing of the past, but instead remains a rock upon which national progress has struggled and still founders today. *The Color of Politics* explains that state of affairs.

Brian D. Behnken
Iowa State University
Ames, Iowa

Acknowledgments

The number of people who contributed to this work is significant, and I will invariably omit somebody, so I apologize in advance for anyone I overlook. I would like to thank Kim Kennedy-White at ABC-CLIO and Praeger Press for helping make this book possible. A special thanks to Brian Behnken, the series editor, who is my oldest friend in academia from our days as teaching assistants in the Department of History at the University of Houston.

At my place of employment, Montana Tech of the University of Montana, this book would not have been possible without the help of the amazing staff at the library and its interlibrary loan, so special thanks go to Debbie Todd and Ann St. Clair for their role in creating this work. Thanks also go to my dean, Douglas Coe, and my former department chair, Jack Crowley, who both supported a course reduction that aided me greatly in finishing this manuscript. John Ray, Tech's political science professor, also deserves thanks for reading and commenting on one of the chapters. Thanks as well to Jeffrey Cass for providing me with a copy of his conference paper on Barack Obama and the birther movement.

My mother Nancy deserves the most thanks and mention here since the love and support she has given me throughout this project have proven immeasurable, and it would not have been possible without her.

Introduction

In all manifestations of racism from the mildest to the most severe, what is being denied is the possibility that the racializers and the racialized can coexist in the same society, except perhaps on the basis of domination and subordination.[1]

George Frederickson, the historian who wrote the abovementioned quote, defined racism as marked by the two key concepts of difference and power. A racialized minority group, which in many historical cases is a majority, is regarded as a "them" or "other" by the dominant racial group, the "us." This could manifest itself anywhere from social discrimination to outright genocide, with numerous variations within the range.[2] For African ns in the United States, this racism first expressed itself as forced enslavement during colonial times, which gradually gave way with emancipation after the Civil War to government-sponsored discrimination and denial of political rights. This state of affairs slowly began to erode in the mid-twentieth century with the decline of global white supremacy (in the form of decolonization) and the mobilization of the civil rights movement at home. For Latinos, the discrimination was less severe, since it did not include enslavement, but the effects of social discrimination and segregation in the wake of the U.S.-Mexican War were no less real for them then they were for black Americans.

Ever since the peak of the civil rights movement in the 1960s and the end of legally sanctioned, or *de jure*, segregation, commentators, the media, and the general public have spoken about the end of racism. So pervasive is this notion that efforts by governments and other institutions to remedy past racial imbalances through affirmative action programs have been called reverse racism. Even academics refer to the period after 1968, the year of Martin Luther King, Jr.'s assassination and the passage of the Fair Housing Act, as the post–civil rights era. Yet the prevalence of racial struggle and conflict has continued, as has been seen in legislative battles over extensions of the Voting Rights Act and racially based redistricting, as well as in literal battles of racial turmoil like the Los Angeles riots of 1992.

While the rhetoric of racial intolerance faded with the civil rights era, it became replaced with the coded words of the "southern strategy" of Richard Nixon and other white conservatives, who sought to win the votes of whites, southern and non-southern, with appeals for "law and order" and against "forced busing" and welfare. Meanwhile, the two opposing factions of the civil rights movement—black southerners and white segregationists—were gradually absorbed into the Democratic and Republican Parties. The partisan realignment of the South toward the Grand Old Party (GOP), or what political scientists Earle and Merle Black labeled the "Great White Switch," helped with the election of conservative presidents like Ronald Reagan and George W. Bush.[3]

While conservatives adopted what scholars have called a color-blind ideology, a more cynical label might be color-blind racism, since the conservatives of the New Right ignored institutional racism and backed policies like social welfare cuts that while ostensibly color-blind, disproportionately hurt people of color.[4] Institutional racism, or the prevalence of racism in governmental policies and larger society, was reflected in a variety of areas by the 1980s, but probably nowhere was this clearer than in the "war on drugs" and the mass incarceration of African-American youth for non-violent drug offenses. A moral panic over crack cocaine led to a bipartisan effort to combat drug use, with a heavy focus on interdiction and prosecution over treatment, in effect criminalizing a public health problem and bringing a disproportionate police response to inner-city ghettos. The political effects have been felt in areas like black voting, where criminal records from drug prosecutions have hindered the ability of black men and women to vote in some states that bar convicted felons from the franchise.

The most extreme forms of racism are confined to the far right of the political spectrum and often are not involved in electoral politics at all; instead, they are manifested in violent groups like neo-Nazis, militias, and other white supremacist groups. But in the political mainstream, some overt manifestations continue, from Jesse Helms's race-baiting ads in his 1990 Senate campaign to the unsuccessful gubernatorial candidacy of former Klansman David Duke in Louisiana. The route most white conservatives have pursued, however, is one of attacking controversial programs like affirmative action as "reverse racism" while avoiding criticism of more popular civil rights laws like the Voting Rights Act and instead quietly supporting their renewal.

The new century exposed a number of continuing problems of race, or more accurately, the media "discovered" the problem and reminded white

Americans of it. The major example of this was Hurricane Katrina, which showed the continuing and growing intersection of race and poverty in the United States, coupled with the federal government's lax response to black suffering. White hostility to black displaced residents of New Orleans further revealed the strong antipathy many whites still felt toward African Americans. The other seminal event, the election of Barack Obama to the presidency in 2008, triggered predictions of a "postracial" United States, since many white voters had now voted for a black candidate, pushing aside fears of a nationwide "Bradley effect," in which white voters give lip service to a black candidate but then vote against him or her. Yet the rise of the Tea Party, which combines antitax and antigovernment activism with occasionally racist vitriol against the new president, showed such predictions of a postracial United States to be misguided. The backlash against immigration, also linked to the Tea Party, showed that racism in the modern United States was far from a simple black and white issue.

It would be an error to label the continuation of racism in U.S. politics as simply a conservative phenomenon. While the Democratic Party has turned from its segregationist past to embrace black voting, this does not mean that all white Democrats have become full-blown antiracists. The support that Democratic politicians like Bill Clinton have given to policies like welfare reform, which hurt low-income African Americans, indicated a readiness of centrist Democrats to take black voters for granted while pursuing an agenda designed to appease white voters. Outside of the Democratic Party, extreme voices like Louis Farrakhan have attempted to politically mobilize black Americans with antiwhite and anti-Semitic rhetoric. Controversial programs to address institutional racism, most notably the reparations movement, have also added to racial polarization and put white liberals on the defensive.

This book seeks to show the continuation of racism in U.S. politics, in particular in the events described earlier in this chapter. Chapter 1 deals with the continuance of racism in the United States after the end of legal segregation in the 1960s, with the decline of overt racism but the continuation of institutionalized racism and its prevalence in national politics. The increasing assimilation of African Americans into politics did not translate into a decline in racist attitudes, any more than that same mainstreaming reduced black poverty. Chapter 2 examines the history of racial issues in elections, especially racial "dirty tricks" and the way that racially polarizing wedge issues kept race in national and state politics even in the "post–civil rights" era. Chapter 3 discusses historical cases of the Bradley effect and analyzes the conditions that help convince a white voter to back a black candidate. Chapter 4 deals with the hot-button issue of illegal immigration and the role of nativism in elections. Chapter 5 examines the controversial issue of legal barriers that hamper minorities' full access to the right to vote, from voter ID laws to felony disfranchisement. Chapter 6 charts the political rise and election of Barack Obama to the presidency, a landmark event in breaking racial barriers in U.S. politics, but one that did not diminish racial antagonisms in the body politic. Chapter 7 charts one of those combative organizations that emerged during Obama's first term, the Tea Party, and whether the conservative political movement is primarily motivated by racist opposition to the first black U.S. president.

Chapter 1

Race, Racism, and Left- and Right-Wing American Politics

Richard Nixon once told his speechwriter Pat Buchanan that "you have to give the nuts twenty percent of what they want."[1] While Nixon was not talking specifically about race, this quote accurately describes the approach that recent politicians have had to take when courting white voters with racist sentiments. Openly racist rhetoric was unpalatable, but coded appeals were acceptable. Repeal of civil rights legislation, which would be tantamount to rolling back the civil rights movement, was out of the question; however, policies that protected white privilege and undermined black gains while being on the surface nonracial were doable. This became the political approach of many Republican politicians as well as some Democrats at the end of the twentieth and beginning of the twenty-first centuries. It has its origins in the mainstreaming and institutionalization of the civil rights movement, which created the paradox in U.S. government and society of antiracist policies existing alongside institutional racism and the prevalence of racially polarized voting. Since the 1970s, both political parties have adjusted themselves to the realities of massive black political participation, as well as the resulting white backlash. The result has been changing expressions of racism in the United States, but not an alteration of its fundamental desire to maintain white supremacy and limit the participation of racial minorities in the U.S. political arena.

The 1950s and 1960s were marked by utterances of crude racist discourse by white politicians, mostly in the American South as white segregationist Democrats fought the civil rights movement. Alabama Governor George Wallace and Mississippi Senator James Eastland became some of the most famous of the gallery of demagogues who openly castigated racial integration and linked it to interracial marriage and other ills they said would destroy the white race. While the expressions of racism occasionally dealt with other racial groups, such as opposition from southern Democrats to admitting Hawaii as a state due to its large Asian population, the racial conflict of the period was literally framed in black and white terms.[2]

The mass movement of African Americans in the 1950s and 1960s that scholars call the civil rights movement ended most public displays of racist discourse. The organizing efforts of groups like Martin Luther King, Jr.'s Southern Christian Leadership Conference (SCLC) combined with the legal activism of the National Association for the Advancement of Colored People's Legal Defense Fund (NAACP-LDF) pressured the federal government to support civil rights legislation. The most notable example of this occurred in Birmingham, Alabama, where the SCLC campaign to desegregate the city's downtown business district triggered a violent white response and forced President John F. Kennedy to introduce what eventually became the Civil Rights Act of 1964. The bottom-up pressure in Birmingham, Selma, Alabama, and other places led to the passage of the aforementioned act as well as the Voting Rights Act of 1965, both of which were signed into law by President Lyndon Johnson. These two landmark pieces of legislation dismantled the legal structure of segregation in the South and ended the mechanisms used by southern states to prevent black voter registration. When the Supreme Court struck down state bans on interracial marriage in *Loving v. Virginia* in 1967, the United States was, at least on paper, a society that did not officially discriminate based on race.[3]

Yet the legacy of racism remained, even if the law was silent on racial difference. Lyndon Johnson said in his Howard University commencement address in June 1965 that "you do not take a person who, for years, has been hobbled by chains and liberate him, bring him up to the starting line of a race, and then say 'you are free to compete with all the others,' and still justly believe you have been completely fair . . . we seek not just equality as a right and a theory but equality as a fact and equality as a result." Johnson inaugurated the War on Poverty as part of his plan to link economic rights to political ones, a federal version of what Martin Luther King pushed for with his Poor Peoples' Campaign. However, King's vision of economic equality was more radical and egalitarian than Johnson's program, which rejected income redistribution and pursued a top-down, heavily bureaucratic approach that ultimately did little to fight poverty. Johnson even rejected the proposal of Sargent Shriver, the director of the Office of Economic Opportunity (OEO), to raise cigarette taxes to fund a jobs program, which in the view of historian James Patterson, "thus ended the possibility that the War on Poverty would do much to produce jobs (or enhance income) in the present."[4]

This institutional racism, which meant that programs and governmental institutions that were superficially color-blind negatively and disproportionately impacted racial minorities, undergirded Johnson's comments at Howard University. Indeed, Johnson's own antipoverty programs reinforced rather than challenged existing structures of racism. In his programs related to public housing, for example, resistance from white communities to both new public housing sites and attempts by the Department of Housing and Urban Development (HUD) to integrate public housing by limiting free choice for applicants (called tenant selection) led the federal government to back down. Federally funded urban renewal programs like Model Cities added to the problem, as developers displaced low-income minority residents in favor of commercial properties. Such relocation—or Negro removal, as critics called it—fueled the Newark, New Jersey, riots of 1967. With public housing increasingly confined to inner cities and loans from the Veterans' Administration and Federal Housing Administration financing homes in overwhelmingly white suburbs, racial segregation continued in fact even as it was dying in law. Middle-class white Americans, and by extension the federal government, were willing to wipe away legal segregation and voting barriers but not link economic rights to citizenship. In Martin Luther King's assessment, "the paths of Negro-white unity that had been converging crossed at Selma, and like a giant X began to diverge."[5]

The end of legal segregation and the growing visibility of black Americans in U.S. life led to the decline of overt expressions of racism. Saying racial slurs in public or in mixed company became increasingly unfashionable and even taboo. Sometimes this new sensitivity about race could backfire on well-meaning whites if blacks perceived condescension in their rhetoric. This famously happened in 1965, when Daniel Patrick Moynihan, an assistant secretary of labor, issued his paper *The Negro Family: The Case for National Action*, which became known as the Moynihan Report. The report outlined Moynihan's controversial analysis of the black ghetto, in which he argued that high unemployment led black men to abandon their families and create impoverished, female-headed households, a condition of black family weakness that allegedly had its origins in slavery. The result was poverty, family breakdown, welfare dependency, school dropouts, and youth crime, all of which widened the income gap between black and white families and created a "tangle of pathology," one of the more controversial statements he made in the report. Although he proposed traditional liberal solutions of public spending on jobs and family income supplements, the report generated a firestorm of controversy. First, the August 1965 Watts riot in Los Angeles eroded white support for new antipoverty programs that focused on race. Second, the release of the report that same month came just as the new self-assertiveness and pride of the black power era began to emerge. Black civil rights activists denounced the report as an example of white liberal interference in the black family, with critics accusing Moynihan of a range of sins, from elitism to sexism to racism. The Johnson White House dropped the report, and Moynihan soon departed the administration, an early example of the political correctness that swung to the opposite extreme of the racist rhetoric of the 1950s and early 1960s.[6]

Yet race did not disappear completely from public discourse; only *overt* racism did. What emerged in its place was a new subtlety about race and public rhetoric, where white politicians now made coded appeals to race to win over white voters uncomfortable with integration. Richard Nixon refined many of these appeals in the 1968 election, when the urban race riots and black power of the previous summers triggered a white backlash. Welfare criticism became a large part of this backlash, since the heavy post–Moynihan Report media focus on the rising rates of black illegitimacy led to increased criticism of AFDC (Aid to Families of Dependent Children) welfare rolls, which also rose in the late 1960s. Welfare was further linked to race in the minds of many white Americans with the activism of the National Welfare Rights Organization (NWRO), an advocacy group of largely poor and black activists who engaged in sit-ins and occupations of welfare offices to gain increased benefits. Rising crime rates were part of the backlash as well, which Nixon exploited in campaign ads. The Supreme Court, already a target by members of the archconservative John Birch Society and southern segregationists over its civil rights rulings, created new critics on the racialized issues of crime and welfare with various rulings protecting the rights of the accused and access to welfare. These rulings involved famous cases like *Gideon v. Wainwright* (1963) and *Miranda v. Arizona* (1966), which provided for the right to court-appointed counsel and the right to remain silent during interrogation, as well as lesser-known cases like *Shapiro v. Thompson* (1969) and *Goldberg v. Kelly* (1970), which protected the rights of welfare applicants against state restrictions.[7]

Yet Nixon's call for "law and order" and other appeals in 1968, as the inner cities burned and student unrest plagued U.S. universities, shaped much of the new racial rhetoric. Nixon famously made an appeal to the "forgotten Americans—the non shouters, the non demonstrators." He in particular criticized the busing of students, usually by judicial order, to achieve racial desegregation of schools. While much of this was part of the president's "southern strategy," of appealing to segregationists, Nixon was helped by the independent presidential candidacy of Alabama Governor George Wallace, an outspoken segregationist whose bombastic rhetoric, mostly directed against antiwar protestors and "hippies," allowed Nixon to cast himself as a centrist candidate between the extremist Wallace and the liberal Hubert Humphrey, whose speeches focusing on stopping the causes of the riots made him appear to be excusing criminal behavior. At the same time, Nixon's running mate selection of Maryland Governor Spiro Agnew, who freely used ethnic slurs and in the words of one writer, could "out-Wallace Wallace," siphoned votes from the Alabamian's base.[8]

This new subtlety—which thanks to people like Agnew could often be very unsubtle—did not mask the continuation of raw racial issues in the 1970s. One of the most contentious issues was the development of affirmative action, which ironically owed a lot to Richard Nixon. In 1969, Labor Secretary George Schultz, with Nixon's approval, established the Philadelphia Plan. The plan required construction unions that worked on government contracts to set up "goals and timetables" for the hiring of black apprentices. By 1971, the program was extended to all federal hiring and contracting, which meant that it impacted over one-third of the country's labor force. Predominantly white labor unions in the American Federation of Labor-Congress of Industrial Organizations (AFL-CIO) saw this as an attack on their apprenticeship systems and bitterly objected to the plan. The NAACP, which perceived the plan as a ploy by the Republicans to divide the key Democratic constituencies of labor and African Americans, also opposed it.[9]

This charge had some truth to it; White House domestic advisor John Ehrlichman endorsed the plan mainly for being "anti-labor and pro-black," but it was also part of Nixon's plan to promote "black capitalism" and thus woo black voters (especially middle-class ones) to the Grand Old Party (GOP) using new initiatives such as the Office of Minority Business Enterprise. The Philadelphia Plan was in fact originally a Johnson administration plan that Arthur Fletcher, a black Republican and assistant secretary of labor under Nixon and Schultz, came across and successfully pitched to Nixon and his Cabinet. Yet the Philadelphia Plan worked, creating parity between minorities and whites in apprenticeship training and increasing minority participation in the labor force covered by the plan to 17.4 percent by 1979.[10]

The adoption of racial preferences as "affirmative action" owes heavily to the actions of Nixon and his subordinates, for the phrase was never meant to favor one race at the expense of another, even a significantly more privileged ethnic group. In fact, the words initially had no clear meeting at all. The Civil Rights Act of 1964 established the Equal Employment Opportunity Commission (EEOC), part of Title VII of the act, which banned job discrimination. Under its description of unlawful employment practices, the act said that a court could order "affirmative action as may be appropriate, which may include reinstatement or hiring of employees" in cases of intentional discrimination by employers. During the Senate debate over the act, Edward Kennedy rejected charges that enforcement would lead to reverse discrimination, and Hubert Humphrey famously declared that he would begin "eating the pages one after another" of the bill if anyone could find language endorsing racial quotas.[11]

President Johnson also used the phrase "affirmative action" in his 1965 executive order that created the Office of Federal Contract Compliance (OFCC), which enforced job nondiscrimination in any company receiving a federal contract. Johnson's efforts to avoid alienating labor unions meant that affirmative action lacked a clear definition until Nixon's enactment of the Philadelphia Plan. Symbolizing the early confusion over the term and enforcement, one company lawyer said in the mid-1960s that "when the government tells what affirmative action is then we'll comply." Like the Johnson administration, Nixon and his Labor Department avoided using the term "quota," since that was prohibited by the 1964 act, so Schultz instead used the term "goals," a semantic dodge at best since Schultz in 1970 ordered that the "rate of minority applicants recruited [for employment] should approximate or equal the rate of minorities in the population in each location." Despite the linguistic gymnastics, racial preferences were clearly in place by the end of the Nixon administration and steadily increased the rate of minority participation in labor unions.[12]

The adoption of "goals and timetables," "ranges," "set-asides"—indeed *any* word except "quota"—became increasingly common in U.S. institutions after 1970. Corporations and unions that depended on federal contracts adopted them either in response to the demands of the Labor Department or the Supreme Court. In 1971, the court cited the Civil Rights Act of 1964 and ruled in *Griggs v. Duke Power Co.* that intelligence tests and other ostensibly neutral exams used by employers, unless they directly related to the jobs in question, could not be used if they disproportionately barred minority applicants. To allow such exclusion, the Court unanimously ruled, would " 'freeze' the status quo of past discriminatory practices." This increased further the use of quotas and statistical parity by employers, since now failing to consider the historical burden of discrimination became in effect discrimination by the employer against the employed. In this way, executive and judicial actions by 1971 had changed the meaning of affirmative action from its congressional intent in 1964.[13]

Although affirmative action began with employment, it rapidly expanded to other areas, especially in the wake of *Griggs*. One author equated *Griggs*'s impact on employment policy to *Brown v. Board of Education*'s on public education. After *Griggs*, height and weight requirements in police and fire departments were abolished for being discriminatory against Hispanic, Asian American, and female applicants, and airlines abandoned age limits for flight attendants. Nearly every form of hiring, testing, promotion, termination, and other conceivable employment condition faced scrutiny for racial or gender discrimination.[14]

With the federal government vigorously enforcing court interpretations and programs to promote racial diversity and minority access, it was only natural that higher education became a key part of affirmative action as well. Universities, including law and medical schools with their limited enrollments, adopted set-asides for minority admissions, beginning such programs in the 1960s in response to the activism of student radicals. By the early 1970s, the Department of Health, Education and Welfare (HEW) provided additional federal sanction and support for such programs. Ironically, quotas were once part of U.S. higher education, but had been used earlier in the twentieth century in the opposite fashion by elite universities like Harvard to exclude and set limits on Jewish applicants to schools. For this reason, some Jews opposed minority set-asides. One Jewish law professor, Alexander Bickel of Yale Law School, took up the banner of opposition in the 1970s. Bickel was a former liberal and civil rights advocate now turned neoconservative, and he contributed to the Jewish magazine *Commentary*, a journal headed by fellow Jewish liberal-turned-neoconservative Norman Podhoertz. Bickel wrote a brief for Marco DeFunis, a Jew rejected by the University of Washington Law School. Bickel argued in his brief, written in 1973 for the Anti-Defamation League, that the school's minority admissions program discriminated against DeFunis by favoring "less qualified" candidates on racial grounds. The Supreme Court declined to hear the case of *DeFunis v. Odegaard* in 1974, and the Nixon administration did not take a stand in the case.[15] Still, the opposition of some Jews to affirmative action showed, like the split between labor and blacks over job quotas, the problems of holding together a liberal consensus on racial issues.

While Jewish neoconservatives, or Jewish former leftists who swung to the far right, were best remembered for their opposition to Henry Kissinger and his détente polices with the Soviet Union during the Nixon and Ford presidencies, opposition to affirmative action was also a major component that splintered some Jews from liberalism. Much of the Jewish opposition came because of fears of quotas, and with American Jews constituting only 2.7 percent of the population, neoconservative Jews feared that Jews would suffer from affirmative action in higher education, given that they were overrepresented in many professions. While Jews had been strong support-ers of the civil rights movement, the quota issue added onto already existing tensions between blacks and Jews from the 1960s, over such issues as the anti-Israeli rhetoric of and support for the Palestinians that Black Power militants declared after Israel's victory over the Arab states in the Six-Day War of 1967. Clashes between Jewish teachers and black parents in New York City public schools added to hostility between the two ethnic groups. While most Jews stayed loyal to liberalism and the Democratic Party, the affirmative action controversy added to divisions in the Ameri-can Jewish community in the 1970s.[16]

It took a gentile rather than a Hebrew to create the legal challenge that became the best-known Supreme Court decision involving affirmative action. Allan Bakke, a middle-class white man of Norwegian ancestry, had been educated as a mechanical engineer and served as a Marine captain in Vietnam. After earning a master's degree at Stanford in the late 1960s, he then worked as an aerospace engineer for the National Aeronautics and Space Administration (NASA) in California, where he lived with his wife and three children. His real desire, however, was to become a doctor, so after taking the proper prerequisites, he applied to a dozen medical schools in 1973.[17]

Every school turned him down, apparently for being too old at age 33. But the University of California–Davis rejected him twice, and he was incensed when he found out through an assistant dean that his test scores were higher than some of the minority applicants admitted. Davis had a special admissions program that set aside 16 out of 100 places in its new admissions for minority students, namely blacks, Mexican Americans, and Asians. Bakke responded by filing suit against the school and demanded that he be admitted. In September 1976, after a poor defense by the university, the California Supreme Court ruled against Davis and ordered Bakke's admission. The court said the program of aiding what Davis called "disadvantaged" students violated the Fourteenth Amendment's Equal Protection Clause, since it used race as a sole means of admission. This was bolstered by evidence that Davis had never admitted a white student who claimed to be disadvantaged, even though over 200 white applicants had labeled themselves as such.[18]

The university regents admitted Bakke at the state court's request but delayed ending the program pending an appeal to the U.S. Supreme Court. The Supreme Court took up the case shortly after President Jimmy Carter took office in 1977. The case attracted major public and media attention, with a record 58 "friend of the court" briefs filed. Defenders of the university included the Carter administration, civil rights groups, liberal religious organizations, and labor unions, with the notable exception of the AFL-CIO, while Bakke received support from conservative and Jewish groups. Supporters of the university argued that the set-asides were at worst "benign discrimination," while opponents called it "reverse discrimination."[19]

The *Bakke* case seemed to strike at the heart of hard work, individualism, and fair play, terrorizing white Americans with the ghosts of a racist past. One man, Allan Bakke, seemed to be sacrificed in favor of liberal collectivism, social leveling, and group rights. The end result was the application of quotas to all aspects of American life and the creation of a proportional society, or at least that was how it became oversimplified in the court of public opinion by opponents of affirmative action. Universities always considered other factors beside merit, such as preference for athletes, military veterans, and other groups, so race was just another factor, defenders of the set-asides argued. Also, diversity became a worthy reason for the set-asides, since minorities would raise awareness of minority health issues with white doctors. Also, since white doctors were unlikely to set up practices in minority communities, minority doctors were needed for health care access, a critical issue in 1970, when black life expectancy was 7.1 years less than that of whites.[20] Yet Bakke's clearly higher test scores were a hard argument for defenders of the university to overcome.

For President Carter, *Bakke* was a political minefield. Whites heavily opposed affirmative action, but Carter had also won his narrow victory with 82 percent of the black vote. Civil rights groups were already criticizing Carter for his refusal to introduce new antipoverty programs, all while nonwhite unemployment rose. Yet Jews, who always had high voter turnout, voted 75 percent for Carter. After some vacillation, Carter, facing intense pressure from black congressional representatives and the NAACP, sided with Davis.[21]

In June 1978, the Court in *Regents of the University of California v. Bakke* sided with the California Supreme Court, upholding Bakke's admission and invalidating the Davis set-asides. Yet the Court then compromised, reversing the state court's ban on *all* race-conscious admissions programs. In short, race could be considered, but it could not be the sole or primary factor. The Court's own confusion was reflected in the six separate opinions the justices issued. Lewis Powell's decision became the most cited, with his defense of the ideal of diversity over remedying past discrimination as a rationale for affirmative action. While some civil rights leaders, such as Jesse Jackson, deplored the decision as "a devastating blow to the civil rights struggle," others saw optimism. Since the Court allowed race to be considered with other factors, Vernon Jordan, head of the National Urban League, called it a "green light" for some affirmative action programs. *Time* magazine summed up the mixed decision by declaring "QUOTAS: NO/RACE: YES" in its cover story on the ruling.[22]

For all of its media exposure, *Bakke* had little impact on affirmative action. Allan Bakke went to medical school, and most university affirmative action programs survived. To get around the decision, many schools simply kept their policies informal and unwritten, which is exactly what Harvard College—whose special admissions program Powell had praised—already was doing. Bakke won, but so did affirmative action, which had been upheld for the first time by the Supreme Court.[23]

Affirmative action became even more entrenched as part of the U.S. mainstream in 1979 with another court case. The case, *United Steelworkers of America v. Weber*, involved Brian Weber, a white technician at a Louisiana chemical plant who had been excluded from a training program that had set aside half its openings for black workers. The plan had been created in 1974 as part of an agreement with Kaiser Aluminum and Chemical Corporation and the United Steelworkers of America. Prior to this, only 1.83 percent of the skilled craftworkers at the company were black, out of workforce that was 39 percent black. Weber seemed a David fighting the twin Goliaths of big business and big labor, both of which had negotiated this agreement, and unlike the shy Allan Bakke, he relished the publicity. He won in both the district and appeals courts, but the Supreme Court reversed the lower decisions in a 5–2 ruling in June 1979, citing that the plan had been negotiated by private interests and not dictated by the federal government. While civil rights leaders were predictably thrilled, so were employers, who cited the ruling as a clear guideline from the Court on what kinds of affirmative action were permissible, the kind of rules that the federal government lacked in the 1960s.[24]

While affirmative action was clearly rooted in U.S. society by the end of the 1970s, the other controversial racial issue of the decade, busing, was not. Busing, or assigning schoolchildren to other districts with the goal of integration and racial balance, addressed the same question as affirmative action: Should people today have to compromise or atone through social policies for the sins of the nation's racist past? Like affirmative action, busing involved the entire country, not just the South. Yet since it involved children, busing was even more emotional and volatile a political issue than affirmative action, and unlike affirmative action, the passions it aroused frequently became violent.[25]

Busing originated from two key Supreme Court decisions. The first was *Green v. County School Board of New Kent County* (1968), out of New Kent County, Virginia. The Court ruled against the county for maintaining a system that segregated 85 percent of the black students into an all-black school. The Court said that school boards had an "affirmative duty to take whatever steps might be necessary to convert a unitary system" that would eliminate racism "root and branch." The ruling paved the way for further suits in which court-ordered integration through busing came to locales ranging from rural Mississippi to major cities like Denver. The other major ruling, *Swann v. Charlotte-Mecklenburg Board of Education* (1971), involved the sprawling Charlotte-Mecklenburg school system in North Carolina, which encompassed 550 square miles and 84,000 pupils, with a 29 percent black population concentrated in the northwestern portion of the city. The Court's unanimous ruling led to the district becoming one of the most integrated in the nation.[26]

Students, of course, had always been bused in modern education, and busing had been used prior to the civil rights movement to *segregate*, not integrate, by sending black children miles away from their homes so that they would not attend closer white schools. The expansion of busing and school desegregation to the North and West, however, exposed the complexities of racism in cities within these regions. Unlike the legal racial segregation in the South, which had been written into the law, all-black schools arose in nonsouthern cities from a plethora of factors, including deliberate zoning patterns by white governments, discriminatory real estate and lending practices, and other factors that were either ostensibly nonracial or carried out by private entities.[27]

Opposition to busing became perhaps the most violent in Boston, where busing between two poor urban neighborhoods with low educational achievement—black Roxbury and white, Irish American South Boston (or Southie, as the locals called it)—erupted in violence in the mid-1970s. Demagogues arose to stir up working-class white resentment, mostly notably Louise Day Hicks, a schoolteacher who provided a respectable face to an antibusing movement that often saw its members hurling racial epitaphs at and attacking black residents. Hicks deplored violence and racist rhetoric, but instead employed the now-commonplace coded language used by respectable opponents of integration, calling for "neighborhood schools for neighborhood children" and criticizing "civil rights infiltrators." While other Boston neighborhood schools integrated with little violence, white students from South Boston and Charlestown schools attacked and harassed black students from Roxbury. Black students responded in kind against whites, and the long-term result was massive white flight from the Boston public schools.[28]

Busing was unpopular nationwide, with most whites and many blacks. A Gallup poll in October 1971 indicated that whites opposed it by a 3-to-1 ratio, while black respondents opposed it 47 percent to 45 percent. Politicians such as Richard Nixon made it part of their re-election campaigns, and finally the Supreme Court put limits on the practice. The Supreme Court, in a 5–4 decision, ruled against busing across district lines in Detroit, a decision that meant that busing between separate suburban and inner-city districts to achieve racial balance was invalidated. The ruling, *Milliken v. Bradley* (1974), reaffirmed existing patterns of school segregation created by housing discrimination patterns and hastened white flight to the suburbs. Since it allowed only intradistrict busing as a remedy to achieve racial balance (which was what Boston was doing), white parents could avoid busing by moving out of the district altogether.[29]

While affirmative action and busing guaranteed that racial issues would remain in the political arena, black political power itself grew in the 1970s. Much of this growth was in urban areas, both northern and southern. In Cleveland, Ohio, Carl Stokes, a black lawyer and former state legislator, launched a bid for mayor of that city. White flight in the previous decades actually aided Stokes's campaign, a trend that would assist other black mayoral candidates. Cleveland lost 300,000 of its white residents between 1930 and 1965, while during the same time period the black population had increased by over 200,000. Blacks were still a minority as 34 percent of the population, but due to voter registration drives during the 1964 presidential election, they constituted more than 40 percent of registered voters. This had meant that earlier white Democratic mayors relied on black support and 10 of the 33 city council seats were held by black politicians. Stokes emerged as a candidate in 1965 to challenge the white Democratic incumbent, Ralph Locher, who alienated black constituents with his stands on civil rights issues. Stokes lost in a four-way race but won 85 percent of the minority vote.[30]

When Stokes ran again in 1967, he made sure he had white support, since black voters were not a majority. He built coalitions with white business leaders, who supported his candidacy because of worsening racial tensions in Cleveland in 1966, including a race riot and a hardline "law-and-order" approach by Locher. The white business community hoped Stokes's election would ease tensions in the city and promote long-term development. Stokes beat Locher in the Democratic primary and then went on to defeat his Republican opponent with only 50.3 percent of the vote. He won with overwhelming black support and the support of the white business elite, but not the mass of white ethnic working-class voters, who switched to vote Republican in the election.[31]

Stokes became the first black mayor of a major American city, but his administration showed that black political power had its limits and would not be a cure-all for black poverty and racial inequality. During his two terms in office, he delivered antipoverty programs to black constituents, but strikes by municipal workers and a series of scandals weakened him, and he declined reelection in 1971. His black electoral base splintered, and a white Republican succeeded him.[32]

The other notable black victory that occurred during this same time period was in Gary, Indiana. White flight in this steel-producing center had created a 55 percent black majority by 1967, but whites still made up 52.3 percent of registered voters. Civil rights organizations and community activists helped create a grassroots political base in the black community, and this led to the political career of Richard Hatcher. A lawyer and county prosecutor, Hatcher provided legal counsel for some of these community groups and used those connections to win a seat on the city council in 1963. He stayed an activist on the council, alienating the Democratic Party machine that had backed him and that had expected him to be satisfied with a share of patronage, the traditional way it placated black officials. In 1967, he launched his own bid for mayor, and grassroots black organization and voter registration yielded a high black voter turnout that won him the Democratic primary. He was also aided in the primary by two white candidates who split the white vote. Yet Hatcher's maverick strategy meant that the Democratic Party organization in Gary refused to aid him against his white Republican opponent that fall, and even unsuccessfully tried to purge voter registration lists of black names. Hatcher won a narrow victory of 1,389 votes, built on strong support from Jewish voters as well as the expected black support. Unlike Stokes, Hatcher solidified black supporters and won re-election for the next two decades.[33]

In both these cities and others, white flight aided the chances of black candidates, which ironically underscored the continuance of racially polarized voting rather than most whites accepting and supporting a black candidate. Yet as the 1970s began, black mayoral candidates took these victories as encouragement and sought to win control of other cities. In Detroit, Coleman Young, a Democratic state senator who had a history of civil rights and union activism going back to World War II, ran for mayor in 1973. White flight in the Motor City had been hastened by bloody racial riots of 1967, and blacks made up 43 percent of the population by 1970. By 1973, the number of black registered voters surpassed the number of white voters in the city. Like Stokes in Cleveland, Young narrowly triumphed over his white opponent by promising an integrated, diverse city government, rhetoric designed to alleviate white fears of a black "takeover" of city hall. That same year, Tom Bradley won a more decisive victory in Los Angeles, winning against Mayor Sam Yorty with 56 percent of the vote. Bradley, who had lost to Yorty four years earlier, managed to pick up almost half the white vote and a majority of the Latino vote, as well as overwhelming black support. Los Angeles was primarily white, so such coalition-building was even more essential for a black victory than it had been in Cleveland and other cities.[34]

These victories were not just confined to northern and western cities, either. In the South, the registration of black voters under the Voting Rights Act and its extensions in 1970 and 1975 created both urban and rural political power. In southern cities, the victory of Maynard Jackson in Atlanta received the most publicity. Atlanta, long a self-described model for moderate civil right reform, had given its black community limited influence in the 1960s, but only after black voters had shown their strength at the polls. In 1968, black voters put white moderate Sam Massell in office and elected Jackson as vice mayor. Jackson soon broke with the mayor when Massell settled a strike with black sanitation workers to the detriment of the workers. In 1973, he challenged Massell for the mayor's office and won. White flight was once again a key reason for his victory, as Atlanta had become a black-majority city by 1970, growing 37 percent in its black neighborhoods while losing 20 percent of its whites. Massell's racially charged rhetoric, which included predicting the "death" of the city under a black mayor, also backfired and stimulated a higher black voter turnout than white. Jackson's victory came only a year after Andrew Young, a former aide to Martin Luther King, Jr., won election to Congress in a district only two-fifths black.[35]

Jackson delivered to his black constituents, reforming the police department to be more responsive to the black community and adopting an affirmative action program for municipal employment and contracts. Over the opposition of the white business community, he awarded 25 percent of the contracts for construction of a new international airport to black-owned firms, and by 1978, black businesses received about 38 percent of the city's municipal contracts. Yet Jackson maintained a close relationship with the white business elite, a political reality that most black mayors had to deal with. When the predominantly black city sanitation department went on strike in 1977, Jackson, in a remarkable show of irony, rejected the workers' demands for higher wages and fired the strikers, even though they had not received a pay increase for three years. While black Atlanta had a burgeoning middle class that benefited from affirmative action, with at least 6 percent of black households earning $35,000 or more annually by 1980 (approximately $98,000 annually in 2012 dollars), one-third of black families still lived below the poverty line. Nor was Jackson alone in this behavior. Coleman Young, even though he had once been a member of the National Negro Labor Council, allied with the Ford Motor Company after his election in Detroit and lowered corporate property taxes while at the same time reducing city services and funding for public educational and social programs. The end of the civil rights movement and the attainment of black political power began to expose the class divides in the black community, with the black poor increasingly left out.[36]

Even in rural areas of the South, where white resistance to black equality during the 1950s and 1960s was often the strongest and most violent, black candidates made gains by the 1970s. In both rural and urban areas, white-controlled governments tried to dilute the black vote and defeat black candidates through gerrymandering, annexation, and at-large elections. These measures had some success and triggered ongoing voting rights litigation by black plaintiffs.[37] Black candidates, not surprisingly, tended to win in black-majority areas, where vote dilution schemes had less effect. Still, the underrepresentation was hard to ignore. By 1980, blacks were 20 percent of the southern population but only 7 percent of its state legislators, with most of the officeholders in Texas, Tennessee, and the Deep South (South Carolina, Georgia, Alabama, Mississippi, and Louisiana). This statistical reality needed to be taken into account when one looked at the 2,601 black elected officials in the South, the number that held office in 1982. While an impressive number, most of these offices were on the municipal or county level and thus had minimal impact on state-level decision making. Probably the most powerful black offices in the South were in the region's four black-majority cities of Atlanta, Richmond, Birmingham, and New Orleans, each of which had a black mayor by the early 1980s.[38] In most of the South, white politicians still held the reins of power, even with the changes wrought by the Voting Rights Act.

Despite these limitations, black political power in the 1970s had reached the point at which it was definable and tangible on both the local and national levels, even if black representation was lower than their percentage of the population. Prior to 1972, the only black congressional represen-tatives came from northern states, and these northern black members of the House formed the Congressional Black Caucus (CBC) in 1971. The CBC had arisen from an informal organization of the House's nine black members in 1969, under the leadership of Representative Charles Diggs, Jr., of Detroit. The CBC joined with white liberal lawmakers to pre-serve civil rights legislation and block efforts by Richard Nixon and his conservative allies to stymie school desegregation, voting rights enforce-ment, and other issues of racial equality. The CBC gave life to the first National Black Political Convention in Gary, Indiana, a meeting of black elected officials, which attracted 3,500 delegates in March 1972. Splits between integrationists and black nationalists weakened the convention and its subsequent meetings, and it had little long-term impact. The CBC continued to grow, however, and received its first southern members when Barbara Jordan of Houston and Andrew Young of Atlanta won election to the U.S. House, the first black representatives from the South since the nineteenth century.[39]

The election of Ronald Reagan in 1980 after the slow gains of the 1970s seemed to herald a reverse of gains made by blacks since 1965. Certainly black Americans seemed to have little positive to expect from a Reagan presidency. The former governor of California, who emerged politically as a supporter of the anti–civil rights Barry Goldwater in 1964, had a long history of opposing federal civil rights laws and enforcement, and he even supported the repeal of his state's fair housing ordinance in the 1960s. He had a history of pandering to white racists with antiwelfare sentiments, including repeated references to an anonymous "welfare queen" who had children to collect more benefits and at least one reference to a "strapping young buck" who allegedly cheated the system. Reagan had openly appealed to the white conservative vote in the South during the 1980 campaign, mostly famously in Philadelphia, Mississippi, at the Neshoba County Fair, where he endorsed "states' rights." Despite these comments, Reagan did make a sustained outreach to the black vote and attracted a few high-profile black endorsements. Much of Carter's own problems with his black political base hurt him in 1980, most notably his dismissal of UN ambassador Andrew Young, who met with officials of the Palestinian Liberation Organization (PLO) in violation of U.S. policy. While Carter won 82 percent of the black vote to Reagan's 14 percent, Reagan won enough white votes for him easily defeat Carter.[40]

Reagan owed little to black voters, and he targeted in his budget social programs that benefited the poor and African Americans. In his first full month in office, he ordered $47 billion in reductions, most of that coming from antipoverty programs. His 1981 budget made cuts in public assistance, inner-city aid, food stamps, job training, and Social Security disability programs. The reduction in food stamps alone was $2 billion, with another $1.7 million taken from child nutrition programs. The latter issue even led to the administration's highly publicized—and quickly retracted after much ridicule—attempt to cut school lunch costs by classifying catsup and pickle relish as "vegetables." Federal housing took an especially hard blow, with a budget that fell from $30 billion in 1981 to $8 billion in 1986, leading to a sharp drop in available public housing in minority neighborhoods. The cuts, combined with the continuing recession that helped Reagan get elected, deeply affected the black community. In 1981, the real median income of all black families declined by 5.2 percent from the previous year. The share of black families below the poverty line moved up from 32.4 percent to 34.2 percent.[41]

In civil rights enforcement, the news was similarly bleak for proponents of federal enforcement. As part of his general program of business deregulation, Reagan proposed a weakening of affirmative action that would require employers to submit written affirmative action policies only for contractors with 250 or more employees and a government contract worth at least $1 million. The previous standard was 50 or more employees and a $50,000 or higher contract. Reagan's "hit man" on affirmative action was William Bradford Reynolds, a scion of the Du Pont family and corporate lawyer who Reagan appointed to be assistant attorney general for civil rights, the top civil rights enforcer in the Justice Department. Reynolds intervened to overturn affirmative action plans in numerous states and municipalities, even though these plans had been approved and even developed by previous administrations.[42]

Reynolds in particular opposed affirmative action because he believed it awarded benefits to entire groups and not individuals who had actually suffered discrimination. This view led him to oppose class-action discrimination suits as well. Perhaps his and Reagan's most controversial action was their 1982 defense of Bob Jones University, a South Carolina college with a long history of racial discrimination. Bob Jones had been denied tax-exempt status by the Internal Revenue Service (IRS) under guidelines approved by President Nixon in 1970. The Justice Department sided with the university in its lawsuit against the IRS, but the Supreme Court upheld the IRS decision in May 1983.[43]

In voting rights, the Reagan administration also attempted but failed to secure a rollback. The Voting Rights Act had been renewed in 1970 and 1975, and was due to expire in 1982. Reagan had called the act "humiliating to the South," and Reynolds pushed the president to veto the renewal bill. Recent actions by the Supreme Court also added to the worry of civil rights advocates. In 1980, the Court dismissed a suit by Wiley Bolden, a black plaintiff in Mobile, Alabama, who had sued over Mobile's at-large election system for its city commission. The system allowed white majorities to outvote the black minority and keep an all-white government, even though the city was 35 percent black in 1970. The Court sided with the city in *City of Mobile v. Bolden*, with Justice Potter Stewart declaring that "the Fifteenth Amendment does not entail the right to have Negro candidates elected."[44]

Civil rights advocates worried for the future of the landmark law. Yet the growth of the black vote since 1965 had compelled white Democrats, the traditional opponents of civil rights legislation, to support federal oversight of southern election laws. In 1975, a majority of white Democrats in the House had voted for final passage of the Voting Rights Act extension, a shift brought about by their increasing reliance on black votes. While southern Republicans, elected with white conservative votes, sought to end the act, they soon found out that opposition to the well-established law had its limits. Reagan received that message loud and clear from Mississippi in 1981. In a special election in southwestern Mississippi, Wayne Dowdy, a white Democrat and local mayor, defeated his Republican opponent by only 1,200 votes. Dowdy had rallied black voters by becoming the first white congressional candidate in Mississippi to openly endorse extension of the Voting Rights Act, something his opponent did not. The loss of the seat, previously held by a Republican, cooled White House opposition.[45]

Civil rights forces, composed of over 150 organizations, crafted a well-organized campaign for renewal, one the opposition could not match. When the House passed a renewal that was even stronger than the current act, Reagan did not support Attorney General William French Smith's hard line against it. Many Republicans even helped pass the act, for example, when Senator Bob Dole of Kansas crafted a compromise bill that extended section five of the act, the portion that required preclearance of new voting laws, for 25 more years. Most importantly, Dole also inserted language to circumvent the *Mobile* decision, the "totality of circumstances" clause (which became known as the results test), which allowed discriminatory *effect* to be considered in voting cases. This was considerably wider than discriminatory *intent*, as was the case in *Mobile*, which limited the plaintiffs to proving deliberate racist intent in voting discrimination. Now even a law that was passed without racist intent but that still had a negative effect on minority voters could be challenged.[46]

As Reagan signed the act into law, federal enforcement of voting rights seemed as mainstreamed as affirmative action. Unlike affirmative action, there was widespread bipartisan support for voting rights enforcement, something that civil rights attorney Frank Parker called the "national consensus on voting rights." Parker argued that there was greater support for preserving access to the ballot than more controversial civil rights issues like busing and affirmative action, and cited the extension of the Voting Rights Act under Republican presidents as proof of this bipartisan support. This support extended to all three branches of government, for the Supreme Court in 1986 accepted the more expansive results test in the case of *Thornburg v. Gingles*, a North Carolina redistricting case.[47]

The consensus even attracted some surprising participants. Although he had opposed renewal of the act, William Bradford Reynolds used the strengthened Voting Rights Act to expand black representation. In 1983, he overturned 36 county redistricting plans in Mississippi, which led to revised plans that doubled the number of black county supervisors in the state. This was done over the bitter objections of white officials in a state whose white voters strongly supported Reagan.[48]

With the Voting Rights Act preserved, black political power continued to expand into the national mainstream in the 1980s, despite the negative effect Reaganomics had on the black community. By 1990, there were 316 black mayors in the country. The expansion of black big-city mayors continued, and voters in Washington, D.C., sent Marion Barry, a former organizer in the Student Nonviolent Coordinating Committee (SNCC) during Freedom Summer, to the mayor's office in 1978. In Chicago, the voters elected their first black mayor in a narrow and divisive race. Harold Washington, a black state senator and congressional representative, challenged incumbent mayor Jane Byrne in the Democratic primary in 1983. Byrne had been elected with black support in 1979, unseating the incumbent who enjoyed the backing of the political machine of the late Richard Daley, who had ruled Chicago with an iron fist for 20 years. She had been the outsider candidate but quickly reconciled herself to machine politics and actually reduced the number of black appointees in her administration. Numerous community groups and black political activists mobilized in opposition to the mayor, including Jesse Jackson's Operation PUSH (People United to Save Humanity). This led to an increase in black voter registration over white registration. Washington rode this wave of mobilization, winning the primary and then facing a white Republican who stoked racial animosity in his campaign advertisements. Washington won through a coalition of black and Hispanic votes, since many white Democrats defected to the GOP.[49]

In Philadelphia, a similar pattern emerged under W. Wilson Goode, who had served as the city's managing director. He challenged two-term incumbent Frank Rizzo, who had alienated black voters during his administration. Goode won with 53 percent of the vote and then defeated two white candidates in the general election. In both cities, black voters made up around 40 percent of the electorate, indicating that the victors received some white support; but in both cities, the bulk of the traditionally Democratic white ethnic voters—Italians, Irish, Polish, and others—were hostile to the idea of a black mayor and willingly voted Republican to try and stop it.[50]

It was not big-city black mayors that proved to be the major black political movement of the twentieth century, but the presidential candidacy of Jesse Jackson. Jackson, a minister and aide of Martin Luther King, Jr., had spent most of his adult life in Chicago, where he worked as leader of Operation PUSH in the black community and supported—and often upstaged—Harold Washington. He lacked electoral experience, working primarily as a community activist linking protest and politics and continuing the tradition of the civil rights movement. While often viewed as self-aggrandizing and headline-grabbing, Jackson was an example of how the activist strains of the 1960s had become thoroughly mainstreamed into the modern Democratic Party. Even many of the more radical elements of black power had been tamed by electoral politics and liberalism, seen in such elections as Winston-Salem, North Carolina, in 1974 and 1977, when a member of the local chapter of the Black Panther Party ran in the Democratic primary for city alderman.[51]

The resentment of many black Americans against the Reagan administration and the extension of the Voting Rights Act galvanized civil rights organizations, and the NAACP and other groups ramped up voter registration efforts. Three million African American voters in the South were still unregistered in 1980s, a critical bloc that could have denied victory to Reagan. Jackson built his bid for the 1984 Democratic nomination on his Southern Crusade, a voter registration push in southern states he began in the summer of 1983. This included cajoling William Bradford Reynolds to come the Mississippi Delta, where he convinced the conservative lawyer that problems existed in the state's county redistricting plans and even with basic voting access. The centerpiece of Jackson's campaign was his Rainbow Coalition, an interracial coalition of progressive activists modeled after 1960s efforts like Martin Luther King, Jr.'s Poor Peoples' Campaign and the Students for a Democratic Society (SDS). Jackson benefited from an increase in black voter registration from 1980 to 1984 in the South, with an average gain of 14 percent in the region.[52]

Jackson was not the consensus choice of the black leadership, however. Jackson's rise after King's assassination in 1968 had been controversial, with Jackson falsely claiming he had cradled the dying civil rights leader in his arms and then later appearing before the Chicago City Council wearing a shirt he claimed was stained with King's blood. By 1983, while Jackson was undeniably popular with the mass of black voters, many black big-city mayors and civil rights leaders opposed his candidacy, with the head of the Congressional Black Caucus charging that Jackson was a lot of talk but not much action.[53]

Jackson revived the rhetoric of Dr. King and attacked the three "isms"—racism, militarism, and materialism—criticized Reagan's foreign policy and budgets, and called for peace abroad linked to economic justice at home. Richard Hatcher, still serving as mayor of Gary, Indiana, ran Jackson's campaign. While many viewed the campaign as symbolic, he outlasted several better-financed Democrats, including Ohio senator and former astronaut John Glenn. Jackson won three southern state primaries and took half of Mississippi's delegates. Jackson's two main rivals were Walter Mondale, the establishment liberal who had been elected as Carter's vice president, and Gary Hart, a Colorado senator who ran as a moderate. Jackson crafted a specific platform and policy proposals, but his campaign suffered when his supporter Louis Farrakhan, a minister in the Nation of Islam, attacked Judaism as a "gutter religion." Jackson added to the anti-Semitism when he made an off-the-record comment to a black reporter calling Jews "Hymies" and New York City "Hymietown." This seriously hurt his credibility and not surprisingly cost him any real Jewish support. His open support for Yasser Arafat of the PLO only added to the charges. Jackson also struggled with Hispanic voters and received little support from working-class whites, exposing a racial divide in the Democratic base. Jackson finished third in the primary race, with 21 percent of the vote.[54]

Jackson's 1984 candidacy was nevertheless the first major showing in a presidential race by an African American candidate, and he forced the Democratic establishment to take him seriously. He directly challenged racialized images of welfare recipients perpetuated in the Reagan era, reminding people that "Reagan has been able to put color on the face of poverty, but most poor are white women, infants, children, and old people." Jackson's campaign built the groundwork for his next run in 1988.[55]

Ironically, Mondale, the eventual nominee, had a long record as one of the strongest pro–civil rights senators to ever hold office. A protégé of Hubert Humphrey, Mondale had as a Minnesota senator helped pass open housing legislation in 1968, the last major legislative civil rights victory of the decade. He had been a strong supporter of busing but tempered his position as white backlash against it grew in the 1970s. He had argued strongly for Carter to back University of California–Davis in the *Bakke* case when it looked as if Carter was going to side against affirmative action. Yet Mondale's problem became that he had to recognize and procure Jackson's support while at the same time not alienating white and Jewish voters. Mondale and Jackson reconciled in time for the convention, but the Jackson delegates, in an ugly intraracial rupture, booed civil rights veterans like Andrew Young and Coretta Scott King for their chastisement of Jackson.[56]

The Reagan campaign, meanwhile, completely wrote off the black vote in 1984 and focused on securing the white vote. Reagan's black outreach was limited to public endorsements from a few black sports celebrities like Muhammad Ali. In fact, the influx of new black voters before and during the Jackson campaign resulted in an upsurge of white voter registration in the South. The 1,342,000 new southern black voters found themselves outvoted by 3,078,000 new southern white voters, in registration drives orchestrated by southern Republican state parties. This racially polarized voting further undercut the Democrats in the South, who were increasingly identified as the "black" party. Mondale lost to Reagan in a landslide in November, with 59 percent of the popular vote going to the Republican.[57]

For the South, the 1984 election showed just how far the partisan realignment of the region had changed since 1965. The once-solid Democratic South was now Republican territory. Lyndon Johnson had famously said after he signed the Voting Rights Act into law in 1965 that "we just delivered the South to the Republican Party for a long time to come." The first "Great White Switch," as the political scientists Earl and Merle Black called it, occurred in the 1964 election when southern white Democrats voted for Barry Goldwater and then continued with votes for Richard Nixon in 1972. Yet they still identified as Democrats and continued to vote for Democratic politicians on the state and local levels. The second Great White Switch came in the 1980s when Reagan received overwhelming white southern support, and southern whites began to change their partisan identification to the Republican Party. With 80 percent of southern white voters going for Reagan in 1984, that switch was well underway. This reality also mirrored the fact, that the overwhelmingly majority of black voters now identified with and supported the Democratic Party.[58]

Still, dissatisfaction with Reagan arose in his second term, even among southern whites. His administration's agricultural polices proved to be unpopular in the South. That ended up enabling a notable election victory in 1986 in the Mississippi Delta, the successful campaign of Mike Espy in Mississippi's second congressional district. Espy, a black lawyer from a well-to-do Delta family, hoped to become the first black congressman in Mississippi since Reconstruction. Twice before, a black Democrat had failed to win the seat in the black-majority district, but Espy benefited from a low white voter turnout due to disgruntled Delta farmers and edged out the two-term white incumbent. His election broke another major racial barrier in Mississippi, integrating the state's congressional delegation.[59]

Reagan's hostility to civil rights did not wane in his second term. In 1985, William Bradford Reynolds began an effort, backed by Ed Meese, the new attorney general, to overturn Lyndon Johnson's 1965 executive order that required government contractors to adopt affirmative action guidelines. Reynolds found himself opposed by both William Brock, his secretary of labor, and much of the business community, who had long since reconciled themselves to affirmative action. Reynolds challenged a now deeply institutionalized affirmative action, effectively part of the racial status quo. He dropped his campaign in 1986.[60]

Although the case dealt with sex discrimination, the Supreme Court decision in *Grove City v. Bell* (1984) also created civil rights headaches for Reagan. The case involved Title IX, which related to sex discrimination and funding for women's sports at universities. The Court limited the effects of Title IX by declaring that federal agencies could not withhold funds from colleges and other agencies guilty of discrimination; rather, it could withhold funds only from those specific departments that had violated the law. Civil rights forces rallied in Congress to amend the decision, and in 1988 passed the Civil Rights Restoration Bill to overturn *Grove City* and extend antibias laws in race, sex, and other categories. Reagan vetoed the bill, making him the first president in modern history to veto a civil rights bill. His veto was overridden, with many Republicans joining in the override. Reagan also experienced another override on a racial issue, when in 1986 he vetoed congressional sanctions against the racist apartheid regime in South Africa, with which his administration had enjoyed relations through a policy he called constructive engagement, which included major business ties and investments with its anticommunist government.[61]

By the time of the 1988 election, after eight years of Reaganomics, it seemed unlikely that the GOP would be able to make any serious inroads with black voters. The 1988 election, however, would become one of the most racially charged ones in U.S. political history. The Republican nominee was Vice President George Herbert Walker Bush, a moderate who had a mixed civil rights record, though it was better than Reagan's. He had been a race-baiter early in his political career, initially opposing the Civil Rights Act of 1964, but as a congressional representative from Houston in the 1960s he supported civil rights legislation. He had largely avoided the affirmative action battles of the Reagan years.[62]

The Democrats still had racial problems, however. Many black Americans felt that the party had not forcefully opposed Reagan budget cuts in the 1980s, and in fact many white southern Democrats had supported them. With Reagan's strength with white voters, the Democrats increasingly were attracted to the idea of nominating a conservative or moderate white Democrat to win the "Reagan Democrats" back to the fold. The white backlash against Jackson only contributed to Democratic support for a centrist white candidate, which meant that black votes were going to be taken for granted. This indifference to black concerns spelled potential trouble for the Democrats, since the number of blacks during the Reagan years who identified themselves as independents rose from 9 to 22 percent.[63]

Of course, the Democratic establishment's bigger racial problem was the return of Jesse Jackson. In 1988, the Jackson campaign was better organized, and Jackson had spent the previous four years strengthening the Rainbow Coalition. Most of that time was spent building up white outreach, especially with whites negatively affected by Reaganomics. He appeared at plant closings, farmers' meetings, and other areas where he connected with unemployed and marginalized white workers. At the same time, he polished and moderated his message, integrated his campaign staff, and in the process alienated some of his black supporters from 1984.[64]

Jackson did better in the primaries, winning over 20 percent of the vote in overwhelmingly white states like Maine and Vermont, and taking 27 percent of the vote in 14 southern states on Super Tuesday. After Super Tuesday, Michael Dukakis, the governor of Massachusetts, and Al Gore, a U.S. senator from Tennessee, came to be seen as Jackson's two main rivals. His white support was clearly greater this time, and his black support remained strong. Jackson then won a decisive victory in the Michigan primary, putting him slightly behind Dukakis in overall delegates. Yet his showing faltered after he lost to Dukakis in Wisconsin and Connecticut, and the governor sewed up the nomination after a clear win in New York.[65]

Dukakis was the son of Greek immigrants, and had built a distinguished record reforming his state's government and presiding over a booming economy. Yet the governor's bland speaking style contrasted sharply with Jackson's oratory and passion. Since Massachusetts had a small black population, Dukakis had no notable record on civil rights issues, a marked contrast from every Democratic nominee since John F. Kennedy. Unlike previous Democratic nominees, he had no real ability to connect with black audiences. This carried over into his dealings with Jackson, and he falsely led Jackson, mostly to stroke the minister's ego, to believe he was a contender for the vice presidential ticket. This led to a row between the candidates that was not healed until the convention.[66]

The racial poison of the 1988 election went well beyond Democratic Party squabbles. The political climate of 1988 was set almost entirely by one man, Lee Atwater, a southern political consultant who specialized in negative campaigning. Atwater used a skillful update of Nixon's southern strategy to stoke racial fears among white voters. The wedge issue Atwater seized on was the furlough program in Massachusetts, begun by a Republican governor and continued by Dukakis. Under the furlough program, William Horton, a black convicted murder, had been granted a pass and promptly kidnapped and raped a white woman in Maryland, and assaulted her fiancé.[67]

In campaign stops, Bush began hitting Dukakis on the furlough program but did not mention Horton's race. However, that was unnecessary, since supposedly independent political action committees (PACs) released flyers and television ads featuring Horton's mug shot, and one PAC even put Horton's victims on a speaking tour. While the Bush campaign did not directly release any material highlighting Horton's race, some state Republican organizations had no problem doing so. These PACs were independent in name only, as the mug shot ad's creators had previously worked for the Bush campaign. The media picked up on the "Willie Horton" ad, giving it extensive coverage beyond the airtime the PACs purchased. To highlight the furlough program, the Bush campaign ran its own ad featuring a revolving door of inmates at a prison. Although most of the actors in the ad were white, the widespread replaying of Horton's mug shot by the media and Republican proxies made in unnecessary for the Bush campaign to mention race.[68]

Dukakis's poll numbers dropped, and against the advice of his advisors, he refused to aggressively counterattack. Adding to his problems, Dukakis failed to effectively rally black voters to his cause. He rarely campaigned in black areas and focused on trying to win white Reagan Democrats back into his fold, which influenced his choice of Lloyd Bentsen, a Texas senator from the party's conservative wing, as his vice-presidential running mate. Perhaps the highlight of the governor's racial disconnect was his visit to the Neshoba County Fair in Philadelphia, Mississippi, the same area that saw the Freedom Summer murders of 1964. Dukakis listened to the advice of white Mississippi Democrats and in his speech there, he did not mention the murders, thus omitting any mention of one of the most infamous crimes of the civil rights movement. Throughout his campaign, he took black voters for granted, a particularly obtuse action given the strong challenge Jackson gave him in the primaries. Black voters experienced only a 44 percent turnout on Election Day, and white voters, especially higher-income ones, voted for Bush. Total voter turnout in the country was below 50 percent, and the vice president won with 54 percent of the vote.[69]

By the beginning of the 1980s, the civil rights movement had been firmly institutionalized in the mainstream of U.S. society, from voting rights protections to the widespread adoption of affirmative action in the public and private sectors. The resilience of these institutions could be seen by the consistent failure of the Reagan administration and conservatives to repeal or even significantly weaken them. Yet as the racial polarization and negativity of the 1988 campaign showed, along with the persistence of black poverty and income disparities compared to whites, that racism and racial difference still remained firmly embedded in U.S. society. It had become unfashionable to be called a racist, and many who advocated polices that hurt African Americans denied they were racist, instead adopting the rhetoric of "fairness" and "equality."

If one of the legacies of the civil rights movement was the creation of a system of racial preferences to remedy past discrimination, then another was the notion of a color-blind society, or one where privileged whites used this rhetoric of equality and fairness. On its surface, the notion of such a society brings to mind white conservatives opposed to affirmative action as "reverse racism" and ignoring racial inequality. It is true that conservative commentators and scholars, such as William Bradford Reynolds, emerged to challenge many aspects of racial preference that they felt hindered true racial equality, and a minority of scholars in academia emerged to give legitimacy to these critiques. Raymond Wolters, a conservative historian at the University of Delaware, criticized the implementation of school desegregation and even its legal foundation. In his 1984 book *The Burden of Brown*, Wolters criticized the judicial interpretation of desegregation as racial balance via court-ordered busing, which is what resulted from the *Green* decision in 1968. He called it "discrimination in order to achieve racial balance" and saw it stemming from the original *Brown v. Board of Education* ruling, in which the court moved away from a strict color-blind interpretation and instead embraced psychological evidence suggesting that segregation harmed black children. He argued a strict constructionist perspective and insisted that judges had "arrogated the right to make social policy," creating in effect through *Green* an affirmative action policy to integrate schools. In his examination of the original five districts that were part of the *Brown* lawsuit and decision, he criticized the integration plans, and blamed progressive education and disruptive black students for a decline in educational standards and school discipline. Wolters called integration a failure and sided with critics who argued that the Equal Protection Clause of the Fourteenth Amendment did not prohibit racially segregated education.[70]

Not surprisingly, liberal critics who defended integration counterattacked. David Garrow, a historian who had written two books on the civil rights movement, called Wolters's book "clearly racist in tone and sentiment," a charge that received coverage in major newspapers due to Wolters's book winning the Silver Gavel Award from the American Bar Association. Garrow amended his charges in a later review of Wolters's book but still said its bias voided "any and all affirmative scholarly values that such a book might pretend to possess."[71]

Another prominent critique of liberal civil rights policies emerged from conservative writer Dinesh D'Souza. D'Souza, a native of India, criticized established civil rights organizations in his 1995 book *The End of Racism* and argued for what he called "competing versions of minority progress," which included a defense of nonwhite conservatives but also a rejection of the bell curve argument that low IQ scores hindered blacks. He echoed the Moynihan Report when he argued that "pathologies" in the African American community, such as high crime rates, legitimize what he called rational discrimination by whites. While he recognized that these cultural problems developed in response to historical discrimination against black Americans, he said that liberal policies like affirmative action only masked black failure and perpetuated racial inequality by promoting diversity over merit. D'Souza criticized, often using provocative language, the spectrum of civil rights policies, including redistricting, but focused more on cultural issues than electoral politics.[72]

Yet the idea of a color-blind society is far too complex to simply dismiss out of hand as a conservative utopia masking or ignoring racial inequality. William Julius Wilson, a black sociologist currently at Harvard University, published the highly influential book *The Declining Significance of Race* in 1978. Then a faculty member at the University of Chicago, Wilson argued a theme similar Moynihan's of 13 years earlier. He said that after the removal of barriers to all African American advancement during the civil rights era, what then occurred was a widening of class divisions in the black community. Educated black men and women were able to enter new positions of prestige in corporations, academia, and other institutions, but the black underclass did not enjoy such gains and actually saw a decline in its position, or "class subordination." The reasons for this, according to Wilson, were the deindustrialization of U.S. cities and the national shift to a service economy, which meant that urban African American workers suffered rising unemployment as the industrial base disappeared. This occurred even as black politicians won political power in major U.S. cities, leading to political control of areas that were increasingly irrelevant. Wilson did not deny that racism still occurred; he argued that racial conflict had to do with noneconomic issues like schools and residential areas rather than jobs. Wilson summed up his argument for the importance of class in the postracial era by declaring that "the problem for blacks today, in terms of government practices, is no longer one of legalized racial equality. Rather the problem for blacks, especially the black underclass, is that the government is not organized to deal with the new barriers imposed by structural changes in the economy."[73]

Manning Marable, a black Marxist, echoed Wilson's focus on class stratification in the black community. Marable argued that the black elite were the prime beneficiaries of the civil rights movement, since they already had the economic resources and education to take advantage of affirmative action programs and the desegregation of higher education. As a result, income inequality between higher-earning blacks and whites mostly disappeared by the end of the 1970s. However, this elite made up only about 7 to 10 percent of the total black population in the United States. For the mass of black Americans, economic inequality, unemployment, and poverty continued. In fact, things worsened in the 1970s with the rise of black-on-black violence, which invited programs of mass arrest and incarceration from the government that targeted black Americans. Here Marable broke with Wilson's argument that race was declining, insisting that "for the unemployed, the poor, and those without marketable skills or resources . . . 'race' continued to be a central factor in their marginal existence."[74]

With its publication in 1994, the controversial best-selling book *The Bell Curve* added to the contentious debate over racism and a color-blind society. The authors, psychologist Richard Herrnstein and political scientist Charles Murray, authored a study of intelligence and its role in U.S. life. The most controversial portion covered ethnic difference and intelligence, in which the authors examined the real differences between blacks and whites on IQ tests. They dismissed the influence of cultural bias and socioeconomic status on the divergent scores but noted the narrowing gap in areas like Scholastic Aptitude Test (SAT) scores between whites and blacks. After examining both environmental and genetic effects on intelligence, the authors concluded that "the major ethnic differences in the United States . . . may well include some (as yet unknown) genetic component, but nothing suggests that they are entirely genetic." While the authors never argued that genetics played a dominant role in racial difference, their entertaining a partial genetic explanation and their dismissal of cultural bias triggered a firestorm of controversy in the media and academic community. Murray's status as a conservative critic of welfare programs, outlined in his 1984 book *Losing Ground*, added to the political fury.[75] It also marked a conservative departure by some in the notion of a color-blind society—most conservatives accepted the notion of racial equality and criticized what they saw as well-intentioned but flawed governmental programs that perpetuated inequality. Few publicly admitted any belief that genetics might indicate fundamental racial inequality, since it went against conservative notions of "rugged individualism" that one could better himself or herself through hard work, education, and diligence.

The small by vocal number of black conservatives that had emerged by the 1980s provided much intellectual respectability to the conservative defense of a color-blind society. Many of these black intellectuals, most trained as economists or social scientists, found employment in think tanks, foundations, or the Reagan administration. They included Samuel Pierce, who served as Reagan's Department of Housing and Urban Development (HUD) secretary, Thomas Sowell of the Hoover Institution, and Glenn Loury of Harvard University. These new black conservatives rejected affirmative action and social welfare programs, and called for black Americans to embrace entrepreneurial capitalism. The intellectuals' program also included calls for African Americans to join the Republican Party, or at least leave the Democratic Party and become independent.[76]

Clarence Thomas became the most famous black conservative to emerge in this era. Thomas, a product of a broken home in rural Georgia, had risen to graduate from Yale Law School. Mentored by Senator John Danforth of Missouri, Thomas entered the Reagan administration and was named to head the EEOC in 1982. Thomas shared the ideological hostility to affirmative action that his associate William Bradford Reynolds held. He stopped using class action suits in employment discrimination cases and also allowed over 10,000 allegations of age discrimination go uninvestigated. This lax enforcement of civil rights law prompted Congress to act instead and pass the Age Discrimination Claims Assistance Act of 1988.[77]

By the end of the 1980s, despite the vocal rhetoric of some of these black conservatives, the majority of black Americans identified as and voted for Democrats. Even the more activist strains and radical elements of the black community had incorporated to varying degrees into the party, such as some of the Black Panthers in the 1970s and elements of Louis Farrakhan's Nation of Islam into the Jesse Jackson campaign. The right wing of

American politics, including the former segregationists and white supremacists who opposed the civil rights movement, had tempered their rhetoric and found a home in the Republican Party. Just as progressive activists and African Americans like Jackson often found themselves frustrated by Democratic centrism, so too did the racial conservatives in the GOP, who were unable to gut affirmative action and voting rights enforcement in the 1970s and 1980s. A radical fringe of conservatism, represented in the 1990s by the nearly all-white militia movement and its hostility to the federal government, sprang up and even engaged in armed clashes with government agents (most notably the Minutemen in Montana). Few mainstream conservatives embraced the militias, due to their extremism and associations with neo-Nazi movements like the Aryan Nation, even if these same conservatives shared the militias' anxieties over immigration, multiculturalism, and internationalism.[78]

Yet although black Americans were in the political mainstream by the 1980s, what effectively had happened was that black Americans were taken for granted by the Democratic Party, as Dukakis's poor black outreach showed in 1988. The fact that Democratic leaders did this was because the Republicans provided only lip service to wooing black voters but little in terms of programs or legislation to address their interests. Black voters in America then found themselves in much the same position in the Democratic Party that religious conservatives had in the Republican Party—they were mobilized to win elections, but many of their concerns were largely ignored or only symbolically endorsed. Malcolm X predicted this state of affairs in U.S. elections when he called 1964 "the year when all of the white politicians will be back in the so-called Negro community jiving you and me for some votes. The year when all of the white political crooks will be right back in your and my community with their false promises, building up our hopes for a letdown, with their trickery and their treachery, with their false promises which they don't intend to keep."[79] By the 1990s, this state of affairs, only now with black politicians as well as white, seemed to be firmly entrenched in the two-party system.

Despite—or perhaps because of—this mainstreaming of racial opposites into the two-party system, the politics of race and character assassination with racial attacks continued. As the Willie Horton episode showed, race was still a potent factor in modern American political campaigns. Regardless of the accuracy of racial charges, they carried a potent force to unite whites by playing to their fears and anxieties. The Horton ad, as the next chapter shows, was not the first and would not be the last such attempt to play racial "dirty tricks" in U.S. political campaigns, presidential or otherwise.

Chapter 2

The Role of Race in American Political Campaigns: Willie Horton, Harold Ford, and Other Dirty Tricks

The role of race in U.S. political campaigns is as old as U.S. politics itself. As far back to the early republic, when most black Americans were the property of white Americans, political opportunists stoked the fires of racial fear and anxiety to burn their opponents. One of the earliest examples of this occurred in the first years of the nineteenth century, when James Callender, a sensationalist newspaper reporter, exposed President Thomas Jefferson's relationship with Sally Hemings, his slave and the half-sister of his late wife. Callender referred to Hemings as Jefferson's "concubine," with whom he had fathered five children (but only two survived infancy). In the 1804 election, the opposition Federalist Party (Jefferson was a Democratic-Republican) publicized the relationship in its newspapers, mocking him for keeping a mistress they dubbed "Black Sal" or his "dusky Sally." Even John Quincy Adams, the future president, got in on the act, writing anonymous poems mocking Jefferson and Hemings. Yet the charges made little impact in 1804 with the voters, especially since Jefferson had secured the support of much of his base in the South and the West with the Louisiana Purchase.[1]

In the dirty, bare-knuckles world of antebellum politics, slandering an opponent's lineage with allegations of interracial sex was also fair game. In the 1828 presidential election, Charles Hammond, the editor of the Cincinnati *Gazette* and a supporter of incumbent John Quincy Adams, published editorials accusing Adams's opponent Andrew Jackson of being of a mixed-race background. This alleged parentage came from his mother, whom Hammond slandered as a common prostitute who "married a

MULATTO MAN, with whom she had several children, of which number General JACKSON is one!!!" A Kentucky newspaper levied similar insults against Jackson's wife, comparing her to a "dirty, black wench" for cohabiting with Jackson before her divorce from her first husband was finalized.[2]

As the accusations against Jefferson and Jackson show, white Americans had (and still do) deep anxieties about interracial sex, which gave such charges potency. For some Americans—many (but not all) of them located in the South—these anxieties became a lurid obsession bordering on the pornographic, with vivid nightmares of black men assaulting white women, forcibly marrying them, and producing hordes of mulatto children that would overwhelm and destroy the white race. Of course, a blatantly hypocritically double standard existed from the era of slavery through the civil rights movement, whereby black men had to be kept from white women at all costs, but white male rape and sexual access to black women in slavery and freedom became a perk of being part of the "ruling race" of white Americans.[3]

This racialized and sexualized rhetoric continued as the United States almost committed national suicide over slavery. The sectional crisis over the expansion of slavery in the 1850s, which eventually led to the Civil War, produced extremely toxic and racist political rhetoric. Much of this was directed by proslavery Democrats against the newly emerging Republican Party, which had been officially founded in 1854 as an antislavery party in the wake of the collapse of the Whig Party over northern opposition to the Kansas-Nebraska Act. Proslavery politicians exploited the widespread antiblack prejudices of white voters to accuse the Republicans of desiring black equality, citizenship, and interracial marriage. The label "Black Republican," simultaneously evoking evil and race, became a common epitaph hurled at Republicans, seen in 1854 when Lawrence Keitt, a proslavery Democrat from South Carolina, started a brawl in the House of Representatives by calling a Republican representative a "Black Republican puppy."[4]

The most famous expressions of the racial rhetoric of the era occurred in 1858 during the famed Lincoln-Douglas debates in Illinois. Abraham Lincoln challenged Senator Stephen Douglas, a Democrat, during the 1858 elections. The debates came in the wake of the Supreme Court's decision in *Dred Scott v. Sandford* (1857), in which Chief Justice Roger Taney defended the right of slaveholders to take their slaves into free territory, declaring that blacks were not citizens and had no right to sue in federal court, since they were "so far inferior, that they had no rights which the white man was bound to respect." Lincoln and the Republican Party opposed the decision, and Douglas hammered Lincoln relentlessly over it with a single-minded passion, since the entire seven debates were devoted solely to the issue of slavery. Douglas played to white fears of interracial sex, accusing the "Black Republicans" of thinking that "the negro ought to be on a social equality with your wives and daughters." He declared that that "the signers of the Declaration [of Independence] had no reference to the negro . . . or any other inferior and degraded race when they spoke of the equality of men." The white audience ate up Douglas's attacks and cheered him on. When Douglas asked them if they were "in favor of conferring upon the negro the rights and privileges of citizenship" and if they wanted neighboring Missouri to abolish slavery and "send one hundred thousand emancipated slaves into Illinois" the crowd shouted "down with the negro," "no, no," and "never."[5]

Lincoln, while opposed to slavery, was put on the defensive by Douglas's forceful attack and replied by pandering to white voters, an understandable strategy given that black men could not vote in Illinois. While he privately complained about Douglas's race-baiting, he clearly told the audience that he was "not, nor ever have been in favor of bringing about in any way the social and political equality of the white and black races." He went on to state that he was opposed to black men serving as jurors, voters, and office-holders, and he also affirmed his opposition to interracial marriage. He declared that "physical difference" between whites and blacks "will for ever forbid the two races living together on terms of social and political equality." On political rights like voting, he indicated that those were state, not federal matters. Unlike Douglas, Lincoln did nuance his position and said that despite his belief in black inferiority, "in the right to eat the bread, without leave of anybody else, which his own hand earns, he is my equal and the equal of Judge Douglas, and the equal of every living man."[6] This position went beyond Douglas, who—keeping in line with the *Dred Scott* ruling—gave no indication that he felt black people should have any rights at all.

Lincoln's attempt to carve out a more moderate position than Douglas on race helped him little in the race, for Douglas ended up winning re-election to the Senate when the Democrats held control of the state legislature. But the debates made Lincoln a national spokesperson for the Republican Party and helped him win the Republican nomination in 1860.[7]

The 1860 presidential election, essentially a referendum on whether the southern slaveholding states would stay in the Union, represented the peak of racist rhetoric in the antebellum era. With slavery having torn the country almost in two over the previous decade, the question of black rights and citizenship became even more volatile. Democrats charged that the Republicans were "a party that says 'a nigger is better than an Irishman.'" A Democratic float in a New York City parade carried a banner saying that "free love and free niggers will certainly elect Old Abe," while the *New York Herald* used the reliable standby of race mixing, declaring that a Lincoln victory would mean "African amalgamation with the fair daughter of the Anglo Saxon, Celtic, and Teutonic races." The Republicans had few effective responses to this rhetoric, and instead focused on regional and economic issues in their campaigning.[8]

Of course, the election of Lincoln in 1860 did not bring immediate emancipation or send a flood of ex-slaves north to ravish white womanhood, but his victory still prompted secession, the formation of the Confederate States of America, and four bloody years of civil war. Lincoln, under pressure from abolitionists and his own generals, issued the Emancipation Proclamation in 1863 and made abolition of slavery a war aim, but this action gave the Democrats even more racist ammunition for the 1864 election. The Democratic candidate was George McClellan, the former commander of the Army of the Potomac whom Lincoln had twice fired. McClellan pushed a negotiated peace to end the war, in sharp contrast to Lincoln's insistence on the Union and emancipation. The Democrats had won votes in the 1862 mid-term elections by tarring the Republicans with the brush of racial equality, and they ramped up the charges in 1864. Such rhetoric had consequences far beyond the ballot box, fanning an intense Negrophobia amongst Irish workers in New York City that led to the shocking violence of the draft riots of 1863, where black New Yorkers were lynched in the streets. The *New York World*, a Democratic newspaper, invented a new word—"miscegenation"—to describe the sexual union of the races and their mixed offspring. The paper said that a Republican victory in 1864 would lead to "the blending of the white and the black." Democratic cartoons showed grossly caricatured black men kissing and dancing with white women, and editorials spread lurid, unconfirmed stories about floods of mulatto children born in areas under Union occupation. "Abraham Africanus the First," the Democrats anointed Lincoln, a "widowmaker" who "loves his country less, and the negro more." This base language prompted many black abolitionists and black voters in the North to rally behind Lincoln and support him, especially since he resisted intense political pressure to water down or revoke the Emancipation Proclamation.[9]

Such race-baiting did not work, however. Eleventh-hour Union victories on the battlefield saved Lincoln's re-election chances and preserved abolition as a war aim. With the ratification of the Thirteenth Amendment in 1865, which outlawed slavery, the question during the era of Reconstruction after the end of the war and Lincoln's assassination shifted from freedom to citizenship and voting rights for the freedmen. The ratification of the Fourteenth Amendment in 1868 and the Fifteenth Amendment in 1870 granted citizenship rights to black Americans and extended the right to vote to black men. In the postwar South, black voters elected black men to public office and formed coalitions with white Republicans to bring self-empowerment and political rights to the freedmen.[10]

Not surprisingly, the specter of granting black men rights equal to those of whites—unimaginable just a few years before—became the political mantra of the Democrats, continuing on their earlier anti-Lincoln hysteria. The 1866 elections were the first time civil rights for blacks played a central role in a political campaign, a reality brought about by the end of slavery the previous year. With the debate over the Fourteenth Amendment as the major issue, racial appeals by the Democrats and their standard-bearer, President Andrew Johnson, failed to unite white voters against black rights. These white voters favored punishing the defeated Confederacy and thus voted for a congressional majority that favored black suffrage in the South (but not the North).[11]

This single-minded opposition to Reconstruction and the enfranchisement of black men continued as a central theme of the 1868 presidential election, which pitted Horatio Seymour, the Democratic governor of New York, against the hero of the Civil War, General Ulysses S. Grant. Seymour's running mate, Frank Blair, publicly lambasted Republicans for yoking the South to the political rule of "a semi-barbarous race of blacks who are worshippers of fetishes and poligamists [sic]" and wanted to "subject the white women to their unbridled lusts." Blair's rhetoric kept race central to the campaign, what one historian referred to as "the last Presidential contest to center on white supremacy." In the South, white vigilantes led by groups like the Ku Klux Klan unleashed a reign of terror against the Republican Party and its black supporters. The tactics helped Seymour in the South but nationally, revulsion against the Democrats and Grant's celebrity status ensured a Republican victory and the continuation of Reconstruction.[12]

Yet the hearts of voters are fickle, and the 1870s proved no exception. Northern disinterest in Reconstruction grew during Grant's scandal-plagued administration, and the financial calamity of the Panic of 1873 put economic concerns at the forefront. The Republicans lost control of the House of Representatives in the 1874 elections, and soon the retreat from Reconstruction was in full swing. White violence in the South secured Democratic control of southern statehouses, with scant federal intervention. The antiracist sentiment of Reconstruction that had helped the Radical Republicans amend the U.S. Constitution to guarantee racial equality and voting rights was always fragile, and now collapsed. With the election of Republican Rutherford B. Hayes to the presidency, part of the Compromise of 1877 that the Republicans brokered with southern Democrats, federal enforcement of the rights of the freedmen in the South, came to an end. As a Kansas Republican said succinctly, the new administration policy was "niggers take care of yourselves."[13]

With the nation retreating from the promise of racial equality, black political participation in the South declined under the new Democratic governments, which came to power promising to "redeem" the old Confederacy of "Negro domination" and other ills. Southern state governments after 1877 relied on legal maneuvering such as gerrymandering, election supervision, as well as outright fraud to curb black influence at the polls. White Democrats also utilized violence, although not as intensely as they did during Reconstruction. The black vote, as well as much of the Republican Party in the South, began to disappear from southern elections.[14]

The last gasp of interest in black voting on the federal level came in 1890, when Representative Henry Cabot Lodge of Massachusetts sponsored an elections bill in the House of Representatives that would have provided federal monitoring of congressional elections in the South, in response to continuing reports of the intimidation and harassment of black voters. Southern Democrats blasted Lodge's bill as the Force Bill and rallied against it. The Lodge bill passed the House but failed to overcome a Democratic filibuster. With the death of the bill came the end of efforts by the GOP to protect what was left of black suffrage in the former Confederacy.[15]

The Lodge bill scared the South and prompted the final phase of ending the black vote, the formal adoption of disfranchisement and segregation under the Jim Crow laws of the 1890s and early 1900s. Mississippi, arguably the most antiblack state in the Old Confederacy, led the way in 1890. Its Constitution of 1890 enacted a variety of mechanisms, on their face nonracial, to purge black men from the voting rolls. S. S. Calhoon, the president of the constitutional convention, made the racial nature of the gathering clear, however. "Let us tell the truth if it bursts the bottom of the Universe," he declared. "We came here to exclude the negro. Nothing short of this will answer." Using a poll tax, a literacy test, a list of disqualifying crimes (which was composed of property crimes, not violent ones), and an "understanding clause" that allowed white registrars to use their discretion to bar voters, black voter registration dropped sharply. Other southern states followed, using parts of the "Mississippi Plan" to effectively nullify the Fifteenth Amendment. The Supreme Court soon gave its approval to Jim Crow as well, upholding segregation in public facilities with *Plessy v. Ferguson* (1896) and specifically upholding the Mississippi Constitution of 1890 with *Williams v. Mississippi* (1898).[16]

Part of the reason for this burst of political prejudice in a comparatively short period of time had to do with the Populist movement. The Populists, or Peoples' Party, emerged in the early 1890s as a third party devoted to the interests of small farmers and working-class Americans, and in the South, some white Populists tried to form cross-racial coalitions of poor blacks and whites. This led to some remarkable efforts by white Populists to eschew racial rhetoric and make common appeals based on class and economics. Thomas Watson, a Georgia Populist, told black and white farmers that "you are kept apart so that you may be separately fleeced of your earnings. You are made to hate each other because upon that hatred is rested the keystone of the arch of financial despotism which enslaves you both." Although the Populist commitment to racial equality can easily be overstated—Watson was also on record as opposing "social equality" between the races—the effort alarmed white Democrats, who increased their rhetoric of white supremacy and appeals to white voters to stay loyal to the Democrats. Not surprisingly, the Democrats then backed disfranchisement of blacks as a way to remove this potential threat of a class-based alliance.[17]

Ironically, the removal of black men from politics did little to tone down the toxicity of the racial rhetoric of white southern Democrats. While racial issues ceased to be a major issue in presidential elections by the 1890s, having been eclipsed by economic issues and foreign policy, segregationists on the state level continued their appeals to white supremacy. This rhetoric was linked to the rise in lynching in the South, were white mobs tortured, mutilated, burned, and hanged hundreds—eventually thousands—of black men (and some women, too) in ghastly fashion to maintain white supremacy, and in particular to discourage any contact between black men and white women. The widespread toleration of lynching by state authorities accompanied open expressions of support for the practice, which is not surprising given the total loss of political rights for southern African Americans during this time. Some of the rhetoric became so violent and brutal that it bordered on the genocidal. James K. Vardaman, a governor and senator from Mississippi, declared in 1907 that "if it is necessary every Negro in the state will be lynched; it will be done to maintain white supremacy." Rebecca Lattimer Felton, a journalist with the *Atlanta Journal*, said publicly that "if it takes lynching to protect women's dearest possession from drunken, ravening human beasts, then I say lynch a thousand a week if it becomes necessary."[18]

Even President Theodore Roosevelt, hardly an upholder of racial equality, faced the wrath of white southerners when he invited federal black officeholders and their wives to the White House in 1903. Vardaman, then running for governor of Mississippi, called Roosevelt a "little, mean, coon-flavored miscegnationist" who had by his actions made the White House "so saturated with the odor of the nigger that the rats have taken refuge in the stable."[19]

Both main parties paid little attention to the concerns of black Americans, but even left-wing political parties showed a remarkable blind spot concerning the role of race in the United States. The Socialist Party, which received almost 1 million votes in the 1912 presidential election, contained black members and supported biracial labor unions but did little to address the violent racism of the era that specifically afflicted blacks. In fact, some socialist leaders appealed to crude racial stereotypes, for example, Victor Berger told his colleagues in 1902 that "there can be no doubt that negroes [sic] and mulattos constitute a lower race," and he argued that black men were predisposed to rape. The Socialist Party's leader and presidential candidate, Eugene Debs, criticized racial prejudice but viewed race as essentially a problem created by capitalism and class antagonism. In 1903, he said that "there is no 'Negro problem' apart from the general labor problem," and in an article that same year wrote that the party "had nothing specific to offer the negro, [sic] and we cannot make special appeals to all the races. The Socialist Party is the party of the working class, regardless of color."[20] Such comments could hardly have encouraged black workers who faced lynching and race riots, a phenomenon not seen with the same intensity towards other U.S. ethnic groups.

As Jim Crow laws effectively removed African Americans from politics, the racial question ceased to play a major role in the early twentieth century. African Americans, at any rate, received little encouragement regarding race relations on the federal level. Woodrow Wilson, elected as a progressive Democrat in 1912, had asked for and received black support for his candidacy, but upon taking office, he reversed course to appease his fellow southern Democrats and instituted racial segregation in federal agencies, firing workers who objected. Needless to say, black leaders were dismayed, especially when Wilson rebuffed their appeals.[21]

Occasionally, presidents would speak out against racial violence, which is what the Republican Warren G. Harding did in 1921 when during a speech in Birmingham, Alabama, he condemned lynching. While he made the usual statements opposing social equality, he directly criticized Jim Crow discrimination and the denial of suffrage, making it the strongest presidential address on black civil rights since Reconstruction. Harding's support for an antilynching bill could not overcome Democratic opposition in Congress, however. The revival of the Ku Klux Klan in the 1920s gave racist, anti-Semitic, anti-Catholic, and anti-immigrant expressions even more legitimacy in public life, as state and local politicians—many in nonsouthern states—joined or actively sought the support of the so-called "invisible empire" of the KKK. The resurgent Klan contributed to the xenophobia against the Democratic presidential nominee in the 1928 election, New York Governor Al Smith, a Catholic and the son of Irish immigrants. A variety of factors worked to defeat Smith, and he lost to Herbert Hoover, the Republican nominee.[22]

The re-election of Franklin Delano Roosevelt (FDR) as president in 1936 began the slow process of bringing racial issues back into national politics. The Democratic Roosevelt, as part of his New Deal, constructed a political coalition that included urban blue-collar ethnic workers, white southerners, and (a first for the Democrats) black northerners. Roosevelt appointed more black Americans to federal posts and agencies than any previous administration, and his relief policies aided jobless and impoverished African Americans. First Lady Eleanor Roosevelt in particular cultivated the goodwill of African Americans. They responded by breaking from the GOP and heavily favored FDR in the 1936 election, a reversal from 1932 when most black northern voters favored Hoover.[23]

Of course, not all black Americans benefited from FDR's reforms. Some New Deal polices, such as the National Recovery Act (NRA) and Agricultural Adjustment Act (AAA), displaced black workers and farmers. Some New Deal projects, like the Tennessee Valley Authority (TVA), practiced racial segregation. Most notably, not a single piece of civil rights legislation passed Congress during Roosevelt's four terms, and he refused to intervene on behalf of a National Association for the Advancement of Colored People (NAACP)–backed antilynching bill, since it would cost him critical white southern support for his New Deal legislation.[24] Yet Roosevelt's New Deal, for all of its mixed results, began the slow process of breaking black Americans from the Party of Lincoln and increasing the national influence of blacks in American politics.

In retrospect, it is not surprising that at this point in history, black voters began to shift to the Democrats. But in the 1930s, the historical pull of Lincoln and emancipation still lingered, and it took the extreme hardships of the Great Depression, and Republican opposition to New Deal policies that benefited African Americans, to overcome switching support to a Democratic Party that relied heavily upon its white supremacist southern wing. None of this meant black Americans robotically shifted their allegiance from one party label to another. Black Americans still acted in their own organizations and mobilized economically and politically, most notably in the Brotherhood of Sleeping Car Porters (BSCP), which became the most powerful black labor union in the country. Its leader, A. Phillip Randolph, formed a coalition of black organizations and successfully pressured Roosevelt with a threatened March on Washington into creating a federal agency, the Fair Employment Practices Commission (FEPC), to investigate racial discrimination in defense industries that received federal contracts.[25]

The Great Depression and the belief of many Americans that capitalism was beyond repair produced one of the strongest periods of radical support for left-wing parties, most notably the Communist Party. Communists helped extensively with unionizing industries under the Congress of Industrial Organizations (CIO), and workers were organized biracially. The Communist Party also won black support for its outspoken opposition to racial discrimination and its spirited defense of the Scottsboro Boys, eight young black men who in 1931 were convicted of rape in Alabama and sentenced to death. Still, the Communist Party was a class-based party, and despite its direct appeals to African Americans, it fell into the same downplaying of race that the earlier Socialist Party did. Oscar Hunter, a black party member in Chicago, was criticized by white members for making racial appeals when he organized black workers for the party. When Hunter referred to black people as "my people," white party leaders sent another black member to severely chastise him and declare that "there's no such god damn thing."[26]

The influence of black voters grew because hundreds of thousands of African Americans migrated to northern and western cities during World War II looking for work. Black Americans had been migrating out of the South since the Exoduster movement to Kansas in the 1870s, which was a western migration of ex-slaves hoping to become independent farmers, but during World War I, over 300,000 blacks migrated to northern cities to look for jobs in defense and related industries. During the 1940s, the migration exceeded 1.5 million as World War II and the draft created a demand for laborers in the North and West. By 1940, 22 percent of black Americans lived in the North, up from 10 percent in 1910.[27]

These migrations had a noticeable effect on the Democratic Party as southern black migrants exercised the franchise and supported the New Deal. The first major evidence of this change came in the 1944 presidential election, when Roosevelt was looking for a nominee to replace his vice president, Henry Wallace, who party leaders regarded as too liberal. One of the leading candidates, Senator James Byrnes of South Carolina, was vetoed by Ed Flynn, the powerful Democratic Party boss for the Bronx. Byrnes had led a filibuster against an NAACP-backed antilynching bill in 1938, and he condemned the NAACP for its lobbying, declaring that "the Negro has come into control of the Democratic Party." For that reason, Flynn said that Byrnes would cost the Democrats 200,000 black votes in New York City alone. Flynn pushed for—and got—the eventual nominee, Missouri Senator Harry S. Truman, who would eventually succeed to the presidency. Black voters that fall gave Roosevelt a margin of victory in eight states, including Michigan and Maryland. This was a substantial break with the Republican Party, since the GOP nominee, Thomas Dewey of New York, had while he was governor signed into law the first state regulation prohibiting racial discrimination in employment.[28]

A major shift had occurred, with the black vote not only helping to decide a national election, but also determining the vice president (and as fate would have it, the next president). Truman succeeded to the office when Roosevelt died in April 1945, and when facing a tough election campaign against Dewey in 1948, he firmly threw his support behind civil rights forces. Partly his move was political expediency, and partly it was genuine concern over a wave of southern racial violence in 1946. That year, Truman appointed a committee to make civil rights recommendations, and the committee released a report, *To Secure These Rights*, calling for vigorous federal action and legislation against lynching, racial segregation, and disfranchisement. Truman endorsed these recommendations, but none passed the coalition of southern Democrats and conservative Republicans who controlled Congress.[29]

Still, Truman became the first president since Warren Harding to publicly endorse civil rights, and unlike Harding, he did not nuance his comments with nods to opposing "social equality." He spoke before the NAACP in 1947, a first for a U.S. president. Most significantly, he issued Executive Order 9981, which desegregated the U.S. armed forces. This open endorsement of the rights of black Americans enraged white southern Democrats, some of whom bolted from the national party to nominate a States' Rights, or "Dixiecrat" ticket as a third party. Their candidate, Governor Strom Thurmond of South Carolina, showed that although the racist rhetoric of the national parties had declined, it had not inside the South. Thurmond declared at his acceptance speech in Birmingham, Alabama, that "there's not enough troops in the army to force the southern people to break down segregation and admit the Nigra' race into our theaters, into our swimming pools, into our homes, into our churches." His ticket won four traditionally Democratic states in the South, but Truman held enough of the rest to prevent the Dixiecrats from acting as a spoiler in the election.[30]

Truman's election meant that openly endorsing rights for black Americans was not an electoral kiss of death. However, the anticommunist hysteria of the Red Scare and McCarthysim stymied the rhetoric for racial equality in the 1950s. The witch hunts for suspected communists devastated liberal organizations that supported civil rights. Groups like the NAACP purged their membership of alleged communists, which had the effect of deradicalizing much of the civil rights movement. This self-policing did little good, however. Southern segregationists tarred civil rights supporters with the brush of anticommunism to discredit and destroy the movement. In 1950 John Rankin, a Democratic representative from Mississippi, called civil rights activities "part of a communistic program, laid down by Stalin approximately thirty years ago."[31]

Both parties did little to stand up for racial equality in this period. The Republican standard-bearer was Dwight Eisenhower, the hero of World War II who served two terms as president. Eisenhower publicly supported and signed into law the Civil Rights Act of 1957, the first such bill since Reconstruction, but one that did little to register black voters in the South. He sent federal troops to enforce a court order to integrate Central High School in Little Rock, Arkansas, but only after much hesitation and the threat of mob violence. Nor were the Democrats any better. Eisenhower's opponent in both elections was Adlai Stevenson, the Democratic governor of Illinois. Despite his reputation as a liberal, Stevenson chose John Sparkman, an Alabama senator, as his running mate and both men deferred civil rights questions to the states. This timidity was largely to avoid another Dixiecrat walkout, and it meant reversing most of Truman's strong civil rights platform of 1948. Stevenson had better civil rights credentials in in 1965 when his running mate was Estes Kefauver, a liberal senator from Tennessee who, along with fellow senators Albert Gore and Lyndon Johnson, refused to sign the Southern Manifesto, a political declaration of southern senators and representatives who by signing pledged to oppose the *Brown* decision. Neither stance helped Stevenson win against the popular Eisenhower.[32]

It took the mass mobilization of African Americans, on their own and with only limited white support, to keep the issue of racial justice in the spotlight. So began the civil rights movement—even before the *Brown v. Board of Education* ruling by the Supreme Court in 1954, which declared segregated public education unconstitutional. Beginning with lawsuits and boycotts against segregated transportation and culminating in the legislative victories of the Civil Rights Act of 1964 and the Voting Rights Act of 1965, the activists in the civil rights movement used bottom-up pressure and direct action in their mass organizing to force first John F. Kennedy and then Lyndon Johnson (who was more willing than Kennedy) to dismantle legal Jim Crow, bring black Americans into the political mainstream, and end most of the openly racist rhetoric of the segregationists.[33]

As mentioned in the previous chapter, the shift now went toward nonracist rhetoric and the coded language of race, such as Richard Nixon's appeals to "law and order" and Ronald Reagan's denunciations of "welfare queens." But even though racist rhetoric declined and became politically and socially unpalatable, racial "dirty tricks" related to this coded language continued and became part and parcel of modern electioneering.

As mentioned previously, perhaps the textbook example of the modern racial dirty trick came in the 1988 presidential election with the Willie Horton and other related ads involving the Massachusetts furlough program, which GOP strategists effectively used to drive white voters away from Michael Dukakis and into the camp of George Herbert Walker Bush. For the central role that race played in the ad campaign and the cynical way it influenced later election tricks, it merits a thorough examination.

Although the long history of white obsessions over the alleged sexual aggressiveness of black men toward white women laid much of the context

for the effectiveness of the furlough ads, more recent historical develop-
ments also played a role. One of these was anxiety over crime in the
1980s. There had been an undeniable rise in crime in the United States
since the 1960s, and between 1965 and 1970, the number of reported
crimes rose from 4.7 million to 8 million; the number of violent crimes
almost doubled, from 387,000 to 738,000. By 1980, more than a million
violent crimes were reported each year.[34]

Not surprisingly, people blamed everything from poverty to television
for the crime increase. The Supreme Court became a favorite target as it
strengthened the rights of criminal defendants in a series of rulings in the
early and mid-1960s, part of the broader "rights revolution" that included
establishing the right to privacy, upholding the recently passed civil rights
legislation, and striking down racially discriminatory laws. These decisions
predated the rise in crime as well as the urban race rioting of the later
1960s, which led many Americans to make a causal connection linking
the liberal Warren Court, black rioters, and violent crime. These criticisms
of the Court added to already-existing hatred for the justices by southern
segregationists for the *Brown* decision, so these rulings gave them additional ammunition to appeal to Americans on a nonracial issue. Yet race
intertwined with the issue of crime and contributed to the racially coded
law and order rhetoric of Richard Nixon and other conservatives. Race also
became linked to the crime issue by mostly white police departments, for
example, in Detroit in the 1970s, when the affirmative action imposed by
Mayor Coleman Young met severe criticism from the white-dominated
police union, who linked it to Detroit's skyrocketing homicide rate.[35]

Public opinion reflected these worries about crime. By 1969, three out of
four Americans thought the courts were too lax with accused criminals,
and by 1974, that number rose to 82 percent. A growing majority supported the death penalty as well. Adding to the racial tensions over the
issue was the participation of young black men in crime. The Justice
Department's 1974 crime statistics indicated that victims blamed black
men for three out of 10 cases of aggravated assault, four out of 10 rapes,
and six out of 10 robberies. Black men were six times more likely to commit
murder than whites. All of those pointed to an undeniable rise in crime, but
the reality was that the vast majority of the victims of black crime were
black people themselves. Of the 223 murders in Boston in 1973 and 1974,
only 24 involved black men killing whites. Much of the high rate of
black-on-black violence was related to the drug trade in the deteriorating
inner cities, but white politicians exploited the specter of black criminality

to frighten white constituents. In Boston, for example, these fears played into white opposition to court-ordered busing. And just as the split between blacks and organized labor and blacks and Jews over affirmative action played into the hands of conservatives and weakened liberalism, so too did liberals' attempts to rationalize crime and lawlessness with poverty and other sociological explanations.[36]

By the 1980s, black violence and drug use were inseparably linked in the nation's perception of crime. The "war on drugs" actually began during the Nixon administration, in response to rising drug use on college campuses, inner-city neighborhoods, and even the Army in Vietnam. In 1969, Nixon pushed for legislation that created mandatory sentencing guidelines, but much of his proposals were watered down in Congress. He then declared a national drug emergency in June 1971 and focused more on enforcement than treatment. On the state level, Nelson Rockefeller, the liberal Republican governor of New York, embraced mandatory life sentences for drug traffickers, a sign of things to come.[37]

By the early 1980s, the drug war took on added intensity under Ronald Reagan. Federal law enforcement agencies received massive increases in their budgets for narcotics enforcement, while treatment and education programs received major cuts. Much of the administration's focus was on marijuana, but cocaine use had been rising steadily since the mid-1970s, and by 1985, an estimated 25 million Americans had tried it. But it was crack cocaine that became the focus of the 1980s drug war. The cheap high of crack caught on in impoverished black and Latino inner-city neighborhoods, and the drug hit while the ghettos were experiencing a steady drop in blue-collar manufacturing jobs along with high rates of poverty and unemployment. In 1985, the media began to run sensational stories on crack that led to massive—and exaggerated—news coverage by 1986. As crack grew in popularity, urban violence associated with gangs and dealers as they fought over drug markets also rose. While crack use became racialized like welfare and other hot-button political issues, white Americans feared that the drug was spreading out of the ghettos. Media outlets like *Newsweek* claimed that drug use was spreading into white middle-class suburbs. In September 1986, in the midst of this media panic, Congress passed tough antidrug legislation that the president soon signed into law. The new legislation established mandatory minimum sentences determined by drug weight, which included penalizing possession of crack cocaine far more heavily than the same amount of powder cocaine. Congress strengthened the penalties further in 1988. The result was an increase both in incarceration for black men and President Reagan's poll numbers. Meanwhile powder cocaine, associated with suburbia, Wall Street yuppies and other affluent whites, received little attention.[38]

This hysteria over drugs and crime, marinated in age-old perceptions of black criminality and violence, became the national context for the introduction of race into the 1988 presidential campaign. The man largely responsible for manipulating this context was Lee Atwater, a Republican political consultant on George Bush's campaign staff. Atwater, a native of South Carolina, had come of age during the civil rights era. He grew up in segregated Columbia and graduated from all-white high school in 1969. An avid fan of practical jokes, he took this love of trickery to increasingly mean-spirited depths in his career. His political education began in 1971 when he interned for Senator Strom Thurmond, the former Dixiecrat-turned-Republican. His less savory schooling in dirty tricks began in 1973, when he met a young Texan named Karl Rove, who, among other things, stole a political opponent's stationary and sent out falsified letters on it.[39]

Atwater met George Bush when he was still in the College Republicans and Bush was chairman of the Republican National Committee (RNC), beginning a political relationship that would last the rest of Atwater's life. Other political associations he developed in the early 1970s included Harry Dent, the architect of Nixon's "southern strategy." He managed his first major political campaign in 1974, the unsuccessful bid of Carroll Campbell, a Republican state legislator in South Carolina, to become the lieutenant governor of the state. He was more successful two years later, when he managed Campbell's election to the South Carolina state senate.[40]

Atwater's experience was shaped by the difficulties Republicans had in winning elections in the 1970s South, when many conservative Democrats and segregationists had not yet switched their allegiance to the GOP. He said, "Republicans in the South could not win elections by talking about issues. You had to make the case that the other candidate was a bad guy." He honed this negative campaigning, albeit in a nonracial way, when he served on the campaign staff for Strom Thurmond's successful 1978 reelection.[41]

Atwater's first real use of a dirty trick involving race and religion came in 1978, when Campbell ran for the fourth congressional district in South Carolina against Max Heller, a Democrat and the popular mayor of Greenville. An independent candidate emerged who got on the ballot via a petition. The third candidate was Don Sprouse, a high school dropout

and tow-truck driver who had been legally feuding with Heller's administration over the city's refusal to contract his wrecker service. Sprouse
focused his attacks entirely in Heller, and two days before the election, he called a press conference, blasted Heller for refusing to "believe
Jesus Christ has come yet," and declared that a Jew should not represent
the district. Sprouse even defended Campbell, mentioning his Episcopalian
faith. Campbell won the election.[42]

Campbell, who publically condemned Sprouse's statements, had com-
missioned a poll that summer indicating that that specifically worded
charge—that Heller did not believe in Christ—would cripple Heller's campaign. Atwater denied any involvement with Sprouse, but he reportedly
bragged years later that he leaked the poll to him, even though Campbell
and Sprouse denied the charge. The anti-Semitism was particularly vicious
since Heller had been born in Austria and fled his Nazi-occupied homeland
in 1938. Lee Bandy, a political writer for the *State*, a South Carolina
newspaper, said that "none of us believed" the denials and that "Lee
Atwater did not leave his fingerprints on his dirty tricks."[43]

Sensing how effective the issues of race, religion, and ethnicity were to
voters, Atwater made his attacks more direct in the 1980 congressional
elections. Atwater worked as a pollster for Representative Floyd Spence, a
Republican running for re-election in the second district in South Carolina.
His opponent was Tom Turnipseed, a state senator and former George
Wallace aide who had shifted toward liberalism in the years since the
1968 election. Atwater utilized telephone "push polling" techniques that
suggested Turnipseed was a member of the NAACP. These "push polls"
were leading questions designed to raise unsubstantiated, often blatantly
false doubts about a candidate in voters' minds, such as asking, "Would
you be more likely to vote for this candidate if you knew he belonged to
the NAACP?" Turnipseed had high negative ratings and was likely to lose
the election anyway, but Atwater added to his infamy with an exchange
he had with the Democrat concerning the polling. Turnipseed had run in
the Democratic gubernatorial primary in 1977 but withdrew for health reasons. He publicly revealed he had received treatment for depression as a
teenager, including electroshock treatments. While his treatment was public knowledge, it did not stop Atwater from illegally obtaining Turnipseed's
medical records from the University of North Carolina Hospital. During
the 1980 campaign, when Turnipseed publicly accused Atwater of the push
polling, Atwater responded, "What do you expect from someone who was
hooked up to jumper cables?" Although it had little outcome on the

election, which ended in Spence's re-election, the "jumper cable" remark added to Atwater's unseemly reputation and overshadowed the push-polling that Atwater used against Turnipseed.[44]

Atwater came on the national scene after Ronald Reagan's 1980 election victory, when Thurmond used his influence with James Baker, Reagan's chief of staff, to give Atwater a job in the Office for Political Affairs. His job was funneling loyal campaign workers into political patronage jobs, which built him a base in the administration. This included black appointees, even black Democrats whom Atwater passed off as Republicans. His political education continued as he befriended former president Richard Nixon, perhaps the epitome of the political dirty trickster.[45]

Atwater's conception and use of race as political force came into focus for the 1984 campaign. Borrowing from fellow South Carolinian Harry Dent, Atwater developed his own strategy for 1984. He outlined it in March 1983 in a 72-page single-spaced memo entitled "The South in 1984." It involved uniting white voters, specifically two traditional white groups in the South, the country-club set of Republicans and the populists, who leaned Democratic. His goal was to get the populists to vote for the GOP and not ally with the third group, black voters, who would vote Democratic. Black outreach would take a back seat—if any seat at all—in the 1984 election, and the focus would be entirely on building up a solid bloc of white voters to carry the South. The unstated implication, of course, was that racial appeals would be the glue to hold these two different social classes of whites together. After all, that is what Nixon did to undercut Wallace in the South in 1968, with the Republican's attacks on court-ordered school desegregation plans.[46]

Atwater showed a key ability to micromanage the most minute and seemingly trivial racial details, recognizing that in the era of television and the mass media, visual symbolism mattered. For example, when Reagan appeared in San Antonio, Texas, in May 1983, Atwater wrote a memo indicating that if the president ate a tamale, it should be dehusked before being given to him, to avoid an embarrassing repeat of President Gerald Ford at the Alamo in 1976, whom Atwater felt had alienated Latino voters when he attempted to eat a tamale still wrapped in its corn husk.[47]

Atwater's political education included being schooled by political masters like Nixon and Dent, but as he came into his own in the Reagan White House, he also began to associate with the next generation that would benefit from his expertise. This included his early association with Karl Rove, as well as not one but two future presidents. His relationship with George

Herbert Walker Bush began when Atwater was in college, but it grew in the 1980s. Bush himself had little solid political ideology, a fact that was famously shown in 1980 when he reversed himself on abortion rights to become Reagan's running mate. Distrusted heavily by Reagan conservatives, Bush was by no means a certainty for the 1988 nomination. Atwater's courting of Bush developed in full after the 1984 re-election of Reagan, when Bush began building the staff he needed for his 1988 campaign. This political partnership led to George W. Bush being appointed to Atwater's staff, beginning another political relationship that would have a long-term influence on U.S. politics.[48]

As the 1988 campaign began, Atwater had help from other operatives in the Bush campaign. One who would play a major role was Roger Ailes, who had worked on the Nixon campaign in 1968. Ailes had reinvented Nixon for television in that campaign, and 20 years later, he was brought on to work with Atwater to do the same for the vice president. Atwater told a reporter that Ailes "has two speeds. Attack and destroy." Ailes demonstrated his ruthlessness when he and Atwater went negative against Bob Dole, the Republican Senator from Kansas and Bush's main rival in the GOP primaries. Ailes created the negative "Straddler" ad, which portrayed Dole as waffling on key issues, especially tax increases. The ad likely did not make a key difference in the race, but the media perceived that it helped defeat Dole in the New Hampshire primary and derail his campaign, an image reinforced when Dole angrily told Bush on live television to "stop lying about my record."[49]

With two seasoned political operatives on the Bush team, both skilled at creating negative, disabling ads, the only thing missing was an issue. When Michael Dukakis won the Democratic nomination, Republican aides scoured his home state of Massachusetts to find any morsel of controversy in the governor's record and life history—and in his wife Kitty's as well—to exploit. What they found was a local political issue that would soon become the ugliest racial controversy of the election and make the 1988 campaign the most racially charged in 20 years.[50]

The story of William R. Horton Jr., for purposes of the election, began October 26, 1974, when during an armed robbery he stabbed a 17-year-old gas station attendant named Joseph Fournier to death in Lawrence, Massachusetts. Horton, a black man, served 10 years for first-degree murder and then fled the state while out on a weekend furlough. In April 1987, he broke into the home of Clifford Barnes and Angela Miller, an engaged white couple in Maryland. He assaulted Barnes, tied him up, and then raped Miller twice. After being terrorized by Horton for 12 hours, Barnes escaped and contacted the police. Horton was arrested after a chase and shoot-out. He was charged by the state of Maryland with 18 crimes, including rape and kidnapping. He received two consecutive life terms and 80 additional years.[51]

In the wake of Horton's crime spree, four women, including Fournier's sister, began a petition drive to ban furloughs for first-degree murderers. Dukakis had not begun the furlough program; it was actually initiated by Republican governor Francis Sargent in 1972. Dukakis did support the program, and in 1976 vetoed a bill that would have banned furloughs for first-degree murderers, thus paving the way for Horton's own weekend pass. Massachusetts newspapers ran stories on the petition drive, which was gaining momentum as 1988 began. One of the newspapers, the *Lawrence Eagle-Tribune*, even won a Pulitzer Prize for its coverage of the Horton story. The publicity convinced Dukakis to reverse himself and not oppose a ban on furloughs for murderers. He did not help his image in the press when he handled poorly public confrontations with furlough opponents, including the mother of a murder victim.[52]

The reality of the furlough program was less cut and dried then it seemed. On the surface, it seemed as if Massachusetts was a bastion of liberal permissiveness on the issue of violent crime. Yet first-degree murderers in Massachusetts served on average over 19 years, as opposed to the national average of 11 years for a first-degree murderer. Massachusetts did not have the death penalty but did have life without parole, which was responsible for the increase in time served. In another state, Horton would likely have already been paroled for the 1974 murder. Forty-five other states, as well as the federal government, had furlough programs. The Massachusetts program was in fact modeled after a furlough program that had been signed into law by no less of a conservative than California's Governor Ronald Reagan. Dukakis, who preferred (indeed, epitomized) cool reason in both his administration and political campaigning, resisted calls to end the program and cited academic studies that indicated the furloughs helped rehabilitate prisoners back into society and maintain order in prisons. On violent crime, Dukakis had an impressive record. Violent crime had dropped 13 percent in the state during his administration, drug convictions had increased fivefold, and the homicide rate was the lowest of the major industrial states.[53] But such statistics mattered little compared to the compelling story of a convicted black murderer terrorizing a white suburban couple, a nightmare tailor-made for a Hollywood script.

On the campaign trail, it was not the Republicans who first brought up Horton and the furloughs. That dubious honor went to Senator Albert Gore, Jr., of Tennessee, one of Dukakis's primary opponents in 1988. Gore brought it up at a campaign stop in April in New York, but he did not mention Horton's name or race. However, the story had already been reported in the mass media, so no explicit mention of race was necessary. After the Bush campaign saw the negative reaction that the Horton issue had on two focus groups of Reagan Democrats in New Jersey and Alabama, Bush began in June to mention the furlough program in speeches and referred specifically to Horton's rape and assault on the Maryland couple. Dukakis did not respond, deferring responses to his campaign manager, Susan Estrich.[54]

Bush reportedly was reluctant to use the furlough issue in such a negative way and had to be convinced by Atwater, who showed him tapings of the focus groups. Bush, too, made no mention of Horton's race. Ironically, racial issues were one of the few things that Bush had showed consistency on in his political career. When in 1964 he ran against Senator Ralph Yarborough, a Democrat, he opposed the Civil Rights Act of 1964, which Yarborough had supported. When Bush ran for a U.S. House seat in 1966, he reversed himself, defeated a racist Democratic opponent, and won two-thirds of the black vote in his Houston district. He then firmly joined the pro–civil rights wing of the GOP, working with Democrats on these issues and supporting Nixon's Philadelphia Plan that created federal affirmative action programs. He even defied his constituents on civil rights issues, such as in 1968 when he voted for the Open Housing Act. This vote took considerable political courage, since Bush then had to face a crowd of 400 hostile constituents when he returned to his Houston for a town hall meeting. He defended his vote, reminding the angry crowd of returning black veterans from Vietnam who would then be denied the right to live where they chose. Bush said he "would die first" before supporting such a policy. He won re-election.[55]

Yet when Atwater, Ailes, and others met with Bush at Kennebunkport, Maine, to show him the tapings of the focus groups, Bush's only hesitation did not concern the ethics of using the Horton issue in a racially negative way, but instead his fear that it would backfire on the campaign. The bigger concern was Bush's poll numbers, which showed Dukakis with a 70 percent favorable rating versus Bush's 53 percent. Political expediency won out, and Bush, who had also been hammered by Bob Dole in the GOP primary over the Iran-Contra affair, acquiesced to Atwater and Ailes. Ailes told a reporter that "the only question is whether we depict Willie Horton with a knife in his hand or without it."[56]

As a Republican insider, Bush certainly knew the value of focus groups. Since 1976, the GOP had aggressively pursued and funded market research to determine the public's mood and manipulate the media. This process began with Nixon and advisors like Ailes, but became a science in the post-Watergate era. Between 1977 and 1984, various GOP committees raised $767 million to the Democrats' $201 million, which gave the Republicans a huge fund to draw on to hire media consultants and conduct research. The Democrats spent only $186,000 to conduct four polls from 1977 to 1984, while to monitor public opinion, the Republican National Committee spent more than $100,000 a month in the same period. This included hiring market research firms to conduct focus-group testing to create and gauge the effect of positive and negative advertisements. The disparities were still apparent in 1988, when the Democrats had two staffers devoted to research compared to 35 for the GOP.[57]

For Atwater, though, this was 1988, an entire generation after the civil rights movement and the resulting inability to make crude racial appeals to win white voters. It was not 1964, so any appeals had to be more subtle, using the coded language that developed during the Nixon era. Atwater summed up this situation in an interview he gave in 1981. He said that Reagan's southern strategy did not depend on the old Harry Dent and Nixon approach of opposing the Voting Rights Act. Economic issues, he said, replaced those racial ones, but the message was still there. Atwater declared that:

[B]y 1968 you can't say "nigger"—that hurts you. Backfires. So you say stuff like forced busing, states' rights, all that stuff. You're getting so abstract now [that] you're talking about cutting taxes, and all these things you're talking about are totally economic things and a by-product of them is [that] blacks get hurt worse than whites. And subconsciously maybe that is part of it. I'm not saying that. But I'm saying that if it is getting that abstract, and that coded, that we are doing away with the racial problem one way or the other. You follow me—because obviously sitting around saying, "we want to cut this," is much more abstract than even the busing thing *and* a whole hell of a lot more abstract than "Nigger, nigger."[58]

Atwater had difficulty containing his glee at the racial dynamite of the Horton case and even connected it to racial turmoil in the Democratic Party. The public dispute between Dukakis and Jesse Jackson during the primaries carried over into the selection of a vice-presidential running mate for Dukakis, with Jackson considered but not selected for the spot. Atwater equated Jackson with Horton when the black preacher appeared at Dukakis's home during the selection process, commenting that "maybe he'll put this Willie Horton guy on the ticket after all is said and done." Comments like this, which equated the most powerful black man in the Democratic Party to a rapist and murderer, made Atwater's later comments that the furlough and Horton issues had "nothing to do with race" ring particularly hollow.[59]

One part of the attacks on Dukakis was for Bush to hit the furlough issue without mentioning race, even if Horton's name was mentioned, which Bush did for the first time on June 22 in Louisville, Kentucky. The widespread media coverage of the Horton case, including a *Readers' Digest* story in June on the furlough program, aided Bush in this area. Bush could then claim the issue was crime, not color. To shield the Bush campaign from accusations of racism, Atwater even hired Ray Charles to perform at the Republican National Convention.[60]

The second part of the attacks was the airing of a television ad attacking the furlough program. Sig Rogich, a Bush staffer working with Atwater, flew to Provo, Utah, to oversee the filming of the ad. Using Brigham Young University students in rented prisoner uniforms, Rogich created the famous "Revolving Door" ad, which showed a stream of convicts moving through a revolving door at a prison. The voice-over mentioned Dukakis's vetoes of the death penalty and mandatory sentences for drug dealers, as well as blamed him for "his revolving door prison policy" of weekend furloughs. The ad mentioned Horton's crimes without mentioning him by name, and the final commercial had two black, one Hispanic, and 16 white convicts. But the racial message was still subtly inserted in the ad. The black-and-white ad featured the convicts walking with their heads down, and only one convict—one of the black ones—looked up at the camera to make eye contact with the viewer. As reporter Sam Donaldson noted, the ad "was calculated to emphasize the one African-American here."[61]

The GOP subcontracted out the more overt racial parts of the Horton issue. The allegedly independent National Security Political Action Committee (NSPAC) created two ads on the furlough issue. The ads were created by Larry McCarthy, Floyd Brown, and Jesse Raiford, former Ailes employees now working outside the campaign. One of the ads was the "Weekend Passes" ads, which criticized Dukakis's record on crime and used Horton's mug shot, referring to him as "Willie" Horton, the moniker that the murderer would be known by during the campaign. The ad and its visual reference to Horton's race ran only on cable television for two weeks but received major coverage in the news media, which showed clips from the ad as examples of the campaign's negativity.[62] Of course, this also meant massive (and free) advertising for the Bush campaign.

Another PAC spent $2 million to send Cliff Barnes and Angela Miller, the couple attacked by Horton, on a speaking tour that included appearances on *Geraldo*, the *Oprah Winfrey Show*, and other talk shows. Barnes even starred in a radio ad in which he claimed that "Michael Dukakis and Willie Horton changed our lives forever." While the Bush campaign never officially used Horton's mug shot, some state Republican organizations did, placing his image next to Dukakis's and thus making Horton his de facto running mate. A Maryland GOP fundraising letter asked if Dukakis and Horton were "your pro-family team for 1988."[63]

The claims by Atwater and Ailes that they were independent of these PACs were disingenuous at best. Aside from the Ailes connection, other links existed. Jim Baker, Bush's campaign manager, requested that the PACs withdraw one of the ads, but he did so well into its run. In a postelection investigation by the Federal Election Commission, the head of one of the PACs said that Baker had veto power over their ads. One of Ailes's associates actually passed a copy of the "independent" Horton ad to the television talk show the *McLaughlin Group*, which then aired the ad. Atwater relished any chance to mention Horton, such as when a phone interview with the convicted murderer aired, in which Horton said he supported Dukakis. Atwater spun this as "Willie's endorsement" to reporters, and said, "I don't know if Dukakis would let him out, but I think there would be a better chance." Perhaps the clearest link came from Roger Stone, a GOP operative and Atwater friend. Stone recalled Atwater showing him the independent Horton ad and declaring that he had secured financial backers to air this ad separately from the campaign. When Stone advised Atwater that the ad was a mistake based on its racist tone and pointed out that the furlough issue alone was eroding Dukakis's lead, Atwater dismissed Stone as a "pussy."[64]

Ironically, there *was* a potentially even more damaging crime issue than Horton that the Bush people could have used against Dukakis. In this case, a murderer pardoned by the governor went out and committed another murder. The murderer, however, was white. After the election, *New York Times* columnist E. J. Dionne asked Atwater why he did not use this in an ad campaign, since it involved a murder rather than a rape and did not have the racial element. Atwater claimed he did not know about the case until after the election, and if he had known, he would have used it. Such a claim was hard to believe, given the budget and staff Atwater had at his disposal to accumulate dirt on Dukakis, which included six researchers going through 25 years of Massachusetts newspapers, accumulating 135,000 quotes, and even uncovering an antiwar letter Dukakis had submitted to the Brookline City Council in 1949.[65] For Atwater to claim he knew nothing about the white murderer before the election with that level of research and then to be confronted about it by a newspaper reporter strains credibility. More likely, he passed on using this issue because it *didn't* deal with race. It simply lacked the explosive combination of race, interracial rape, and appeals to white male voters to protect their wives and daughters from the mythical "black beast rapist," a fear that that had compelled white men of previous generations to form mobs to burn, hang, and torture black men to death.

Whatever damage the ads did to Dukakis, his complete lack of damage control made them even more effective in derailing his campaign. He asked fellow governor Mario Cuomo what to do about the ads, and the New York governor advised him to ignore them. Dukakis later said that "was the worst advice he had ever given me." Dukakis's belief that the furlough issue—which had already won a newspaper a Pulitzer Prize before he was even nominated—would not be a major campaign issue was seriously misplaced. Dukakis's lack of response showed on the Pledge of Allegiance, another controversy that Bush and Atwater hammered him with. As governor in 1977, Dukakis vetoed a bill requiring teachers to recite the Pledge in class. He did so because he had been advised by the state's attorney general that such a bill would be held unconstitutional under a prior Supreme Court ruling, but Bush used the issue to portray the governor as an unpatriotic liberal. When Dukakis did respond to these issues, it was often too little, too late. As Atwater said, "we never could have done it without Dukakis."[66]

The media during the 1988 campaign did little to investigate the links between Atwater, Ailes, and the Willie Horton ads. Democratic staffers and politicians, including Tom Turnipseed, urged reporters to investigate the unsubstantiated rumors and links between the PACs and the Bush campaign, but none showed any interest. Moreover, the repeated coverage of the ads by the news media made sure that even a limited-release or regional ad would receive repeated nationwide coverage.[67]

Bush and his team continued to deny during the election that there were any racist overtones to his campaign. When the Dukakis campaign levied that charge in October, Bush angrily denied it and said that the charge of racism was "some desperation kind of move." Bush rather tellingly did not distance himself from the controversial PAC ads and said that he did not mind the ads using his photograph. What aided Bush in his denials of racism was a clumsy attempt by the Dukakis campaign to respond to the furlough ads. The Democratic response was a television ad called "Furlough from the Truth," about Angel Medrano, a federal convict who escaped from a halfway house and murdered a pregnant woman. The ad included pictures of the Hispanic murderer and the victim in a body bag. The ad did not mention Medrano by name, but it still invited a counter-charge of racism as well as hypocrisy. Moreover, the Democrats could not link Bush directly to Medrano's furlough, so the ad did nothing to help Dukakis.[68]

Dukakis's poll numbers collapsed, and his repeated focus on getting the white Reagan Democrats to vote for him was not working, not in the face of the negative ads. He also did little campaigning in black neighborhoods, which kept black voter turnout low. Dukakis was in effect thrown on a double-edged sword of race. He feared making too many overtures to black voters, especially after his squabbles with Jackson, and thus took them for granted. But the negative ads of the GOP disarmed any attempt he might have made to lure white Democrats back to the fold. Dukakis lost to George Bush, 46 percent to 54 percent. The election was marked by the lowest voter turnout since 1924.[69]

After the election, Atwater continued to deny that he had exploited racial fears with the ads, and Bush in later years angrily denied he had run a racist campaign. Bush looked tough and overcame his image as an effete northeasterner, and had in fact turned that label around and stuck it on Dukakis. Bush had now presented himself as the tough-on-crime president and would take that to new heights—or depths—with the drug war. For the Democrats, the lesson was that they needed a candidate who could handle people like Jesse Jackson but not seem to be coddling black people or their interests in an overt fashion.[70]

No one seemed to love the campaign, despite these denials. Newsweek said "anyone who felt good about American politics after the 1988 presidential campaign probably also enjoys train wrecks, or maybe a day at the beach watching an oil slick wash ashore." Atwater was rewarded with the chairmanship of the Republican National Committee. Yet Horton lingered as an issue into 1989 and cost Atwater. When in February 1989 the president of Howard University named Atwater to the board of trustees, students at the historically black college rebelled. Atwater's appointment was part of his plan to mend fences with the black community after the 1988 campaign and reach out to black voters, but it backfired badly. Protests by Howard students, including over 500 who occupied an administration building, forced Atwater to resign from the board.[71]

Bush developed a better record with African Americans than Reagan had, which was not hard given Reagan's indifference to the black community in general. This did not rest on any concrete reversals of Reaganomics but instead came through meetings with black educators and business leaders, as well as increased enforcement of civil rights laws and supporting sanctions against the apartheid regime in South Africa, something Reagan had opposed. Yet Bush's overtures, and Atwater's Operation Outreach to racial minorities, were rocked by continuing racism among the growing southern wing of the GOP. The highest-profile incident of this was when David Duke, a former grand wizard of the Ku Klux Klan, won election to the Louisiana state legislature as a Republican. Atwater opposed Duke and tried to expel him from the party, but the interference backfired and aided Duke's victory. Duke went on to run in Louisiana's open primary for governor, where he placed first with a plurality. In the runoff, he lost to Edwin Edwards by a 61–39 margin, but he still received 55 percent of the white vote.[72]

In other southern political races, Republicans with longer and more credible establishment ties to the GOP also used racial wedge politics to their advantage. Guy Hunt, who won reelection in 1990 as governor of Alabama, used it more subtlety. He ran ads showing his Democratic opponent, Paul Hubbert, with prominent black Democrats, most notably Jesse Jackson. In North Carolina, Republican senator Jesse Helms made far more overt appeals to white voters in his successful re-election. His opponent was Harvey Gantt, the black former mayor of Charlotte. Gantt drew stronger than expected support from white voters, so Helms aired a television ad that showed a white worker crumpling up a job rejection letter and a voiceover declaring that "you were qualified for that job, but it had to go to a minority because of quotas." The attacks on racial quotas and accusations that blacks received preferential treatment differed little from David Duke's own campaigning against affirmative action. Helms had a long history of overt race-baiting, including filibustering both the renewed Voting Rights Act of 1982 and creation of the federal holiday honoring Martin Luther King, Jr.'s, birthday.[73]

Atwater's death from brain cancer in 1991 robbed the GOP of their greatest political strategist, but the presence of people like Helms in the party meant that racial wedges would still be used in campaigns. Atwater's influence lived on in future campaigns, consciously or unconsciously. For the Democrats, that influence meant learning the lessons of 1988. When Bill Clinton, the Democratic governor of Arkansas, announced his candidacy for president in late 1991, he hired James Carville as his top political consultant. Carville utilized the same kinds of dirty tricks as Atwater, for example, planting rumors and using personal issues to drive up an opponent's negatives, which is what he did when he successfully managed Robert Casey's election to the governorship of Pennsylvania. Mindful of the importance of the black vote to the Democrats, he avoided the kind of nasty racial appeals of the GOP, but other issues like gender were acceptable, as was seen when he handled the Gennifer Flowers sexual accusations levied against Clinton.[74]

Bush had his own problems on race that undid any efforts by the GOP at outreach. When Thurgood Marshall, the first black Supreme Court justice, retired in 1991, Bush nominated Clarence Thomas, the conservative protégé of Reagan civil rights head William Bradford Reynolds, to replace him. Replacing the attorney who argued for the *Brown* plaintiffs with a black neoconservative opposed to affirmative action did not increase Bush's appeal in the black community. On that contentious issue, Bush also burned any bridges with blacks to shore up white conservative support. Twice he vetoed civil rights legislation that he said would "lead to more quota hiring of minorities and women." This came at the same time Jesse Helms was running his own controversial ad on affirmative action, which linked Bush even more indelibly to race-baiting. Then in April 1992, the Los Angeles riots broke out after a jury acquitted four white police officers of beating Rodney King, a black motorist. The videotaped beating had been widely played around the world. The verdict triggered rioting in South Central Los Angeles, leading to 60 deaths. Bush vacillated on his response, and some of his aides wanted him to exploit the riots to scare white voters to the GOP, in effect making Los Angeles the Willie Horton of 1992.[75]

Clinton was no Dukakis, however. Unlike the Massachusetts governor, Clinton had grown up around African Americans in rural Arkansas. He also showed shades of Atwater in his own cynical manipulation of race. At a Rainbow Coalition speech in the aftermath of the riots, Clinton addressed comments by Sister Souljah, a rap singer who was one of the other speakers. Souljah had given an interview to the *Washington Post* in which she said, "if black people kill black people every day, why not have a week and kill white people?" Although she was quoted extensively about her other thoughts on the riots and retaliatory violence, it was this quote that received all the attention when Clinton denounced it and compared her comments to the racism of the Klan. He said, "if you took the words 'white' and 'black' and reversed them, you might think David Duke was giving that speech." Ron Walters, a Jackson associate, called Clinton's denunciation of Souljah at Jackson's event a rebuke of Jackson, insisting that "this son of bitch . . . was standing up to the left of his party." The press interpreted it as defiance of Jackson as well, with the *Washington Post* describing Jackson as "utterly taken aback." Jackson called the Clinton statement a "very bad judgment" and that Souljah had been "misunderstood" and deserved an apology. What made Jackson supporters angry was that the attack on Souljah—and by extension Jackson—had been planned by Clinton staffers deliberately to appeal to white voters. It seemed to work, since Clinton received praise in the press for his comments.[76]

Clinton's own racial Machiavellianism aside, the governor received help on burnishing his image as a racial moderate from the far right of the GOP. George Bush faced a strong primary challenge from Pat Buchanan, the conservative television commentator who had first cut his teeth politically in the Nixon administration. Buchanan had a long history of opposition to school desegregation and affirmative action, and he attacked Bush for his indecisiveness on affirmative action, accusing him of supporting quotas. Buchanan had also been on record as supporting white immigration and making comments downplaying the extent of the Holocaust. He made appeals to white voters that cast aside the pretense of coded language and led Bush to believe he would be a fringe candidate, but he stunned the president by almost winning the New Hampshire primary. While much of that was a protest vote against Bush, Bush refused to attack Buchanan as a racist, and when he defeated his challenger, he placated Buchanan with a primetime speech slot at the Republican National Convention in Houston.[77]

Buchanan's speech set the tone of the convention. He attacked Bill and Hillary Clinton for their alleged support for "abortion on demand . . . homosexual rights . . . [and] women in combat units," but his most memorable comment came on the Los Angeles riots. He praised the 18th Cavalry that restored order during the riots with "M-16s at the ready . . . representing force, rooted in justice, backed by moral courage." He then declared that "as these boys took back the streets of Los Angeles, block by block, so we must take back our cities, and take back our culture, and take back our country." Buchanan made no explicit mention of race, but he did not need to, given the televised coverage of the riots and black rioters' highly publicized beating of Reginald Denny, a white truck driver—who was saved from the attack by four black residents of South Central. Bush did not criticize Buchanan for his "take back our culture" speech, and by letting him set the tone for the convention, gave it his approval.[78] The effect was to frighten moderate voters, and unlike the Willie Horton ad in the general election, Bush and his staffers could not deny or explain away any affiliation with Buchanan.

Clinton, running as a New Democrat, continued to distance himself from black issues in the general election. He made appeals to white Reagan Democrats with televised attacks on welfare. Yet unlike Dukakis, Clinton had been raised in the South and had an ease and familiarity with black voters that the Massachusetts governor lacked. Yet what also aided Clinton was Bush's own floundering on race. Without Lee Atwater to manufacture a racial wedge issue out of affirmative action or the Los Angeles riots, Bush largely stayed away from racial issues, possibly due to reporters' increased sensitivity to racial issues after ignoring them in 1988. On the issue of blacks and crime, which so wounded Dukakis in 1988, Clinton erected his own racial shield. Clinton had in fact suffered his own self-inflicted furlough-style defeat when a murderer he released from prison during his first term as governor killed again, contributing to his unsuccessful re-election. When he ran again in 1982, he publicly apologized, won re-election, and seldom allowed early release after that. During the 1992 campaign, he approved the executions of two inmates in Arkansas. One of them, Rickey Ray Rector, was a black man who had shot and killed a black police officer and then shot himself in the head. The unsuccessful suicide attempt left Rector brain-damaged, but the courts ruled him mentally competent. The execution blunted any soft-on-crime charges by Bush. As the head of the Arkansas chapter of the American Civil Liberties Union (ACLU) said, "if you can kill Rector, you can kill anybody."[79]

On Election Day, the three-way race between Clinton, Bush, and Texas billionaire Ross Perot, who ran under the banner of the independent Reform Party, saw Clinton win with a 43 percent plurality. Clinton's tactics did alienate some black voters, as black turnout dropped from 8.3 million to 8.1 million, yet white turnout rose overall. Still, Clinton's victory rested heavily on his ability to keep black voters in his camp, for Bush still won a plurality of white voters. Perot's candidacy was also key to splitting the white vote and letting Clinton win with a plurality in states with higher black population levels, like Ohio, Louisiana, and Georgia. This has generally been credited as the reason for Clinton's win, combined with the black vote.[80] Unlike Mondale and Dukakis, however, Clinton had achieved the notable victory of being able to manage (and marginalize) Jesse Jackson without appearing to kowtow to him.

If one thought that eight years of Clinton would mean a decline of racial rhetoric in American politics, the end of the twentieth century disabused them of that notion. Clinton's support from African Americans grew to unprecedented heights during his presidency. He had pursued policies like welfare reform in his first term, which harmed blacks but shored up white support. Yet he appointed numerous African Americans to prominent positions in his administration and during the Monica Lewinsky scandal in 1998, which led to his impeachment, black leaders and much of the black community rallied around him. The level of black support and Clinton's own ability to easily associate with black Americans led Toni Morrison, the Nobel Prize–winning writer, to call him "our first black president."[81]

In the 2000 election, it remained to be seen whether the Democrat who inherited this mantle would be subjected to a racial wedge to drive away white voters. In the Republican presidential primaries, the politics of race and racism continued unchecked. The two major candidates were George W. Bush, the governor of Texas and son of the former president, and John McCain, the longtime senator from Arizona. Bush, who had successfully made inroads with Latino and black voters in Texas while governor, refused to take a strong position on affirmative action. His "new kind of Republican" approach took a hit when McCain won the New Hampshire primary, which then sent the candidates into conservative South Carolina. There they entered a state controversy over the Confederate flag, which had been flying for five years over the statehouse in Columbia. Whites defended it as an honor to the Confederacy, while blacks saw it is a symbol of slavery and segregation, a feeling enhanced by the fact that the flag was put up in 1962, at the height of the civil rights movement. Bush deferred the issue to states' rights and said "the people of South Carolina can solve the issue." However, one of his supporters, state senator Arthur Ravenal, blasted the NAACP for its boycott of the state over the flag. Ravenal called the civil rights group the "National Association for the Advancement of Retarded People" and then apologized the next day to people with developmental disabilities for comparing them to the NAACP. Bush merely called the remarks "unfortunate." McCain did a similar evasive dance to avoid offending white primary voters. He had first called the flag in a televised interview a symbol of "racism and slavery" but the next day reversed himself and called it a "symbol of heritage," language frequently used by the flag's defenders. McCain's muddling in the politics of Confederate memory and imagery deepened when liberals attacked him for hiring Richard Quinn, the editor of *Southern Partisan*, a pro-Confederate magazine that downplayed slavery and its effects on blacks. Quinn's statements included endorsements of David Duke and attacks on Martin Luther King, Jr., as well as Nelson Mandela.[82]

South Carolina, which Charleston lawyer James Louis Petigru had said was "too small to be a republic and too large to be an insane asylum" after the state's secession in 1860, continued to show how it could have a broad effect on presidential politics even in 2000, no matter how out of step the state was with the rest of the country. Although the flag issue appeared in other southern states and was not isolated to South Carolina, the issue of interracial dating, oddly enough, entered the campaign due to unique local circumstances. Bush delivered a speech on the campus of Bob Jones University, an evangelical private religious college that had been founded by segregationists who preached against Catholicism and Mormonism, and in 2000 still had a ban on interracial dating even though it admitted black students. The furor over the visit, interpreted as a move to appeal to racial conservatives, stuck with Bush well after the primary. After weeks of dismissing the criticism of the visit, he said—well after the primary— that he should have spoken out against the racial and religious policies of the campus.[83]

The racial dirty trick that South Carolina came to be identified with was a smear campaign that brought back memories of 1988. Rumors in the form of phone calls and fliers spread during the primary that McCain had fathered a black child out of wedlock. The calls were push polls, which was what Lee Atwater had used in his campaigns against Max Heller and Tom Turnipseed. Specifically, the caller asked, "Would you be more or less likely to vote for John McCain if you knew he had fathered an illegitimate black child?" The rumors were apparently based on McCain's daughter, a dark-skinned Bangladeshi child that he and his wife had adopted. McCain accused the Bush campaign of creating these rumors, a charge that Bush staffers denied. In fact, McCain's accusations against Bush backfired, including his insistence on a public apology. The name of the individual who made the ads has never been revealed, but Karl Rove, the Atwater protégé and top Bush advisor, became a top suspect. The presence of these ads in South Carolina, Atwater's home state, added to these suspicions, and journalists like Maureen Dowd would refer to the rumors as being handled by "Atwater acolytes in W.'s camp." Years later, the rumors continued to follow Rove, who in 2010 denied that the rumors came from the Bush camp and instead insisted that they came from a professor at Bob Jones University. The scale of the "whisper campaign," which included use of a phone bank, suggested a far higher level of involvement and funding than a simple disgruntled academic. The source was identified as Richard Hand, a professor of the Bible, but he was linked only to sending an e-mail of the smear, not orchestrating a broader campaign. Racial politics ultimately fell in Bush's favor; he won South Carolina with 53 percent of the vote, and then the GOP nomination and presidency.[84]

The 2000 general election, which pitted Bush against Vice President Al Gore, included an attempt by Gore to exploit racial issues to stimulate black voter turnout rather than woo whites. The issue was the murder of James Byrd, a black man killed in Texas by three white men, who dragged Byrd to death behind a pickup truck. Byrd was killed in 1998, while Bush was governor, and the NAACP created an ad that featured Byrd's daughter criticizing Bush for refusing to support hate crimes legislation. She said that Bush's refusal "was like my father was killed all over again." Bush made his own attempts at black outreach during the election, but he won only 8 percent of the black vote, less than his father or Ronald Reagan achieved. He had more success with Hispanics, winning 31 percent of their vote. But the most controversial part of the election both racially and otherwise, would be in Florida, where the highly contested voting process there included allegations of deliberate purging of black voters from registration rolls, faulty voting equipment in black precincts, and reports of black voters being barred and intimidated from the polls. By the time the Supreme Court issued its ruling in *Bush v. Gore* (2000) that gave the presidency to Bush, many black Americans believed that there was a large-scale program of disfranchisement of African American voters.[85]

As South Carolina showed, racial dirty tricks carried a particular resonance in the South. When the candidate who was the target of the ad was black, as Harvey Gantt learned to his dismay, the ad could be particularly potent. In 2006, Harold Ford, Jr., a black congressman from Memphis, won the Democratic nomination for U.S. Senate to run for the open seat being vacated by Republican Bill Frist, the Senate Majority Leader. Ford had served five terms in the House of Representatives, where he accumulated a moderate voting record. He had voted to ban partial-birth abortion and for a constitutional amendment to outlaw same-sex marriage, and he supported the U.S. invasion of Iraq. He had previously shored up his centrist reputation by unsuccessfully challenging Nancy Pelosi for the House minority leader's position in 2002. Much of this centrism was recognition that outside of heavily black Memphis, he needed white support to win, as Tennessee had only a 16 percent black population.[86]

Ford's family proved to be one of his liabilities. Ford came from a privileged background as the son of Harold Ford, Sr., a U.S. representative, and he won election to his father's congressional seat at age 26. He had an uncle under indictment on federal corruption charges, which brought some negative press to his campaign. Despite charges of privilege and family corruption, Ford clearly was not a left liberal like Jesse Jackson. He was affiliated with (and would become chair after the Senate election) of the Democratic Leadership Council (DLC), an organization of centrist Democrats. Back in 1988, Jackson had criticized Delaware senator Joe Biden for his membership in the DLC, calling them "Democrats for the Leisure Class" who "didn't march in the sixties and won't stand up in the eighties."[87]

Ford faced Bob Corker, the Republican nominee and former mayor of Chattanooga, in a state that had not elected a Democrat to the U.S. Senate since 1990 and in a region that had not sent a black man to the Senate since Reconstruction. Corker ran as an "outsider" in contrast to Ford's Washington experience. It was not Washington or Ford's family that became the lightning rod of the campaign, however, but an ad financed by the Republican National Committee that painted Ford as a liberal. The ad featured a series of actors posing as average citizens being interviewed on the street and commenting sarcastically on Ford's positions on issues. The topics in the ad ranged from national security to the estate tax, but it was one segment in particular that achieved notoriety. The segment featured an attractive white woman, bare-shouldered, who said that she had "met Harold at the *Playboy* party!" She closed the commercial by looking into the camera, winking, and saying "Harold, call me." This *Playboy* comment referred to a visit by Ford to a Jacksonville, Florida, party during the 2005 Super Bowl.[88]

The ad drew swift condemnation. William Cohen, a Republican and former secretary of defense, called it "a very serious appeal to racist sentiment." Lincoln Davis, a conservative Democrat from a rural Tennessee district, blasted the ad and said, "tell Karl Rove we don't want this stuff on TV in Tennessee." The *New York Times* criticized the ad as "sleazy" and "resonating with the miscegenation taboos of Old South politics."

Ford, who was single, defended his visit to the party and said, "I like football, and I like girls." He denied he had ever been to a party at the Playboy mansion, however.[89]

What was generally overlooked in the uproar over interracial sex was the ad's subtle insulting of black voters' intelligence. The only African American in the ad was an actress who began the spot by saying, "Harold Ford looks nice, isn't that enough?" The comment played to white beliefs that black people were superficial voters who supported a candidate based on skin color and appearance, not on substantive issues. The belief that black people were not intelligent voters, which was used in the era of Jim Crow to disfranchise them through literacy tests, understanding clauses, and other mechanisms, continued into the present day. William Mounger, the finance chairman for the Mississippi Republican Party, wrote a letter to Ronald Reagan in 1981 urging him to oppose renewal of the Voting Rights Act. Mounger declared that "black votes are only for sale through government handouts," a statement at once making demeaning generalizations about black voters and tying them to welfare, which in itself was a racialized issue.[90] The RNC ad perpetuated this lingering stereotype of African Americans as easily manipulated voters, although any criticism of that point was overshadowed by the ad's sexual innuendo.

Corker distanced himself from the ad and asked that it be pulled from TV stations. A spokesperson for the Corker campaign called it "tacky, over the top." Ken Mehlman, the chairman of the RNC, defended the ad, declaring that he saw nothing racist about it. In a further blurring of the relationship between "independent" groups and the GOP, the RNC had paid for the ad, but it had been produced by an "independent expenditure group." Thus Melhman claimed he did not have the power to remove the ad. Despite Melhman's claims, the RNC pulled the ad, but it had already received, like the Horton ad, free nationwide coverage.[91]

Ford dismissed the ad, declaring that "you know your opponent is scared when his main opposition against you is, 'My opponent likes girls.'" Despite Ford's bravado, the ad hit anxieties that white Americans—especially white southerners—had about interracial dating. John Geer, a professor of political science at Vanderbilt University, said the ad "makes the Willie Horton ad look like child's play." And like the Horton ad, it had an effect. The election proved to be close, with Corker edging out Ford 51 percent to 48 percent.[92]

The common theme of the ads in the Michael Dukakis and Harold Ford campaigns—black men and white women, whether it be rape or consensual sex—struck the right racial nerves of white voters, as the results of those races show. Yet the opposite, white men and black women, carried far less ability to inflict wounds in a campaign, even in the far more racist days of Thomas Jefferson. Much of this has to do with racial and sexual double standard, whereby access to black women did not threaten the racial and sexual order of white male patriarchy, while black men having access to white women did. Another factor, however, was likely white male titillation about and admiration for a white man enjoying sex with a black woman. As one historian of Jefferson and Sally Hemings noted, despite Federalist anger at Jefferson's relationship with Hemings, it was "highly probable that stories about the president and his beautiful young mistress made many men in the country secretly admire more than revile him."[93] While in racially conservative areas like South Carolina this tactic was less likely to work, as with the McCain rumors in 2000, in a national election the charge of white man and a black woman seemed less threatening to whites, especially white men.

One racial issue in this chapter deserves to be examined separately, away from the chronological narrative and analysis of dirty tricks and campaigns. This issue is a uniquely regional racial issue, specifically the role of the Confederate battle flag and other Confederate imagery in political campaigns. Yet as the South Carolina primary of 2000 showed, the issue could have a significant impact on the national political landscape. However odd it may seem to nonsoutherners, the iconography of the Confederacy—in a region that includes states that honor Robert E. Lee (e.g., Alabama) or still have the Confederate battle emblem on their state flags (e.g., Mississippi)—resonates emotionally with many white southerners and can prove decisive in political contests.

The Confederate battle flag—the blue St. Andrew's cross on a red flag, which is distinct from the Stars and Bars, the standard used by the Confederate government—was never an official flag of the Confederacy. The battle flag, or "rebel flag," became identified with opposition to the civil rights movement in 1948, when delegates from the Dixiecrats, or States' Rights Democrats, gathered in Jackson, Mississippi, and in Birmingham, Alabama, to oppose President Truman's civil rights proposals and nominate segregationist politician Strom Thurmond as their presidential candidate. While not adopted as an official standard of the splinter party, it did become widely identified with the segregationist platform of the Dixiecrats through rallies and use by southern state delegations.[94]

The Ku Klux Klan made heavy use of the flag in the 1950s and 1960s, which added to its association with white supremacy. However, more mainstream white southerners also used the flag as a symbolic image to oppose federal civil rights enforcement, such as its presence during George Wallace's famous "segregation forever" speech and its use by the White Citizens' Councils, composed of middle-class white southerners opposed to the *Brown* decision. Violent resistance to integration, such as the University of Mississippi riot in 1962 over the admission of James Meredith, a black veteran, also included the rebel flag as a central image of that defiance.[95]

It should surprise few, then, that such an image of white supremacy entered political contests, even after the heyday of the civil rights era. Other forms of Confederate imagery also entered political races. In Mississippi in 1982, an open U.S. House race between a white Republican and black Democrat attracted national attention when Webb Franklin, the Republican, released an ad that prominently featured a Confederate statue in front of a county courthouse. The ad included a voiceover that referred to Franklin as a "congressman for us." Franklin insisted that the ad did not have any racist intent, but it was cited after the election—which Franklin won due to high white voter turnout—in a courtroom during a redistricting case in his district as an example of racial bias.[96]

The flag itself became a prominent issue in Mississippi in 2001 during a referendum to change the state flag. The rebel flag had been on the Mississippi state flag since 1894, and after a state Supreme Court ruling in 2001, residents voted in a referendum to keep the old flag or adopt an alternate design without the rebel design. Voters, in a highly charged election that opened up racial and ideological wounds, kept the original 1894 design by a 2 to 1 margin. The issue became a political wedge used by Haley Barbour, the Republican nominee for governor, when he challenged the Democratic incumbent, Ronnie Musgrove, in 2003. Even though Musgrove had remained neutral in the flag debate, Barbour, to win white voters, brought up the two-year old issue, declaring that he was "not in favor of changing it," implying that Musgrove had been. Taking a politically settled issue and reviving it as a racial wedge issue contributed to Barbour's 53-percent victory over Musgrove.[97]

A similar situation developed in Georgia, which had incorporated the rebel flag into its state flag in 1956, during the height of backlash against the *Brown* decision. Governor Roy Barnes worked behind the scenes to convince the legislature to change the flag, a change he pursued to avoid an NAACP-sponsored economic boycott of the state. Barnes worked quietly in hopes of avoiding a nasty and bruising public controversy over the flag, which is exactly what his predecessor Zell Miller experienced in 1993 when he tried to convince the legislature to change the flag. The new Georgia flag that the state adopted in 2001 placed the rebel flag alongside other flags from the state's history, all reduced in size from the size of the rebel flag on the old design. Yet Barnes's hope to avoid fallout from the issue went unfulfilled, as backlash from flag supporters combined with other issues to defeat Barnes and put Sonny Purdue in the governor's office. Perdue, a Republican state legislator, had voted against the flag change and promised voters a referendum on the issue. Perdue's exploitation of the issue gave him support from rural and conservative whites, but he angered supporters of the 1956 flag by introducing a new flag that resembled the old Stars and Bars of the Confederacy but did not restore the St. Andrew's cross. When voters approved the new flag in 2004, the controversy quietly faded away.[98]

As the racial dirty tricks and wedge issues have shown, race can be skill-fully—or crudely—exploited by a candidate or political operative to win white votes. While this strategy was perhaps most famously used against a white man, Michael Dukakis, it also proved effective against black candi-dates by playing to lingering voter discomfort over interracial sex or imply-ing that the black candidate would favor black interests and issues over those of white voters. This latter issue went far beyond racial trickery or wedges, however. The fundamental reluctance of whites to vote for a black candidate, as the next chapter shows, has proven a major obstacle for the viability of black candidates running for office in white-majority areas.

Chapter 3

The "Bradley Effect": Election Outcomes and Race, or Would I Vote for a Black Candidate?

Cornell Belcher, a political pollster who worked on Barack Obama's 2008 campaign, shared a photograph with the *New York Times* at the end of the election. It showed a homemade Confederate flag with the caption, "Rednecks for Obama. Even we've had enough." Belcher said it epitomized a shift he had seen late in the election among white voters who freely admitted racial biases in his polling. These voters moved toward Obama, in effect putting aside their reluctance to vote for a black man out of a deeper concern for the economy and their own pocketbooks. As another pollster put it, "If a house is on fire, the owner does not care what color the fireman is."[1]

Clearly Barack Obama broke a major barrier by becoming the first African American president in U.S. history, a feat he accomplished by winning significant white support. Yet the presence of racial bias among white voters, along with a long-standing historical reluctance by white voters to vote for black candidates, have hampered the election of black officials to statewide offices. While black congressional representatives, mayors, and county and local officials in smaller districts where black populations comprised a majority due to redistricting could win office, the fact that no state had a black majority meant that successful black candidates had to win significant white support. Failure to do so related to the "Bradley effect" or "Wilder effect," after the political campaigns of black politicians Tom Bradley and Douglas Wilder, often in which the candidate's actual vote tally defied polling numbers going into the Election Day, as well as the results of exit polling. In effect, some white voters expressed support for the black candidate to the pollsters but voted for the white candidate in the voting booth. In several well-known races—and in some that were less well known—this phenomenon seems to have held true, but in others it did not. Various factors have historically played in role in the electability of a black candidate, including what *type* of black candidate is running.

In the era of Reconstruction in the 1860s and 1870s, when the first black candidates were elected to office, the victors tended to be in majority black areas. Black political power was concentrated on the local level—in school boards, county offices, and other positions. The only two black U.S. senators of the period, Hiram Revels and Blanche K. Bruce, came from the state of Mississippi, a black-majority state, but at that time state legislatures selected senators. Few blacks served in statewide offices, with the most notable case being P. B. S. Pinchback of Louisiana, who served as acting governor for over a month after the impeachment and suspension of the state's governor in December 1972. Black men nearly always served as junior partners with white Republicans, who held the most important offices. Only in South Carolina, a black-majority state, did black legislators comprise a majority in the state legislature and pick one of their own as speaker.[2]

With the end of Reconstruction and the decline of black political power, the United States did not see viable black candidates return until the twentieth century, especially with the onset of the civil rights movement and mass mobilization of African Americans. But it was not the South, where large numbers of potential black voters resided, where the first black person to win a popularly elected statewide office emerged. That victory occurred in Massachusetts, a state with a small black population. Edward Brooke, who was born and raised in a middle-class black household in Washington, D.C., grew up in that segregated city, graduated from Howard University, and moved to Boston for law school after serving in World War II. He ran twice for the state legislature in the 1950s but lost. Brooke ran as a Republican in heavily Democratic Massachusetts, which proved—along with his race—to be a liability. His identification as a Republican was not unusual for an African American in the 1950s, before the passage of major civil rights legislation and the resulting shift of black voters to the Democratic Party. In 1960, he ran for secretary of state, his first attempt at statewide office in Massachusetts. He lost but won over 1 million votes in a state with 93,000 African Americans. Brooke, since he was running in an overwhelmingly white state, downplayed his race whenever he could, despite being a former National Association for the Advancement of Colored People (NAACP) officer. His image as a deracialized candidate of integration even carried over to his interracial marriage to his Italian wife, who campaigned for him in Italian districts. He criticized fellow Bay State politician Henry Cabot Lodge for publicly boasting that Richard Nixon would appoint the first black Cabinet member if elected.[3]

Brooke made a further name for himself in state politics under Republican governor John Volpe, who appointed Brooke to the Boston Finance Commission, an office he used to attack corruption in the city's politics. Against the wishes of Grand Old Party (GOP) leaders, he then ran in 1962 for attorney general and won his first statewide office. In 1963, he feuded with the NAACP and other civil rights groups over a school boycott they had called against de facto segregation in the Boston schools. While Brooke made it clear to white voters he was not beholden to civil rights groups, he did say that he supported demonstrations if they were within the law and had been trying to mediate between the Boston School Committee and civil rights groups, but the committee, chaired by the soon-to-be notorious anti-integration activist Louise Day Hicks, had spurned his offers. Civil rights activists in Roxbury, a heavily black Boston neighborhood, called Brooke an Uncle Tom, especially when he said that "boycotts, sit-ins, and demonstrations . . . merely intensify the resentment of the population . . . and undermine the best interests of the Negro community." Brooke said that he did support busing due to the racial segregation that plagued Boston schools, but he could not support the boycott because it was illegal. Brooke carved out a stance as a gradualist and pragmatist on racial issues, a strategy that put him at odds with activists but reflected the realities of being a black Republican in a heavily white and Democratic state.[4]

Brooke did secure a solid record on some civil rights issues, such as opposing a ban on busing, supporting abolition of literacy tests for voting, and filing briefs in support of the Fair Housing Law, a Massachusetts law that banned discrimination in renting. He also filed a brief in support of the Voting Rights Act of 1965, a brief that was signed by 19 other states and became part of *South Carolina v. Katzenbach*, the case that upheld the constitutionally of the act. He also opposed the Goldwater Republicans in the GOP and their opposition to federal civil rights laws, lamenting their views for the difficulty they caused black recruitment in the GOP. "We [the GOP] missed a historic opportunity" on civil rights [in 1964], Brooke said. His actions did not hurt his popularity, and he won a comfortable reelection in 1964 despite the Democratic landslide of President Lyndon Johnson that year.[5]

Some of Brooke's success appeared to be due to a "guilt factor" with white voters, or whites voting for Brooke *because* he was black. Carl Rowan, a black journalist, said that for white Bostonians, "electing Brooke is a much easier way to wipe out guilt feelings about race than letting a Negro family into the neighborhood or shaking up a Jim Crow setup." Such sentiment can explain why Brooke won large majorities in the same districts that also elected Louise Day Hicks, who drew her political strength from the antiblack sentiments of working-class whites. Brooke himself accused his opponents of bringing up the race issue and that they "always saw to it" that voters knew the light-skinned Brooke was black. By May 1966, eight in ten Massachusetts voters were aware of Brooke's race. Brooke's efforts to not be "the Negro candidate" carried over to his demeanor and white perceptions about his light skin color, which aided him in not appearing "too black" for heavily white Massachusetts. As a Harvard government professor said, "he's more white than many white persons in this state in appearance, mannerism, and philosophy."[6]

Brooke ran for the U.S. Senate in 1966, and angered conservatives with his endorsements from the liberal Americans for Democratic Action, as well as his opposition to the Vietnam War and support for antipoverty programs and Medicare expansion. He won the GOP nomination anyway and faced Endicott Peabody, a former governor. The campaign received considerable national press coverage due to Brooke's race, and he was forced to deal with a potential white backlash due to the prominence of "black power" as a rallying cry in the media and the resulting anger against it and the "long, hot summers" of racial rioting that escalated in 1965 with the Watts riot in Los Angeles. Reporters picked up on antiblack comments from white voters and ran them as examples of what Brooke had to deal with come November. Being a black candidate, some feared, would cost him Irish American votes in Boston. Yet Brooke's rulings as attorney general had angered civil rights advocates, and some white liberals and black voters had qualms about him for that, and favored Peabody, who came from a strongly pro–civil rights family. But when she campaigned for him in their neighborhoods, his Italian wife helped defuse Italian American voters' hostility towards blacks, or at least towards Brooke. As for federal involvement in civil rights, Massachusetts voters were evenly split on the question of whether the government was doing "too much" or "too little" for black Americans. On more specific civil rights issues, however, the state's voters gave more conservative answers. Most of the voters disapproved of withholding state funds from racially imbalanced schools and opposed fair housing legislation. But when asked specifically if they thought Brooke was doing "too much" or "too little," only 4 percent thought the former and 20 percent the latter.[7]

Brooke complained about the backlash issue and said that he was not "running as a Negro," but he took pains to denounce Stokely Carmichael, the civil rights activist who popularized the black power slogan, when Carmichael came to Boston during the campaign. He also criticized Lester Maddox, the segregationist governor of Georgia, as a "white power" extremist, in effect saying that Carmichael was a racist on par with Maddox. With two pro–civil rights candidates running, other issues received attention, such as the candidates' differences on Vietnam (Peabody was prowar while Brooke was not). Brooke called Vietnam "the most important issue in my campaign," and that the issue of race "was largely unspoken." Brooke was able to win support for his calls for peace negotiations when he won key support from ministers and from a Harvard professor who had run in the primary.[8]

The crime issue, which ironically would be used 22 years later to defeat Massachusetts's own Michael Dukakis in his bid for the presidency, actually helped the black candidate in this case. Brooke's record as attorney general of fighting corruption helped with the voters, but Peabody has his own problems with crime. He had advocated the repeal of the death penalty in the state during a period in which several policemen were killed by criminals, which fed perceptions that he was soft on crime. Peabody's primary contest to get the Democratic nomination also left him with depleted campaign coffers, and he trailed Brooke in campaign expenditures.[9]

Brooke won the election with over 1.2 million votes, 400,000 more votes than Peabody received, and did well in the white ethnic neighborhoods of the Irish and Italians. Brooke did not experience the white backlash that some observers expected since he was running against a white Democrat who had at least as strong of a pro–civil rights record as he did. As one political commentator noted, "Peabody couldn't take advantage of the backlash because his record was even more liberal than Brooke's." While Brooke's conscious efforts at assimilation and downplaying race helped, the specifics of state politics in liberal Massachusetts, a heavily Democratic state, also aided his victory.[10]

As the only African American senator, Brooke served as the de facto senator for all of the nation's minority groups. He supported civil rights measures, worked to defeat antibusing legislation, and cosponsored the Fair Housing Act of 1968 with Walter Mondale. Brooke also served on the President's National Advisory Commission on Civil Disorders, popularly known as the Kerner Commission. The commission investigated the race riots and urban civil disorder of the 1960s and issued its report in 1968 that blamed poverty and white racism for the violence and famously stated that the United States was "moving toward two societies, one black, one white, separate and unequal." He also often clashed on civil rights issues with his fellow Republican Richard Nixon during the latter's presidency. He backed Judge Arthur Garrity's controversial decision to begin court-ordered busing in Boston and helped convince officials in Gerald Ford's Justice Department to not support the antibusing plaintiffs.[11]

Brooke won reelection in 1972, but 1978 proved to be a more difficult challenge. The election year opened with him facing a nasty and well-publicized divorce from his wife, Remigia. Disparities in financial documents in the divorce case and those that Brooke had filed with the secretary of the Senate led to an ethics investigation against him. The Senate Ethics Committee did not file charges, but the bad publicity weakened Brooke. While he had controversially supported busing, other issues such as Brooke's pro-choice stance also hindered him. He faced a primary challenge from Avi Nelson, a conservative radio talk-show host, who raised large sums from out-of-state conservatives. Nelson attacked Brooke for being too liberal on gun control, abortion, and other issues. While Brooke won renomination, he was wounded. He faced Paul Tsongas in the general election, and prominent Democrats—including longtime civil rights supporter and fellow senator Ted Kennedy—campaigned against Brooke, indicating that for Kennedy, party was more important than diversity in the Senate. The reverse was true for Brooke, who received campaign support from Jesse Jackson and Coretta Scott King despite Brooke's Republican affiliation. Ultimately, the fallout from the scandal over his financial records contributed heavily to his defeat, and Tsongas won with 55 percent of the vote.[12]

Brooke did experience a version of the Bradley effect in his defeat. His campaign hired Robert Teeter, a political pollster, to conduct polling for the campaign. Teeter projected a 10-point lead days before the election, although Brooke later said he was skeptical. After the election, the campaign found out that Teeter had skewed the results by hiring young people out of Detroit to make the calls to Massachusetts voters. Brooke said that the callers were "identifiably African American" to the people they called, so many of the respondents said they would vote for Brooke even thought they were not going to. As Brooke explained, "they did not want to appear racist."[13] Whether the voters were voting against Brooke on his race cannot be ascertained, but the exercise showed the problem with polling and its ability to exaggerate poll numbers for a black candidate.

Brooke had been elected largely despite his race, not because of it, and his defeat largely resulted from nonracial issues. The man whom the Bradley effect came to be associated with came from a political background that involved more racial diversity and coalition-building than Brooke had to deal with in Massachusetts. Thomas Bradley, the son of a Texas share-cropper, had been a track star at the University of California at Los Angeles (UCLA) and had worked as both a police officer and a lawyer. He won elec-tion to the Los Angeles City Council in the 1960s, representing a district that was two-thirds nonblack. This meant that from his earliest days in politics, Bradley knew how to reach out to nonwhite voters and build political coalitions. He challenged Sam Yorty, the mayor of Los Angeles, in 1969 in the Democratic primary and lost. Four years later, he developed his "coalition of conscience" of blacks, Hispanics, Jews, and whites, beating Yorty with 56 percent of the total vote. Bradley won 95 percent of the black vote, slightly over half of the Hispanic vote, and almost half the white vote, with strong Jewish support.[14]

Bradley governed Los Angeles in the wake of black power radicalism, and his image as a black moderate helped him keep his coalition together. As the *Wall Street Journal* noted, "Tom Bradley doesn't act like Huey New-ton or an Angela Davis." He hoped to parley his coalition-building skills and nonthreatening demeanor into higher office in California. By the time he decided to run for governor in 1982, two black men had already won statewide office. Mervyn Dymally had won election to the lieutenant gover-nor's office, and Wilson Riles had been elected state superintendent of edu-cation three times. Bradley did not face a major white Democrat in the primary and easily won the Democratic nomination.[15]

Bradley faced George "Duke" Deukmejian, the Republican nominee and state attorney general. He had a relatively liberal record from his time as a state legislator, casting votes for the Equal Rights Amendment and bilin-gual education. This did not bode well for Bradley, since as political scien-tists have noted, black candidates have a much harder time defeating white liberal or moderate opponents than ones who are extremely conservative.[16] Another factor that cast a shadow on Bradley's chances was the range of propositions on the ballot in the general election. These included three propositions to reduce state taxes, as well as bonds for constructing new prisons and other anticrime measures, all of which signaled a potentially high conservative voter turnout in November. Deukmejian, as the attorney general, utilized the crime issue against Bradley, even though the mayor was a former police officer. Bradley's refusal to outline specific programs to fight crime led Deukmejian to hit him as "soft" on crime, and Deukmejian highlighted their respective differences on the death penalty. Bradley also had to deal with unpopular incumbent governor Jerry Brown, who was then running for a U.S. Senate seat against San Diego mayor Pete Wilson. Deukmejian frequently compared Bradley and Brown, especially when they held similar positions on an issue.[17]

Related to crime was Proposition 15, a handgun-control ballot initiative. Bradley supported the proposal while Deukmejian opposed it. This issue, probably more than any other, mobilized high conservative voter turnout in 1982, largely due to a $5 million campaign run by the National Rifle Association (NRA) to defeat the proposal. The NRA campaign included using phone banks where callers reminded voters of Bradley's support for the proposition; in addition, many of the callers made the false claim that Bradley wanted to ban hunting weapons as well.[18]

On the issue of race, the media praised Deukmejian for not using racist tactics, but in the post–civil rights era of 1982, he did use racially charged code words. He frequently said that he was the candidate who "can represent all Californians," which implied that Bradley, as a minority, could represent only minority interests. His campaign also aired radio spots in Southern California that were aimed at older white voters, many of southern U.S. origin. The ad featured the actor Slim Pickens declaring that "Daddy told me never trust a skunk or a politician." "Skunk" is not a well-remembered racial slur today, but it was a derogatory term for blacks used in the South prior to World War II.[19]

Deukmejian's campaign used even more blatant racial material, including ads that foreshadowed future "dirty tricks" like the Willie Horton ad. The racial material included a videotape on crime that featured a black man breaking into the home of a white couple and a black man behind bars. This was released in the guise of an "informational" video by Deukmejian's office of the attorney general instead of as official campaign material. Deukmejian's campaign manager, Bill Roberts, resigned after heavy media scrutiny followed his statement that the Republican would get a 5 percent "race vote," presumably from whites who would vote against Bradley for being black. The final issue came in the last campaign debate, when Deukmejian said that Bradley and Willie Brown, the speaker of the California Assembly, were "allies." While both men were black, they were not close politically and had very different personal and political styles. Deukmejian intentionally raised race as an issue since the confrontational Brown was not popular with many white voters.[20]

Like a lot of black candidates, Bradley had the dilemma of running a campaign that appealed to moderate whites while still holding the enthusiasm of minority and progressive voters. In this area he failed. His moderation and associations with law enforcement and big business made some on the political left in California—a left much stronger in the Golden State than elsewhere—mute their enthusiasm for him. The leftist Democratic Worker's Party (DWP) ran an alternative candidate, Elizabeth Martinez, who pulled 63,000 votes in the general election. With minority groups, Bradley had less-than-stellar support as well. While most Hispanics who voted supported Bradley, many Hispanic voters were not enthusiastic about Bradley and did not vote at all, leading to particularly low Hispanic turnout.[21]

Bradley even failed to mobilize black voters effectively. Here he appeared to make the mistake of taking the black vote for granted as he chased after white voters. He neglected to organize black communities on a grassroots level and did not even bother to open campaign headquarters in many black neighborhoods. He made few speeches directed at black voters or their concerns, and his attempts to avoid race and not address racial issues in the campaign put off many younger blacks. While this was similar to what Brooke did in Massachusetts, he could afford to do since he was in an overwhelmingly white state. In far more racially diverse California, this strategy was a mistake that cost Bradley the high black voter turnout that he needed to win. For example, Alameda County, a strongly Democratic county in the Bay Area, had only a 68 percent voter turnout, and Bradley won it with only 58.9 percent of the vote, no better than Jerry Brown's vote total for the Senate. Postelection surveys indicated only an "average" level of black voting in the contest, and in higher-population black areas, voter turnout even went down from 1978 voting levels.[22]

Still, polls going into Election Day showed Bradley leading by as much as 7 percent. However, 9 percent of the voters fell into the undecided or minor party candidate category, a number that could swing the election either way at the last minute. The Field Institute, which had conducted the poll, also ran an exit survey of 5,000 people as they left the voting stations. Based on these polls, the local media in California projected a win for Bradley, yet Deukmejian won by 93,345 votes out of 7.8 million cast.[23]

The failure of this polling gave birth to the Bradley effect, indicating that majorities for black candidates in pre-election polls are inflated due to white peoples' fears of being considered racist for not supporting a black candidate. What added to the perception of the Bradley effect was that the Field Institute's pre-election surveys for the other statewide elections were all accurate. One problem was the reliance on exit surveys. A large number of older voters in conservative areas refused to give exit interviews on Election Day, which apparently skewed the sample of 5,000 respondents toward Bradley.[24]

The handgun issue has often been cited as the nonracial reason Bradley lost, especially by white Californians eager to deny any charge of racism in the liberal state. Deukmejian supporters and figures in his administration still use this thesis today to deny any racist motivation on the part of any of the white voters in California. They instead portray the election as one of a liberal candidate being defeated, and also point to the defeat of Jerry Brown in the Senate race. While it is true that conservative turnout was mobilized by the NRA campaign, this explanation is overly simplistic. For one, other black candidates did not fare well either in 1982. Wilson Riles, the incumbent state superintendent of education, lost his race to a white opponent, as did two black Republican candidates running for statewide office. Only Allen Broussard, a little-known black candidate, defied the trend and won a seat on the California Supreme Court. Also, white Democrats who supported Proposition 15, such as Democratic attorney general nominee John Van de Kamp, won their elections. In the other Field Institute surveys, the pollsters accurately predicted the outcomes, including the overwhelming defeat of the handgun ban. Only in the governor's election did the discrepancy exist, suggesting race was the differing—or deciding—factor. It became a vicious circle for Bradley, who could not win a majority of white votes, but who alienated his minority supporters by trying to do so. Still, in a state where less than 10 percent of the voters were black, Bradley did not attract a large racially motivated opposition vote. But in a tight race, a low number of white defections combined with only average black voter turnout could make all the difference. Bradley remained in office as the mayor of Los Angeles, and when he ran again for governor four years later, he never enjoyed any polling leads over Deukmejian, and the incumbent easily beat him again.[25]

The following year, Harold Washington launched his successful bid to become Chicago's first black mayor. This election was marred by significant racial tension, unlike the California race. Multiple polls showed

Washington with a 14-point lead over Republican Bernard Epton. Yet Washington won with only 3.4 percentage points because many white ethnics (Irish, Polish, Italians and others) defected to the GOP. Washington's heavy mobilization of the black vote gave him his critical margin of victory, however.[26]

The other political figure associated with the Bradley effect is Douglas Wilder of Virginia, whose own political campaigns and their similarity to Bradley's gubernatorial campaign would change the phenomenon's name to the Bradley/Wilder effect. Douglas Wilder, a grandson of slaves, was born in 1931 and raised in Richmond's segregated Church Hill neighborhood. He graduated with a degree in chemistry from Virginia Union University, was drafted into the Army, and served in the Korean War, where he won a Bronze Star. After the war, he graduated from Howard University Law School and set up a practice in his Church Hill neighborhood. He won election to the Virginia State Senate in 1969 when his two white opponents split the white vote. As an early example of his accomodationist approach, he endorsed a controversial annexation in Richmond that added more white voters to the city, a clear attempt at minority vote dilution. However, his debut on the senate floor was a speech denouncing the state song, "Carry Me Back to Old Virginny," with its references to "massah" and "darkey."[27]

He eventually served 16 years in the state senate, initially pushing a liberal agenda that included fair housing; a state holiday honoring Martin Luther King, Jr.; rolling back the sales tax, and support for Washington, D.C. voting rights and statehood. He also opposed the death penalty and "tough-on-crime" laws that emphasized incarceration. He began to shift in the 1980s to a more moderate position, which critics called an opportunistic shift to win higher office. In 1985, he won the Democratic nomination for lieutenant governor unopposed, which raised concerns that he could drag the entire ticket down that year. Wilder focused on television ads at the expense of campaign staff and direct mailings, and he supplemented this with intensive campaigning across the state. Hoping to avoid a white backlash, he declined an offer from Jesse Jackson to campaign for him and made no mention in his literature of his support for the King holiday. Wilder also undercut racial code words used by his opponents, such as when the GOP nominee for governor called Wilder a liberal, to which Wilder replied that "liberal" was code for "black." His opponent stopped using the term after that. Wilder won with 52 percent of the vote.[28]

As 1989 approached, Wilder sought the office of governor, a far more powerful position than his largely ceremonial post as lieutenant governor. Wilder may have been black, but he did have the advantage of Democratic momentum on his side. Between 1969 and 1977, Virginians elected three consecutive Republican governors but then switched back to the Democrats in the 1980s, giving that party control of the major statewide offices of governor, lieutenant governor, and attorney general. The state's economy was also doing well, which aided the continuation of Democratic rule. Still, a black candidate winning a statewide office in a former Confederate state, as Wilder had done in 1985, was a barrier that had not been broken before in modern times.[29]

Wilder continued his focus on a deracialized campaign and reaffirmed his 1985 decision to not let Jesse Jackson campaign for him. Wilder straddled the fence in relation to legacy of the civil rights movement. He told voters, "I never viewed myself as an activist" but also said, "You fight injustice with every step you take." Still, he told reporters that he did not favor preferential treatment for minorities or other groups, an attempt to distance himself from affirmative action. He avoided any mention of issues of poverty, another attempt to keep himself from being linked to issues that disproportionately affect African Americans. He refused to speak out when black college students were beaten by police in Virginia Beach, instead issuing a "law and order" statement defending the police response, a move that angered some of his black supporters. He even appeared publicly with Confederate flags and called himself a "son of Virginia."[30]

Wilder's Republican opponent, Marshall Coleman, a former attorney general, had not held a political office for seven years and won the nomination only after a bruising primary marked by heavy negative campaigning. He extended this negative campaigning to the general election, focusing on ethical questions from Wilder's legal career. These corresponding ads, which Wilder countered with a focus on positive aspects of his career as well as the issues, ended up hurting Coleman in the general election because they alienated some voters. Coleman was also the standard-bearer for the religious right in the party, which also aided Wilder, since he would not be facing a GOP moderate like Bradley had with Deukmejian.[31]

Coleman's campaign wanted to avoid any appearance of racial pandering to whites, and he issued statements stressing racial equality and fairness. Although this was expected in the post–civil rights movement era, he was also following a long history in Virginia of not using overt race-baiting in electoral campaigns or public discourse, an aversion rooted in Virginia's genteel political etiquette. However, his advisors anticipated a Bradley effect in the election and felt that if Coleman were down no more than five points by Election Day, he would win. The lessons of California, it seemed, inspired confidence—perhaps overconfidence—in Virginia's GOP.[32]

Wilder's shift to the right in the 1980s aided him in the election, allowing him to distance himself from perceptions that he was a black liberal in the vein of Jesse Jackson. To appeal to upper-class whites and to insulate himself against the kind of "soft-on-crime" charges that had crippled Michael Dukakis the year before, Wilder ran in 1989 as a supporter of the death penalty to insulate him against these accusations and head off a drop in voter support. This was a sharp reverse of his earlier position, and he did the same when he declared opposition to statehood for Washington, D.C., even though such a move would have increased federal representation for the large African American population in the city. To win business support, he supported antiunion "right to work" laws. Wilder crafted these positions in an effort to win one-third of the state's white voters, the number he roughly needed combined with high black voter turnout to win; to further aid himself in this endeavor, he avoided heavy campaigning in the black community. Wilder thus took the black vote for granted and expected a high turnout since he was black; by not seeking black votes, he could position himself as a candidate who was not "too black" and one who did not appeal to black pride to win votes. Put another way, Wilder, like Brooke when he ran for the Senate, ran as a governor who happened to be black, rather than a black governor.[33]

Abortion proved to be one of the issues that did not deal with race but was a decisive issue in the election. Earlier in 1989, the U.S. Supreme Court ruled in *Webster v. Reproductive Health Services* that states can set additional limits on abortion beyond those allowed by *Roe v. Wade* (1973). Coleman embraced the decision, called for new restrictions on abortion, and endorsed a constitutional amendment to ban it even in cases of rape and incest. Wilder took a pro-choice stance, even though he himself had shifted from opposing parental consent for abortion in 1978 to supporting it in 1985. Coleman's extreme position on abortion gave Wilder an opening, and in their debates and in advertisements, he attacked Coleman for his position. One Wilder advertisement featured a statue of Thomas Jefferson and accused Coleman of undermining Virginia's long history of individual liberty and "give it [your rights] to the politicians."[34]

Wilder enjoyed favorable press coverage throughout his campaign, from both national and local media. National newspapers gave the race heavy attention since it could result in a black governor, and they focused only on the issues of race and abortion in their coverage. Their coverage was generally positive, stressing the historic nature of his candidacy in a former Confederate state. In the local press, Wilder also received favorable coverage, even though the papers covered more issues than the national media. Coleman, by contrast, received mostly negative (but not exclusively so) attention from the local papers.[35]

Wilder entered Election Day leading in pre-election polls, but like in California, a bloc of undecided voters remained that could easily turn the election. Exit polls, so problematic in the past, added to the inflated estimates of a Wilder victory. A Mason-Dixon exit poll on election night gave Wilder a 10-point victory. However, Wilder won by the slimmest of margins and took just 50.1 percent of the vote. He carried densely populated northern Virginia and the urbanized Hampton Roads area, which overcame Coleman's ability to win a majority of localities in the state. Many of Wilder's voters were "newcomers," or non-native Virginians. The high black voter turnout helped Wilder of course, which was 8 percent higher than the white turnout. The 96 percent of the black vote he won helped him in urban areas over his lagging support in suburban and rural areas. Coleman, on the other hand, failed to energize the white voters in Republican strongholds. Here, Wilder's deracialized strategy and Coleman's weaknesses as a candidate likely played a role. Wilder's pull with white voters was 41 percent, and two-thirds of his total votes came from whites. The abortion issue also gave Wilder an edge with women voters.[36]

Wilder's narrow victory added to belief in the Bradley effect, as political scientists cited what they called "social desirability" in both pre-election and exit polling. Simply put, white voters leaving the polls do not want pollsters, especially black pollsters, to think they are racist when the pollsters ask them about their voting behavior. For example, black interviewers of white voters had an 8.4 percent higher reported preference among their interviewees for Wilder than white interviewers did. One problem with the exit polling was that Mason-Dixon Opinion Research, which conducted the poll giving Wilder a 10-point victory, used exit polls utilizing face-to-face interviews with pollsters. The CBS News/*New York Times* poll, however, used self-administered questionnaires, which showed a lower rate of support for Wilder, especially among white voters. When filling out an anonymous survey, white voters seemed to be more honest than when talking to a stranger—especially a black stranger. The role of social desirability regarding race in skewing the exit poll for Wilder gains credence when the same exit polls accurately predicted the other two statewide races, which featured only white candidates.[37]

Yet the exaggerated poll numbers also, argued political scientist Larry Sabato, aided Wilder. The *Washington Post* projected a Wilder landslide, which Sabato said depressed the turnout of Coleman's supporters in northern Virginia. Mark Rozell, another political scientist who agreed with Sabato's argument, said that liberal bias at the *Post* skewed favorable coverage toward Wilder and noted that the more conservative *Richmond Times-Dispatch* was fairer to Coleman. As Rozell admits, however, it is impossible to know how much this coverage influenced the election and voter behavior. Not all local papers favored Wilder, either. For example, the *Culpeper Star-Exponent*, a small conservative newspaper, ran far more critical stories on Wilder. Like the *Post*, however, the conservative press made only positive, not negative, mentions of Wilder's race, a reflection of the general disfavor open race-baiting would receive from the public. However, Judson Jeffries, another political scientist, suggested that the constant focus on Wilder's race, even while favorable, may have hurt him by reminding voters that he was black, thus encouraging racist white voters to come out against him. Jeffries came to a different conclusion than Rozell and argued that the *Post* ran plenty of critical stories on Wilder, which really just suggests that the perception of pro- or anti-Wilder coverage has more to do with the bias of the academic rather than that of the newspaper.[38]

Wilder's victory did not mean a break from the past, however. Just like Maynard Jackson of Atlanta and Coleman Young of Detroit, who were the first black mayors of those cities, Wilder ran a rather conservative administration. This course reflected his earlier rightward shift and coalition-building with whites, and his own efforts to be a politician who "transcended" race. His own personal style, which was often confrontational, undermined his administration. He angered members of his own party by snubbing them in his appointments to state offices, and soon he fell into feuding with other prominent Virginia Democrats. His relationship with the legislative black caucus did not even enjoy a honeymoon period, and its members were soon alienated from the governor as well. The result in Virginia was an administration like Jackson's and Young's, a conservative one that did little to address the economic concerns of the mass of poor African Americans, key issues such as poverty and joblessness. As historian Manning Marable said of Wilder's victory and subsequent administration, the "triumph" of his victory was "symbolic, rather than substantive," with "little real significance" to the everyday concerns of African Americans. One of Wilder's law partners echoed this and rather tellingly said, "I don't think you'd see Doug leading a mission to impoverished areas."[39]

Nor was Wilder, despite overcoming white reluctance to support a black gubernatorial candidate, able to translate his victory into an even higher office. In 1991, with his state suffering a major fiscal crisis, Wilder announced his candidacy for the Democratic nomination for president. Wilder hoped to capitalize on his run as a "postracial" candidate like he had in Virginia, but also to win overwhelming black support by being a black man himself. His advantage as the only black candidate was confirmed when Jesse Jackson decided well after Wilder's entrance to not make a third run. Wilder positioned himself as a social moderate and fiscal conservative, but his poll numbers dropped among Democrats when they learned he was black. When Jackson decided not to run, Wilder, in another display of political opportunism, tried to become the next Jackson, hiring a former staffer of the black preacher's as his campaign manager and moving left on economics and racial issues. He attacked fellow candidate Bill Clinton for distancing himself from minority issues. Jackson, who disliked Wilder's policies as governor and his refusal to let Jackson campaign for him in 1989, stayed neutral in the race. Wilder ended up with tepid support and faced real competition for black votes from Clinton, and the Virginia governor ended up dropping out of the race before the first primaries and caucuses, with his popularity in his home state dropping to a low of 32 percent.[40]

The other race in 1989 that received significant attention was the election victory of David Dinkins, who became the first black mayor of New York City. Dinkins, who had been president of the borough of Manhattan since 1985, was a graduate of Howard University and entered city politics in the 1950s. He had a reputation as a conciliator, which aided him since New York City was less than a quarter black, so he would need to build a coalition like Bradley's. He challenged the incumbent Ed Koch, who was running for an unprecedented fourth term in 1989. Koch, a Jew, had exacerbated tensions between himself and African Americans in the city when he vigorously criticized and campaigned against Jesse Jackson in the 1988 presidential primary in New York over the preacher's anti-Semitic "Hymie-town" comments. Several incidents had marred race relations leading up to the elections, including the highly publicized Central Park jogger case, in which a white woman was raped and almost beaten to death by what police believed were a group of black and Hispanic teenagers. Dinkins managed to win the Democratic primary, but the results showed sharp racial cleavages, as his strength rested mostly on minority votes while 70 percent of whites supported Koch.[41]

Dinkins impressed many observers by being able to win crossover votes. Some whites felt that a black mayor would help ease racial fears, a notion reinforced by his soft-spoken, nonthreatening demeanor, which had also aided Wilder. Even though Democrats outnumbered Republicans in the city five-to-one, Dinkins was not a shoo-in. Rudolph Giuliani, a former federal prosecutor, ran a vigorous campaign as the GOP nominee and tried to encourage white defections. He played to racial fears, telling voters that a vote for Dinkins would give Jesse Jackson influence in city politics. Dinkins won, but by only two percentage points. This too was in marked contrast to pre-election polls, which put Dinkins anywhere from 14 to 18 points ahead of his opponent. He did experience substantial white defections but managed to hold onto 30 percent of the white vote and a slightly larger percentage of the Jewish vote. His strong showing with black and Hispanic voters, combined with the minority of the white vote, carried the day for him. Like Bradley in Los Angeles, he was able to build a multiracial coalition.[42]

Norman Rice's victory as the first black mayor of Seattle was equally important, but it was largely overshadowed by the victories of Wilder and Dinkins. Seattle had a black population of only 47,000, and election to city offices was city wide. That had not prevented two black men, one of them Rice, from being elected to city council by 1981. Rice served three terms, including president of the city council. He ran for mayor in 1985 and for Congress in 1988, and lost both races. Still, he could claim leadership experience, especially when he helped the city manage the budget crisis brought on by federal budget reductions during the Reagan administration. Rice was reluctant to run again in 1989, fearing white voters would not support him. He changed his mind when Doug Jewett, one of the white candidates for mayor, began pushing to create magnet schools to end mandatory busing in Seattle public schools. This issue and Rice's subsequent entry into the race meant that busing was the dominant issue in the election. Jewett focused on busing while Rice sought to de-emphasize race by discussing crime, public programs, and other issues. Rice and Jewett led in the primary and then faced off in the general election, where Rice focused on a number of issues, especially anticrime programs, to counter Jewett's singular focus on busing and race. Rice dealt with the busing issue by proposing gradual elimination of mandatory busing and working with the school board to improve education. Jewett's lead gradually disappeared as the election drew closer, and high voter turnout, especially of younger voters, aided Rice. Rice won with 58 percent of the vote, a victory not marred by the Bradley effect.[43]

As Wilder's 1989 election victory showed, all black candidates are not created equal. What *type* of black candidate also mattered, since some whites would clearly vote for a black candidate if they were receptive to the candidate's political positions and style. While for some whites the "liberal" label would always be used as their reason to avoid voting for any black candidate, a candidate who downplayed race and ran a deracialized campaign could get a minority of white votes, or as the special case of Edward Brooke showed, a majority. This difference between the type and electability of black candidates was evident in the 1980s in Mississippi's second congressional district. In 1982, Robert Clark, the first black man elected to the Mississippi House of Representatives since Reconstruction, ran in the district, which had been newly created by the federal courts as a black-majority district encompassing the Mississippi Delta. Clark, who ran a markedly more liberal campaign than his white Republican opponent, was associated with the Mississippi civil rights movement (he had first been elected in 1967) that, combined with his race, led to a high white turnout against him. When he ran again in 1984, Clark lost again. Yet in 1986, Mike Espy, a black lawyer and former state employee, ran as the Democratic nominee. Espy was a polished lawyer from a wealthy Delta family, and as a younger man came of age after the civil rights movement. He embraced conservative positions, especially on gun control and the death penalty, and won over Delta business interests. His deracializing of the contest included declining offers from Jesse Jackson to campaign for him as well as securing endorsements from white Democratic politicians. He defeated the Republican incumbent through a combination of his positions and style, high black voter turnout, and low white voter turnout. The latter was largely due to white farmers disgruntled over President Reagan's agricultural policies, but he did increase his support among white voters over what Clark drew in the earlier races.[44]

By the twenty-first century it appeared that the Bradley effect was declining. Aside from a possible decline in racist sentiment among white voters, more accurate polling techniques as pollsters learned from earlier elections may have also played a part. In three governor's races in 2006, pre-election polling approximated the actual totals. In the Ohio and Pennsylvania races, black Republican candidates lost to white Democrats. In Massachusetts, black Democrat Deval Patrick, building on the groundwork laid by Ed Brooke, defeated a white Republican by a 21-point landslide. Still, there were concerns of a nationwide Bradley effect in 2008, when Barack Obama ran for president. Such fears proved largely unfounded, though.[45]

Yet the Bradley effect cannot be buried just yet. While it is most identified with black Democratic candidates, Republicans have also been victims of it. In fact, the Republican does not even have to be black, but only nonwhite or dark-skinned. Such was the case when Bobby Jindal ran for governor of Louisiana as a Republican in 2003. Jindal, a dark-skinned Ivy League educated Republican of South Asian ancestry, actively appealed for black votes and won the endorsement of Ray Nagin, the black Democratic mayor of New Orleans. He lost to Kathleen Blanco, a white Democrat who won with 52 percent of the vote, even though pre-election polls predicted a Jindal victory. In the South, female statewide candidates tended to have more difficulty winning, but Blanco's gender liability was overcome by Jindal's race. The reluctance of white voters to vote for a non-white candidate, compounded by Jindal's special black outreach and the Nagin endorsement, muted the traditional GOP gains of white defections. The "southern strategy" that the GOP had built in the South since Nixon, whereby racial code words were used to appeal to segregationist whites, turned back on the Republicans when they tried to create a more inclusive party. Blanco won the election even when the votes from the solidly Democratic base of New Orleans were removed from the totals. Jindal ran again in 2007 and won, but he benefited from the backlash against state Democrats after Blanco's handling of the Hurricane Katrina disaster.[46]

In summing up the Bradley effect, it is clear that race has been a factor, often a major one, in statewide elections. However, it would be an oversimplification to ascribe a black candidate's defeat solely to this effect. Numerous factors affect each race and can aid in the candidate's defeat or allow him or her to overcome the effect. Each state contest—and more importantly each state—is different and obvious factors, such as the size of the black population compared to the white population, matters. As the elections of Edward Brooke and Douglas Wilder show, a deracialized campaign is key to winning over white voters. To not be too closely identified with black activists like Jesse Jackson or the legacy of the civil rights movement is critical. However, as Tom Bradley found out, to take this approach too far runs the risks of alienating black voters and depressing black voter turnout. Bradley was unable to overcome this dilemma, but Ed Brooke had little to fear from that approach in overwhelmingly white Massachusetts. And as Wilder's election showed, nonracial issues like abortion can introduce other factors like gender to overcome racially polarized voting. Finally, problems with the way the polls themselves are conducted have contributed to the Bradley effect. The shortage of black statewide elected officials, such as the lack of a black U.S. senator today, indicate that black candidates still have difficulty winning when every state in the United States has a white majority. While the Bradley effect may have not completely faded, the small but growing number of successful black statewide candidates, and most importantly the decisive election and reelection of Barack Obama as president, suggests that while there will always be racially motivated opposition to a black candidate, its breadth and appeal are diminishing.

Chapter 4

Immigrants and Political Representation

"Learn to speak Native American or get the fuck out," says a shirt on a popular t-shirt seller's website, which shows an American Indian making an obscene gesture.[1] However profane and irreverent, this statement sums up perfectly the hypocrisy of Americans whose ancestors were European immigrants telling Latino migrants to learn English or leave. Expressions of nativism are older than the republic, and American citizens and policy-makers have argued and debated how much political access and power immigrants should have, as well as how quickly and how many should be made citizens. Not surprisingly, race and racism have shaped these questions of immigration and political representation, and show no sign of abating in the present or immediate future.

As the oft-stated cliché goes, the United States is a nation of immigrants. This goes back to the English treasure-hunters who settled Jamestown in 1607 and even further back to the ancestors of American Indians who migrated across the land bridge of Beringia from Siberia before the last Ice Age separated the continents. The migrations of the colonial era created a diverse, cosmopolitan collection of colonies by the late eighteenth century. Immigrants arrived for a variety of reasons, from the economic reasons of the English indentured servants of Virginia to the French Huguenots of South Carolina fleeing increasing religious persecution in France after King Louis XVI revoked religious toleration in 1685, reversing the earlier Edict of Nantes that had protected the Protestant minority in that country. Many of these immigrants were English-speaking, including the English settlers of Virginia and New England, as well as the Scotch-Irish. The Scotch-Irish originally hailed from the Scottish Lowlands and had been transplanted to Ulster in Northern Ireland during the seventeenth century, where their discontent and conflict with their English land-lords stimulated a large migration in the early eighteenth century; by the time of the Revolution, as many as 250,000 had migrated to the colonies, where they often settled in the frontier hinterlands.[2]

Yet speakers of other languages arrived as well, adding linguistic diversity to the colonies. Aside from the French Huguenots, the Dutch East India Company settled the Hudson River Valley with Dutch immigrants, and this trading colony quickly absorbed the much smaller colony of Finns and Swedes in nearby New Sweden. In 1664, England seized New Netherland, renaming it New York, but the Dutch presence left the colony with a cosmopolitan character.

German settlers from the various German states and the German-speaking cantons of Switzerland arrived and settled, most famously in Pennsylvania (as the misnamed Pennsylvania Dutch), but in colonies to the south as well. And of course one non-English-speaking group, Africans, came involuntarily. The first arrival of Africans on a Dutch ship to Jamestown in 1619 mattered little, since these early arrivals were not treated much differently than white indentured servants. Yet labor demands and hardening racial attitudes in both custom and law meant that after 1660, their status increasingly moved toward slavery, which was already well established in the Spanish, Portuguese, and English Caribbean colonies. In colonies such as Carolina, Barbadian planters migrated directly with the slaves, establishing the "peculiar institution" of African slavery from the outset. During the eighteenth century, as many as 200,000 Africans were brought forcibly to the American colonies, imbedding the institution of racialized slavery in the region.[3]

From the earliest days of settlement, ethnic tensions and nativism flared as the American colonies became settled and developed. The earliest conflicts, of course, pitted English, Dutch, and other European settlers against the Indians whom they expelled or destroyed to gain access to their land. Yet as more immigrants arrived, earlier generations of settlers sometimes resented the new arrivals. In New England, where the homogenous Puritans looked with disfavor on differing religions lest these foreign faiths endanger the Puritans' attempt at a Christian utopia. Because of this belief, Puritan authors like Edward Johnson warned against accepting immigrants. Although colonies like Maryland, Pennsylvania, and New York had religious toleration, the lack of such freedoms in other colonies curtailed Roman Catholic immigration. Even German immigrants, who were largely Protestant, faced prejudice. Benjamin Franklin worried that the "Palatine Boors"—as he called the Germans in Pennsylvania—would side with the French in the event of a war, a fear that prompted the Reverend William Smith to help establish a system of charity schools aimed at Anglicizing the Germans. The scheme faced strong German opposition and failed.[4]

Franklin and Smith's concerns about immigrants' lack of assimilation focused on groups like the Germans and the Scotch-Irish, who formed ethnic enclaves isolated from English communities; but other groups, like the French Huguenots, easily assimilated into colonial society. Colonial authorities alternated between acceptance of immigrants to outright hostility. In areas like South Carolina, white immigrants were welcomed as protection from both Indian attacks as well as slave uprisings. Yet in other areas hostility erupted, such as in 1729 when a mob in Boston rose up to prevent the landing of Scotch-Irish immigrants.[5]

With the end of the American Revolution and the establishment of the United States of America, the young republic moved quickly to define and set limits on which types of people could immigrate and become citizens. Congress enacted the Naturalization Act of 1790, which established a probationary period for new arrivals to undergo training in citizenship, as well as a two-year residency requirement. Aside from providing proof of good character, the applicants for naturalized citizenship had to be "white." This excluded Asian immigrants, African-born slaves who became emancipated, and also specifically American Indians, even though they had been born in the United States. However racist by today's standards, this legislation fit easily into the mainstream racial thinking of the time. Benjamin Franklin called for increasing the numbers of "the lovely White" in America, and Thomas Jefferson said that society should consist of "a people speaking the same language, governed in similar forms, and by similar laws."[6] With the 1790 act, race and citizenship became indelibly intertwined in U.S. history. Interestingly, the law made no mention of religion, leaving a path for white Catholic and Jewish immigrants to become citizens.

In general, the United States had relatively liberal immigration policies during the nineteenth century. The expanding Market Revolution of the early nineteenth century, a period of economic development that spawned growing cities and industrial development, easily absorbed waves of immigrant workers into the developing capitalist economy. Many older immigrant communities, such as the Germans who predated the Revolution, gradually adopted English and assimilated. Still, immigration was not entirely open, as state and local governments held the power to regulate the admission and legal status of foreigners.[7]

Nativism tended to be episodic in nature, marked by outbursts of xenophobia and exclusion, despite the general unease that many native-born

Americans had with immigrants. One famous example of this came in 1798 during the brief period of the Federalist Party's domination of American politics under the presidency of John Adams. The French Revolution spawned a fear of foreign-born radicals operating in the United States, but the Federalists were also looking to deny foreign-born votes to the opposition Democratic-Republicans. First, the Federalist Congress in 1798 lengthened the period of naturalization from five years to 14. Congress then followed the Naturalization Act with the two alien acts of 1798. These laws gave the president the power to arrest and deport resident aliens suspected of subversion. The first, the Alien Enemies Act, never went into effect, since a war with France did not materialize. The second, the Alien Friends Act, was never used due to enforcement difficulties. The more infamous Sedition Act, also passed in 1798, was used disproportion-ately against foreign-born journalists and pamphleteers. These acts either failed to work or backfired, and the resultant swing of immigrant voters toward the Democratic-Republicans played a role in Thomas Jefferson's defeat of Adams in the 1800 presidential election and the repeal of all of the acts.[8]

With the end of the Napoleonic Wars in 1815, immigration rose to even higher levels as regular sea travel resumed and European states swelled with a surplus population. In the 1820s, only 151,000 immigrants arrived; this number rose to 599,000 in the 1830s. Most came for economic reasons, especially in the form of displaced farm laborers and small freeholders impoverished by the rise of large-scale agriculture. However, others came for political reasons, as was the case in 1848 when the revolutions that swept Europe that year were crushed (although the number of migrants fleeing the repression was low).[9]

The most famous episode of pre–Civil War immigration—and the resulting nativism—occurred in the 1840s and 1850s with Irish immigra-tion. Although 1 million Irish had emigrated from the island to the United States between 1815 and 1845, the real catalyst for immigration was the potato blight that struck Ireland in 1845. The fungus rotted the potato stalks and struck annually for the next decade. The Great Famine, which resulted from the blight, killed 1 million Irish by 1855, and the indifference of English landlords, who evicted starving tenants from their lands, hastened the misery and death. Facing death, 1.5 million Irish migrated to the United States in this period, where they moved into low-paying laboring jobs. The Irish influx meant that by the mid-1850s, more than 20 percent of the populations of Boston and New York were foreign-born.[10]

The Irish faced prejudice from native-born Americans, and were often depicted as apelike savages and brutes of low intelligence, similar to the way whites caricatured African Americans. Drunkenness in particular became an Irish stereotype, with one expression declaring, "It's as natural for a Hibernian (Irishman) to tipple as it is for a pig to grunt." Yet much of the prejudice was motivated by the anti-Catholic feelings held by white Protestants, many of whom felt that Catholic immigrants would be loyal to Rome first and thus undermine American democracy.[11]

Ironically, African Americans held some of the strongest anti-Irish views, opinions born largely by competition for low-paying jobs. Black and Irish workers competed at the bottom of the economic ladder in the North and Irish immigrants were even hired in the South by slave owners who did not want to risk their slaves in dangerous work. Irish immigrants quickly learned to play up their whiteness, which gave them an advantage over blacks. Ironically, many Irish cried, "Let them go back to Africa, where they belong!" This competition erupted into violence during the Civil War, when Irish workers feared that Lincoln's emancipation policy would flood Northern cities with freed slaves and depress wages. The New York City Draft Riot of 1863, which began as a protest against the draft, became a four-day antiblack riot during which Irish mobs lynched African Americans and burned black homes as well as a black orphanage.[12]

The treatment of free blacks and Irish immigrants by the American republic highlights the way that race sharply defined who did and did not enjoy the rights of citizenship. Although scorned and subjected to prejudice, Irish immigrants quickly received the right to vote, while northern states largely denied or restricted the ballot for native-born black Americans prior to the ratification of the Fifteenth Amendment in 1870. Foreign status and religion may have been grounds for discrimination from native-born Americans, but whiteness guaranteed citizenship and political rights. The color line led one black journalist to comment that in the United States, "the scum of European society—can come and enjoy the fullest social and political privileges" while "the Native Born American with wooly hair and dark complexion is made the Victim . . . of Social Ostracism."[13]

Among white Americans, opposition to Irish and other foreign immigration materialized in this era in the short-lived Know-Nothing Party, which burst onto the national scene beginning in 1853. Known officially as the American Party, the organization called for restricting officeholding to native-born Americans and extending the naturalization period to 21 years for immigrants. Membership in the party was limited to white

Protestant males, reflecting both racist and anti-Catholic prejudices. The party's influence peaked in 1855, when it elected six governors, controlled several state legislatures, and sent representatives to Congress. The party briefly filled the void left by the collapsing Whig Party and succeeded in altering some state suffrage laws. The more divisive issue of slavery and the defeat of Know-Nothing presidential candidate Milliard Fillmore in 1856 led to the party's decline and created the two-party system of the Democrats and the new Republican Party. One lesson that the Whig Party and later the Republicans learned in this era was that whatever the attraction to nativism, alienating immigrant voters and thus mobilizing high Democratic turnout more than offset any gains with nativist voters.[14]

The twin strains of nativism and racism, while at odds when white immigrants were concerned, came together neatly and efficiently for nonwhite immigrants. The first nonwhite ethnic group to experience this was the Chinese. With the seizure of the territory known as the Mexican Cession (which became the American Southwest) from Mexico in 1848, California passed into U.S. hands. With the discovery of gold there that same year, the territory's population boomed, and western mining and railroad companies sought laborers. Chinese immigrants filled this demand, and 250,000 arrived from 1850 to 1882, with most settling in California. Initially welcomed, the Chinese soon faced hostility from white workers, especially during periods of economic downturn. California began to pass laws restricting the rights of the Chinese, a hardly surprising phenomenon given the already pervasive antiblack, anti-Indian, and anti-Mexican attitudes held by the state's white population.[15]

Congress initially favored Chinese immigration as a way to economically develop the West and secure trading ties with Asian nations. This sentiment led to the Burlingame Treaty of 1868, which encouraged immigration and extended legal protections to Chinese immigrants. But this sentiment proved short-lived. As the nation tired of Reconstruction and the Republican Party retreated from vigorous enforcement of civil rights laws and its commitment to racial equality for African Americans, anti-Chinese sentiment grew as well. In 1870, the Senate defeated an effort by Radical Republicans to remove "white" from federal naturalization laws. In California, the newly formed Workingman's Party, which counted many Irish immigrants among its ranks, whipped up anti-Chinese hysteria and successfully pushed through anti-Chinese laws. By 1879, President Rutherford B. Hayes spoke out against Chinese immigration, and in 1882, Congress passed the Chinese Exclusion Act. Signed into law by President

Chester Alan Arthur, the act suspended Chinese laborers from entering the United States for 10 years, the first time Congress had barred a specific racial group from entering the country. Congress later tightened the restrictions, and the 1880s became notorious for anti-Chinese violence in the West. The act was extended in 1892 with further restrictions, including requiring Chinese immigrants to carry a certificate of residence and prove in court that they had resided in the country prior to 1882. In 1902, the immigration ban was extended indefinitely.[16]

Not surprisingly, Japanese immigrants received similar treatment in the United States. Japanese laborers in California soon became the new focus of anti-Asian sentiment once the Chinese supply was cut off. Although most went to Hawaii, 180,000 Japanese made it to the U.S. mainland between 1885 and 1924. Anti-Japanese sentiment was especially strong in San Francisco, where the school district ordered the segregation of white and Asian schoolchildren. This led to an international crisis, as the Japanese government objected to the segregation and sent a protest to Washington. President Theodore Roosevelt was forced to intervene to avoid alienating the rising power of Japan, which had humiliated Russia two years earlier in the Russo-Japanese War. Roosevelt was able to convince the San Francisco school board to rescind the order and in return, he negotiated what became known as the Gentleman's Agreement in 1908, an understanding with Tokyo that Japan would curtail further emigration of laborers to the United States. The crisis passed, but California still took steps to restrict the rights of the Japanese such as a 1913 ban on owning land.[17]

The racial contrast can again be seen by comparing Asian immigration with European immigration in this same era. European immigration in the late nineteenth century shifted geographically toward migrants from Southern and Eastern Europe. In the decade of the 1870s, over 2 million immigrants from Northern and Western Europe arrived in the United States, while only just over 200,000 were from Southern and Eastern Europe. By the first decade of the twentieth century, the number from Northern and Western Europe had dipped only slightly, but arrivals from Southern and Eastern Europe during this same period of time exceeded 6 million, with Italy and Russia being two of the top countries of origin. This immigration came just as state regulation of immigration receded, specifically in 1875 when the Supreme Court ruled in *Henderson v. Mayor of City of New York* that state regulations like bonds and head taxes on shipmasters and immigrants were an unconstitutional usurpation of Congress's power to regulate foreign commerce. As Congress restricted the admission of Chinese laborers in 1882, the way was set for more federal immigration regulations. Congress passed the most notable—and iconic—legislation of this period, the Immigration Act of 1891, which created a federal bureaucracy within the Treasury Department to process immigrants. This act established Ellis Island as the new federal immigration station.[18]

Nativism again resurfaced in such groups as the American Protective Association (APA), a largely Protestant group that urged stronger barriers for immigration and naturalization, and an end to tax exemptions for Catholic property. The APA echoed the Know-Nothings and appealed to the Republican Party, while the Democratic Party—which depended on immigrant, especially Irish Catholic votes in presidential elections—openly opposed the group. Labor unions were in a more ambiguous position, since they were firmly identified with the proimmigration Democrats but favored restrictions to keep employers from depressing wages with cheap immigrant labor. Like before, xenophobia made little headway on a national scale, at least when it came to white immigrants. Electoral defeat for the Grand Old Party (GOP) in the presidential elections of 1884 and 1892, as well as the midterm elections in 1890, convinced prominent Republicans like William McKinley (who lost his House seat in 1890) to appeal for votes across ethnic and religious lines by focusing on economic issues like the tariff.[19]

While overt bans on white immigration did not succeed, restrictions on these immigrants' political participation made more headway. From the 1890s through the Progressive Era of the early twentieth century, the Immigration Restriction League (IRL), founded by Harvard alumni, gave an intellectual veneer to nativism. Members argued that immigrants were manipulated by political bosses in the urban political machines of American cities, and they called for "electoral reform" to address the problem. The high point of their 1890s activism came with the passage in both houses of Congress of a literacy test for new immigrants, but the bill did not survive President Grover Cleveland's veto. In other areas, restrictionists made more subtle impacts. The widespread adoption of the secret (or Australian) ballot, while on one hand pushed as an anticorruption and vote fraud measure, also had the effect of promoting literacy among voters. Literacy tests made little headway outside of the South until the 1920s, by which time 13 states in the North and West had adopted them. Perhaps the state in which this had the biggest effect was New York, which passed such a law in 1921 in the wake of fears of foreign-born radicals from the

Red Scare. The effect was to disfranchise hundreds of thousands of Yiddish-speaking Jews in New York City and other areas. Pre-election day registration also became the norm in most states. These restrictions did have some impact on immigrant voters, but the Irish political machines of some cities skillfully used the new laws to make it difficult for *other* immigrants to vote and challenge their power.[20]

The restrictionists did not gain a major victory against white immigration until after World War I. Resurgent nativist concerns and doubts about assimilation were heightened by fears of a potential "fifth column" in the event of U.S. entry into the war. In 1917, Congress passed a new literacy test for immigrants and promptly overrode President Woodrow Wilson's veto, despite his own Democratic Party controlling Congress. The Russian Revolution and fears of foreign radicalism in the United States, culminating in the Palmer Raids in 1920, led to a spike in deportations and support even among big business for immigration restriction. This sentiment combined with racist scholarship from the eugenics movement to brand Southern and Eastern Europeans as "undesirable" and unable to be assimilated. This led Congress to overwhelmingly pass the Johnson-Reed Act, officially known as the Immigration Act of 1924. It set quotas for the entry of immigrants, and reserved 84 percent for immigrants from Northern and Western Europe. It also banned Japanese immigration, overturning the earlier Gentlemen's Agreement. Ironically, one of the major exemptions was "Western Hemisphere natives," which allowed Mexican immigration, a nod to agribusiness's labor demands in the South and Southwest.[21]

Meanwhile, to deny them naturalized citizenship, the color line for Asian immigrants became even more rigidly drawn. As early as 1855, the federal district court in San Francisco denied a Chinese man, Chan Yong, citizenship because he was not "white" according to the 1790 Naturalization Law. In 1923, the Supreme Court ruled that Bhagat Singh Thind, a Sikh from British India, was not white in accordance with the 1790 law and denied his appeal for citizenship. Although the children of Asian immigrants received citizenship if they were born in the United States (due to the Fourteenth Amendment and the Supreme Court's interpretation of it in favor of U.S.-born Asians in 1898), their parents could not achieve naturalization. However, as the internment without due process of the American-born children of Japanese immigrants during World War II showed, racial inequality still persisted even though on paper one was a citizen entitled to equal rights.[22]

Limited restrictions on white immigrants show again the salience of race in the American republic. Despite criticism and anxieties from native-born Americans about the massive immigration of Catholic, Eastern Orthodox, and Jewish voters in the nineteenth and early twentieth centuries, almost no serious restrictions on these white immigrants were enacted (at least not until 1924), and most became citizens and voters within a relatively short period of time. This treatment stands in stark contrast to Asian immigrants, who were denied naturalized citizenship and then banned from admittance altogether. It stands in even greater contrast to African Americans, who even though generations removed from Africa found themselves stripped of their basic rights of citizenship in the South and subjected to horrific violence, and American Indians, who despite being the first Americans, suffered a federally sanctioned near-genocide and forced assimilation on a system of bleak, impoverished reservations. An immigrant from Europe may not have been the social equal of an old-stock white Anglo-Saxon Protestant, but his whiteness made him more of a citizen than someone with black or brown skin.

World War II proved to be a major period for shifting and liberalizing the racially restrictive laws and paving the way for future reform. While the fight against the racism of Hitler and Nazism has often been cited as creating a change in race relations in the United States, in reality, racial tensions rose sharply during the war, especially in the areas of African American military service and employment. Jewish refugees fleeing Hitler's Germany found themselves denied entry into the United States, as well as from just about every other nation. Of course, the most glaring example of the inequality was President Franklin Roosevelt's Executive Order 9066, which ordered the relocation of Japanese and Japanese Americans on the West Coast into internment camps for much of the war, all without due process and upheld by the Supreme Court.[23]

Yet the war did lead to immigration liberalization. China became a U.S. ally after the Japanese attack on Pearl Harbor, and the war saw the fortunes of the Chinese in America rise as those of the Japanese fell. Pressure for repeal of the ban on Chinese immigration rose during the war, and maintaining racial barriers on Asians played into the hands of Japanese propagandists. Congress repealed the Chinese Exclusion Act in 1943 but allowed very limited immigration from China. The real breakthrough, however, was the lifting of the ban on naturalized citizenship for Chinese immigrants.[24]

Paired with World War II, the emergence of the civil rights movement in the years after the war was the other major movement that eroded barriers to immigration and citizenship. The Cold War intensified the struggle for the hearts and minds of the world's people, including its nonwhite peoples, which meant that public image became even more important. Racial discrimination highlighted the contradictions between the rhetoric and reality of American democracy, and this gave antiracist activists leverage in some areas. The 1952 McCarran-Walter Act overturned the racial provisions of the 1790 Naturalization Law and extended the right of citizenship to Japanese immigrants.[25]

The act did not overturn the 1924 Johnson-Reed quotas, however. Throughout the 1950s and early 1960s, immigration foes blocked any attempt to reform or abolish these quotas. The connection between hostility to racial progress at home and opposition to nonwhite immigration was obvious, as leading white supremacists in Congress opposed both immigration and antiracist legislation. Senator James Eastland, chair of the Senate Judiciary Committee and its immigration subcommittee, blocked any relaxing of the quotas while at the same time garnering infamy for his opposition to civil rights legislation. Yet in 1964 after meetings with President Lyndon Johnson, the Mississippi Democrat stepped down as chair and made room for Senator Edward Kennedy, a liberal Democrat from Massachusetts who favored immigration reform.[26]

With the passage of the Civil Rights Act of 1964, the federal government was finally on the side of opposing racial discrimination, so the existence of immigration quotas became even more contradictory to the nation's ideals. Vice President Hubert Humphrey called for Congress to "remove all elements in our immigration law which suggest that there are second-class people." After much legislative arm-twisting, Congress passed a bill that abolished the national origins quotas, replacing them with a system of preferences that emphasized family unification and set a ceiling of 120,000 visas from the Western Hemisphere, but without limits or preferences for any country. For the Eastern Hemisphere, immigration was capped at 170,000 visas, with no more than 20,000 from each country, considerably more than the earlier limit of hundreds from Asian countries. President Johnson signed the Hart-Celler Act, known officially as the Immigration Act of 1965, into law in July, before the Statue of Liberty.[27]

The law had a profound and wide-ranging effect on American society. In 1967, immigration jumped to 361,972, the highest in 43 years. The law brought an expected increase in immigration from Southern and Eastern Europe, but it also brought a sharp rise in Asian immigration. Almost 80 percent of the new migrants came from China, India, and the

Philippines. In 1968, when the national quotas of 1924 were phased out under the 1965 legislation, immigration rates soared. During the first few years, on average 400,000 newcomers arrived annually and by the 1970s the number soared to 800,000. By the 1980s, more than 700,000 immigrants arrived per year, even though the number was capped at 270,000. Almost 9 million legal immigrants arrived in the 1980s. By the early 1990s, almost 1 million legal immigrants arrived each year, accounting for almost half of the country's population growth. In all, as many as 40 million legal immigrants arrived in the three decades following the 1965 reforms. Unlike the immigration of the late nineteenth and early twentieth centuries, much of this immigration was from Asia, Latin America, and other non-European regions.[28]

This increase was despite predictions in 1965 that the reforms would have little overall impact on immigration numbers. A major reason for this underestimation came from the Hart-Celler family unification policy, which allowed immigrants to bring spouses, minor children, and parents once the initial arrivals became legal resident aliens. After naturalization, an immigrant could also bring over his or her siblings, and in turn these new arrivals could bring over additional family members. These family arrivals did not count toward the 1965 limits. One arrival, once he or she secured employment and legal residency, could potentially bring over dozens of family members. The Johnson administration had assured Congress that the number of family members would be fewer than 40,000 annually, but the real numbers were double that from 1965 to 1975. In 1978 alone, immediate family members topped 125,000, with most from Asia, Mexico, and Central and South America. The number rose to 138,000 the following year, and under the preferences, Mexico alone sent almost 30,000 family members to the United States every year.[29]

Refugee policy, much of it shaped by the Cold War, also added to immigration numbers. Cuban migrants fleeing Fidel Castro's communist regime received preferences, and by 1990, over 800,000 had entered the United States. The failed U.S. intervention in Vietnam created more migrants, and the fall of Saigon to North Vietnam brought thousands of Vietnamese, Cambodian, and Laotian immigrants to the United States. By 1990, over 1 million Vietnam War refugees had settled in this country.[30]

The flood of immigrants was not all a mass of unskilled, low-wage workers, however. The labor certification provisions of Hart-Celler allowed many skilled Asian migrants to legally emigrate, which brought physicians and engineers along with other skilled professionals from India, the

Philippines, and South Korea, all seeking better wages in the United States. This was in marked contrast to earlier immigration—from 1910 to 1930, only 1.8 percent of immigrants had technical or professional skills, but by 1973 the number was almost 10 percent, and about 20 percent of Asian immigrants in 1973 were considered skilled. This had a profound impact on America's health services, which experienced heavy growth after the passage of Medicare and Medicaid in 1965. American medical schools could not keep up with the demand for new doctors and nurses, so hospitals, especially inner-city ones, brought in professionals from abroad. More than 50,000 doctors and almost 40,000 nurses emigrated to the United States between 1969 and 1973. More than 70 percent of the immigrant physicians came from South or East Asia. However, these doctors and nurses used the family preferences to bring over their own relatives. This trend changed after 1980, as the educational level of Asian immigrants dropped, and the number who lived in poverty increased.[31]

Obviously, Hart-Celler added further to racial, ethnic, and religious diversity in the United States. But the numbers that have been discussed so far largely concern *legal* immigration. Since much of the controversy today over immigration concerns illegal immigration, primarily from Mexico and Central America, the question of both Latino migration and illegal immigration deserves separate mention from the narrative of American immigration presented so far.

The United States' long and contentious history with Mexico goes back to the first half of the nineteenth century. Mexico gained independence in 1821 from Spain and then sought immigrants to colonize its vast northern frontier, especially in the province of Coahuila y Tejas (Texas). Toward that end, the province in the 1820s began to settle U.S. families on the Gulf Coast. Many new migrants came illegally, however, and ignored the requirements set by the Mexican government that the Anglo migrants from the United States become Mexican citizens and Catholics. Ironically, the early immigration history between the two countries consisted of American illegal immigration *to* Mexico.[32]

The Mexican government soon lost control of Texas as Anglo-American settlers, seeking to satisfy their land hunger, flooded into the province. This led to the Texan Revolution in 1836, whereby the settlers rebelled against Mexican control and established the Republic of Texas. The U.S. annexation of Texas in 1845 set in motion the chain of events that led to the U.S.-Mexican War. After invading and occupying Mexico, the United States then ended the war with the Treaty of Guadalupe-Hidalgo in 1848.

This treaty gave the United States much of the present-day American Southwest, including California with its harbors and access to the Pacific. An attempt by some eager expansionists in the U.S. Senate to annex all of Mexico was defeated largely on racial grounds, with many white Americans reluctant to add a large population of racially mixed Roman Catholics to the country.[33]

The newly established international border on the Rio Grande created a migration issue because the Mexican population of the ceded territories—while less than 100,000—had a long history of moving back and forth freely before the creation of the boundary line. With the discovery of gold in California in 1848, thousands of people flooded into the territory to make their fortunes. This included between 15,000 and 20,000 Mexican citizens, mostly from Sonora. The presence of Mexican gold miners angered rival Anglo gold miners, who then resorted to vigilante violence or legal maneuvers such as a tax on foreign miners to expel them from the region. In contrast to California, Texas also saw—and welcomed—an increase in Mexican immigration after 1848 as migrants sought cheaper manufactured goods and higher wages, with many moving into paid labor on ranches and farms. These migrations more than tripled the Mexican population of the United States by 1880 to over 290,000 people.[34]

The policies of Porfirio Diaz, the president of Mexico from 1876 to 1910, added to the migrations. In his quest to modernize and industrialize Mexico, he attracted foreign (especially U.S.) investment, which gave the United States control over much of the Mexican economy. Diaz also began a program of land "reform" that involved displacing hundreds of thousands of peasant farmers by seizing their lands and giving them over to railroad companies and large-scale landlords, with the purpose of encouraging the export of agricultural produce. These policies created a massive surplus population in Mexican towns and cities. This surplus, coupled with high labor demands in the U.S. Southwest in the early twentieth century, led to significant migrations of Mexican laborers to the United States. The United States complied with these realities by maintaining an open border with Mexico, and Mexican immigration became numerically significant after 1905.[35]

The importance of Mexican labor to employers, especially to cotton and sugar beet growers, showed how Mexican immigration was separated from other migration in this era. When Congress began to curtail immigration during and after World War I, Mexican labor was exempted from the restrictions due to the lobbying power of southwestern agribusiness. For example, the literacy requirements for immigrants that Congress passed in 1917 were modified in 1918 to exempt Mexicans, and residents of the Western Hemisphere were not affected by the quotas of the Johnson-Reed Act of 1924. Growers even brought in 83,000 temporary Mexican workers under a contract labor program between 1917 and 1921, of which 21,000 then abandoned their employers and moved to U.S. cities for work and residency.[36]

The growth of Mexican neighborhoods and towns—called *barrios* and *colonias*—also meant increased racism against Mexicans. This included residential and educational segregation. School districts sought to "Americanize" Mexican children, which mostly meant channeling them into industrial or vocational education to make them into reliable laborers. In agricultural areas, where children were used as migrant laborers, school districts reduced and adjusted school seasons according to the harvest so that the children's education would not conflict with the growers' needs for labor.[37]

The Great Depression altered this flow of migration. Widespread unemployment in the United States after the stock market crash in 1929 led to a wave of anti-immigrant sentiment as Anglo-Americans now competed with Mexican laborers for jobs. Local governments and their police forces rounded up Mexicans and in many cases deported them to the border without their families or any means of assistance. In a precursor to what happened to Japanese Americans during World War II, the U.S.-born children of Mexican migrants were deported as well, as few Anglo-Americans made any distinction between Mexican immigrants and Mexican Americans. Many other migrants left on their own rather than face harassment and deportation. More than 350,000 migrants were repatriated to Mexico by 1934.[38]

The arrival of World War II reversed U.S. attitudes toward Mexican immigration yet again, suggesting the cynical nature of the relationship that the United States has with its southern neighbor. Condemned as job stealers during the Depression, Mexican laborers now found themselves welcomed back to satisfy U.S. demand for wartime labor. In 1942, the State Department negotiated the Bracero Program with the Mexican government, which Congress then approved. Guest workers were imported into the U.S. to do civilian labor, with guarantees of fair wages as well as working and living conditions. In reality, the braceros were paid lower wages and endured substandard living conditions. During the war, 300,000 braceros were bought in as migrant farm laborers. The program proved popular with U.S. employers due to the cheap labor, and many Mexicans willingly became braceros despite the abuses so that they could send wages home to their families. In fact, remittances from braceros soon surpassed oil as the major source of foreign revenue for Mexico. As a result of its popularity, the Bracero Program was extended after the war until 1964, with 4.6 million bracero contracts being issued during the program's 22-year history.[39]

The Bracero Program, in the words of one historian, "hastened Mexico's transition into a nation of emigrants." This legal immigration coincided with illegal immigration, however. The U.S. and Mexican governments cooperated in the 1950s to deport undocumented workers. The most infamous example of this cooperation was 1954's Operation Wetback, which resulted in the deportation of 1 million immigrants through military-style dragnets in the Southwest and in Midwestern cities where immigrants worked. Yet it was the increasing number of bracero contracts issued after 1954 that led to the drop in illegal immigration, not stepped-up law enforcement. In fact, enforcement slackened after 1954 as more and more migrants entered the Bracero Program, with 150,000 alone entering California from 1954 to 1958.[40]

Congress terminated the Bracero Program in 1964, largely due to pressure from the American Federation of Labor-Congress on Industrial Organizations (AFL-CIO), which worried about bracero workers depressing wages and the poor conditions they labored under. The Hart-Celler Act of 1965 led to a gradual increase in legal emigration from Mexico, but illegal immigration skyrocketed, going from 161,608 illegal immigrants apprehended by the Immigration and Naturalization Service (INS) in 1967 to over 1 million in 1977. As concern about illegal immigration grew, politicians debated what approaches to take. In one sense, Congress preferred to treat illegal immigration like the "war on drugs"—attack the supply but not the demand. While deportations continued, liberals in Congress (with the backing of labor unions) proposed employer sanctions against businesses that hired illegal immigrants. The growers still had powerful allies in the Senate, like James Eastland of Mississippi, who blocked the legislation. Another reason for lack of support for sanctions was fears by Mexican American groups that these sanctions would lead employers to discriminate against Hispanics. Mexican American opposition to sanctions and other measures against illegal immigration also exposed another potential crack in the liberal coalition, as African American leaders worried about the impact of Mexican migration on black wages and employment.

Environmental groups like the Sierra Club also opposed illegal immigration and called for new restrictions.[41]

Attempts at enforcement also met with controversy. A proposal by the INS in 1978 to build new fences with barbed wire at El Paso, Texas, and San Ysidro, California, triggered objections from the Mexican government and was called by the U.S. press the Tortilla Curtain. The Carter administration ordered the fencing scaled back, but in subsequent years, the INS added more fencing, albeit without the harmful barbed and razor wire designs of the Tortilla Curtain proposal.[42]

By the early 1980s, with illegal immigration higher than ever, Congress finally began to break its deadlock. After several failed attempts, the Immigration and Reform Act of 1986, better known as the Simpson-Mazzoli Act, became law with President Ronald Reagan's signature. The act granted amnesty to undocumented aliens living in the country prior to January 1, 1982 and made allowances for further additions of migrants to work as farm laborers. In a shift from the 1970s, the law did contain some employer sanctions, but they were weakened from the earlier, more punitive proposals. The act's major legacy would be the amnesty provision, which allowed about 3 million undocumented aliens to gain legal residency in the United States.[43]

The Simpson-Mazzoli Act did a lot to legalize illegal immigrants but little to curb illegal immigration. The Reagan and Bush administrations, with their strong probusiness records and corporate base, had little stomach for enforcing employer sanctions. Liberals and labor unions were more concerned about enforcing the antidiscrimination provisions in the act. The judiciary also became involved when the U.S. District Court in Washington, D.C., sided with immigration advocacy groups in *Ayuda, Inc. v. Meese* in 1988 and vacated application denials issued by the Immigration and Naturalization Service (INS), thus widening amnesty further.[44]

Concerns remained in the 1980s about countries that had been penalized under the Hart-Celler Act. Irish Americans and their political allies, like Senator Edward Kennedy, lobbied for more visas for Irish migrants. Others, like Senator Alan Simpson, the Wyoming Republican who coauthored the 1986 reform, wanted to attract more skilled workers. These proposals came together in the Immigration Act of 1990, signed into law by President George H. W. Bush. The act increased legal admissions, especially for employment-based visas, and extended amnesty to immediate family members of aliens who received amnesty under the Simpson-Mazzoli Act. A "diversity" program for Irish and other foreign nationals was introduced. As for illegal immigration, the act contained broader enforcement power and funding.[45]

The acts of 1986 and 1990 represented the last bipartisan successes for immigration reform. Since the 1990s, the controversies over illegal immigration have become increasingly polarized and racialized, even as the Latino population in the United States has grown. Restrictionists on immigration experienced success with grassroots mobilization against illegal immigration in various states, a phenomenon that continues to this day. The highly publicized example was Proposition 187 in California, a 1994 ballot initiative that denied illegal aliens and their children welfare benefits, nonemergency health care, and public education. With the state suffering a budget shortfalls and an economic slump, illegal immigrants became popular targets. The issue became a partisan one when Pete Wilson, California's Republican governor, endorsed Proposition 187 in his re-election bid, and the state GOP did as well.[46]

Proposition 187 coincided with U.S. voters' concerns over immigration. By the mid-1990s, growing numbers of voters expressed concern about both legal and illegal immigration. One-fifth of voters in 1994 ranked illegal immigration as their top concern. After 1992, immigration also became increasingly connected in voters' minds with economic downturns and uncertainty. These attitudes explained the success of Proposition 187, which passed with 59 percent of the vote as Wilson won re-election. However, a federal court immediately issued an injunction against the proposition on the grounds that denial of public education to children of illegal aliens was unconstitutional. This effectively blunted any replication of Proposition 187 in other states.[47]

On the federal level, GOP victories in the 1994 elections and President Bill Clinton's resulting shift to the right did result in more action against illegal immigrants. Clinton endorsed stronger enforcement measures, and signed into law the Illegal Immigration Reform and Responsibility Act (IIR-IRA) into law in 1996, which enhanced federal enforcement of the border and limited immigrant access to public benefits. Immigration also overlapped with the Personal Responsibility and Work Opportunity Act of 1996, the "welfare reform" law that barred noncitizens—including legal immigrants—from many federal benefits.[48] Clinton, running for re-election, did not wish to appear to be coddling illegal immigrants and accepted even legal immigrants becoming scapegoats as a price of his victory.

Race and the question of assimilation was one of the other major reasons beside economics that explained why so many Americans wanted immigration curtailed. Of course, concern about the economic problems that immigrants might cause is cited by some Americans who hold racist views toward Latinos, as it becomes a convenient "nonracial" cover for opposing immigration. The question of assimilation, notably in the area of language, is one raised by immigration opponents. Proposals to make English the national language are routinely brought out by politicians and endorsed in the conservative press (Puerto Rico, where most of the inhabitants are Spanish-speaking and also U.S. citizens, seems to be forgotten in these proposals).[49]

A target that critics often single out for this perceived lack of assimilation is bilingual education. By 1970, twenty-one states required that English be the only language of instruction in school. But in 1974, the Supreme Court in the case of *Lau v. Nichols* ruled that the failure to provide programs tailored to the needs of minority children was a violation of the Civil Rights Act of 1964. The Bilingual Education Act of 1968 had already provided funds for bilingual education, but the *Lau* decision (which involved Chinese students) greatly expanded federal and state funding for bilingual education. The backlash against bilingual education led to the formation of the English Only movement in 1978, founded by Emmy Schafer, a woman who became angry when she could not find an English-speaking clerk in a Dade County, Florida, government office. Another organization, U.S. English, lobbied Congress to make English the official language of the United States. By 1989, both organizations had convinced 17 states to adopt English as their official language. Some prominent politicians, such as Tom Tancredo, a GOP representative from Colorado, have built much of their political career on opposing bilingualism.[50]

The reality does not support this notion of English as a language under assault by Spanish-speaking immigrants. Not surprisingly, as surveys of immigrant-heavy Orange County, California, in the greater Los Angeles area have shown, most first-generation Latinos (76.9%) spoke Spanish at home. Only 20 percent of second-generation Latinos spoke primarily Spanish at home, with half using English almost exclusively at home. By the third generation, the overwhelming majority used only English at home. Studies of Los Angeles have shown similar results. These patterns were also similar when it came to spoken language preferences with friends and especially at work. The rates of English usage were also higher with Latinos who had citizenship or legal residency. This indicates that like previous generations of immigrants from Europe and Asia, Latinos assimilate themselves into American society, including linguistically.[51]

The prevalence of Spanish, of course, is due to the continuing arrival of new immigrants from Mexico and other Spanish-speaking countries. The hostility of the English-speaking majority to Spanish plays a role in its continuation as well. Spanish in the *barrios* remains the language of communication to aid newly arrived migrants and visiting family members. Pride and interest in Spanish heritage and Spanish-language literature coming out of Chicano activism also contributed, and some have cited the negative consequences of Latino generations becoming English-only in an increasingly global and multicultural world.[52]

One area of this growing assimilation is politics. While less than half of all Latinos are registered to vote, the number has been growing steadily. Between 1992 and 1996, 1.3 million Latino voters were added to the nation's voter registration rolls. Federal civil rights measures also aided Latino participation. When Congress renewed the Voting Rights Act in 1975, it included a provision giving language minorities protection under the act, which added new areas outside the Deep South, such as the entirety of the states of Arizona and Texas. The jurisdictions covered under the language minorities clause (which were areas where more than 5% of the citizens were part of a single language minority and had an illiteracy rate higher than the national average) had to provide materials in other languages for the minority voters. This led to an increase in Latino representation in areas like the Southwest, but not evenly or at the same rate as for black elected officials in the South. Stronger gains occurred in local offices like city councils and school boards rather than in statewide or federal offices. In some areas, like New York City, little improvement for minority candidates occurred.[53]

One effect of the Voting Rights Act's extension to Latinos is that jurisdictions were now subjected to review of their redistricting to assess its impact on minority voting strength. This has led to the creation of largely Latino congressional districts, which has added new federal representatives. For example, four new Latino representatives were elected to Congress from the Southwest in 1982 following redistricting from the 1980 census. While a Latino-majority district does not guarantee a Latino representative any more than a black-majority district guarantees a black one, the Voting Rights Act has led to a clear increase in Latino representation. The preclearance provisions of the Voting Rights Act also mean that after every federal census, states with large Latino populations go through the same process of redrawing districts as southern states with black-majority districts do. Not surprisingly, these can become emotionally charged and partisan issues. In Harris County, Texas, Latino elected officials and other leaders recently complained that the proposed redrawn Commissioners Court eroded Latino voting power in one of the precincts, which they feared would lead to no Latino representation in a county that is 40 percent Latino. Their stance also pitted them against black leaders, who were satisfied with black representation in the precincts. Similar controversies accompanied the GOP-crafted redistricting plan for Texas, which did not increase Latino representation despite its growth.[54]

The issue of Latino political representation in elected offices will continue to be a major issue as the Latino population increases. In Texas, Anglo-Americans became a minority in 2004, as the combined black, Latino, and Asian population surpassed them. Latinos are expected to surpass Anglo-Americans in total numbers in Texas by 2020, and Latinos are projected to be the majority by 2040. These growth patterns, contrary to popular belief, are not primarily driven by legal or illegal immigration. The 2010 census indicated that Latinos born in the United States rather than newly arrived Mexican immigrants are now responsible for the bulk of Latino growth. The number of U.S.-born Mexican Americans also widened over foreign-born noncitizens, which carries implications for future Latino voting power. Illegal immigration peaked in the 1990s and has slowed in recent years due to economic downturns and increased border enforcement. Overall, the Mexican American population increased 11.4 percent, with 63 of this growth percent coming from births. Despite these growth numbers, Latinos remain underrepresented in political office, and elected officials are still largely concentrated in municipal and school board positions in the Southwest.[55]

These trends would seem to cause problems for the Republican Party in high-immigrant states, since Latino voters have generally been Democratic voters. This has led to varied approaches by some GOP elected officials, and these tactics fit what one scholar has said is Latinos being publicly—and contradictorily—framed as "America's political darlings and scapegoats." Both parties have been wooing Latino voters for decades, but when roughly 40 percent of Latino voters cast their votes for George W. Bush in 2004, some pundits predicted a long-term shift to the GOP. That election was taken as "proof" that Latino voters were culturally conservative and voted for the GOP largely on cultural values, and thus were being assimilated into American conservatism. Of course, that Latinos are heterogeneous in values, social class, religion, country of origin, and other demographic characteristics gets watered down in this oversimplification, as does the reality that most still voted for Kerry in 2004. For example, non-Catholic Christians, many from evangelical sects, favored Bush, but they make up only 18 percent of the Latino electorate. Catholic Latinos still favored Kerry and the Democrats. Specific factors related to the 2004 election also affected Latino turnout, such as George W. Bush's long relationship with the Latino community in Texas, which led him to develop a more culturally sensitive approach and rapport with Latino voters in Texas than most white Republicans historically have had. A highly effective Latino advertising and marketing campaign by the GOP also produced more effective ads than the Democrats.[56]

What a difference an election cycle makes. Since 2004, the GOP has moved away from Latino voters and threatened to drive them back to the Democrats. First, the rise of armed groups like the Minuteman Project, which formed to patrol the border and fight illegal immigration, has been part of a growing xenophobia amongst some white Americans. The Minutemen Project was established in October 2004 to monitor the Arizona-Mexico border and report to the Border Patrol about migrants crossing. More extreme groups with openly racist agendas have emerged, such as the Minutemen American Defense Fund, a splinter group whose founder, Shawna Forde, was convicted in February 2011 of murdering a Latino man and his nine-year-old daughter. The rise of the Tea Party has further emboldened anti-immigrant conservatives in the GOP. In 2005, H.R. 4437, a House bill sponsored by GOP representative Jim Sensenbrenner called for criminal penalties against illegal immigrants and those who helped them enter the country or harbored them after their arrival, and the GOP-controlled Senate voted to make English the national language of the United States.[57]

Activism by immigrants and their supporters has also heightened the issue of illegal immigration, and has likely fed the nativist backlash. In 2006, thousands of immigrants and their supporters, as well as institutions like the Catholic Church, took to the streets in Los Angeles, Chicago, Houston, and other cities against H.R. 4437. While H.R. 4437 did not pass, its proposal for a 700-mile fence on the border did become law as H.R. 6061, or the Secure Fence Act of 2006. President Bush signed it into law in October 2006.[58]

The real focus of anti-immigration rhetoric and actions in recent years has been on the state rather than federal level, with a return to Proposition 187–style actions by state governments who believe that the federal government was not doing enough about illegal immigration. Russell

Pearce, a state senator in Arizona, sponsored S.B. 1070, an anti-immigration bill that Governor Jan Brewer signed into law in 2010. The law requires local police to enforce federal immigration laws whenever they suspect an individual is an illegal immigrant. Not surprisingly, critics said this would be in effect a legalization of racial profiling of Latinos. Pearce also pushed through another law, which revokes the business licenses of companies that employ undocumented workers. Private efforts to fight illegal immigration along the lines of the Minuteman Project have also emerged, such as another Arizona Republican state senator, Steve Smith, who solicited private donations in 2011 to build a fence to cover Arizona's entire border with Mexico.[59]

The Arizona law became part of a national firestorm over illegal immigration, and a federal court promptly blocked most of the law. Unlike the fate of Proposition 187, Republican-dominated states did not back down from passing similar laws. Georgia passed such a law in 2011 over the opposition of growers in the state, who rely on migrant labor. South Carolina did as well, with both it and the Georgia law empowering police to check immigration status and enforce federal laws. The South Carolina law even made it a crime to knowingly transport or harbor an illegal immigrant, a provision reminiscent of the Fugitive Slave Act of 1850. Not one to be outdone, Alabama passed a law harsher than all the others. Even though only 3 percent of Alabama's population is foreign-born (as opposed to 12.5% nationwide), the law replicated the provisions of the Arizona and Georgia laws, and even barred citizens from giving an illegal immigrant a ride in their car. It also required schools to determine the legal status of pupils' parents, which could discourage parents from enrolling their American-born children. The law was onerous enough that even some conservative ministers spoke out against it.[60]

These laws have had a chilling effect on Latinos, both legal and undocumented, in the affected states. For instance, some Latino students in Alabama stopped attending school in the wake of the law's passage, and some U.S.-born children were denied food stamps because their parents could not prove the children were legal residents. Alabama in particular appears to have done more harm than good with its law. As even legally residing Latino migrants fled the state in the wake of the anti-Latino atmosphere created by the law, businesses and farmers reported the loss of construction workers, roofers, and field hands. They could not find native-born replacements, despite legislators' assurances that the law would reduce the state's 10 percent unemployment. The law also provoked a backlash from

big business, a reliable GOP base, after police stopped and detained two foreign employees working at the state's Honda and Mercedes plants, cases that
attracted embarrassing international attention—not the least because one of
the detained, Detlev Hager, was a visiting executive from Mercedes-Benz
who was arrested for driving with only German identification on him. Business leaders called for revisions to the law, and the Republican attorney general called for the strictest portions to be repealed.[61]

The reaction of GOP leaders in Alabama to this embarrassment
indicates the fundamentally racist nature of these state laws and how their
drafters, despite their claims of color-blindness, are concerned only with
Latino immigrants. When the GOP's corporate base found its interests
threatened by the enforcement of the law, GOP leaders were quick to back
off rather than insist on strict enforcement. Foreign executives and workers
are okay when they work for big companies bringing investment to the
state, but brown-skinned Spanish speakers who labor in menial jobs, and
even their children in public schools, are a racialized "other" that cannot
be tolerated.

The federal government has filed challenges against these rulings,
specifically suing Arizona, Alabama, South Carolina, and Utah, which
means that the Supreme Court would make the final decision in this
federal-versus-state conflict. A federal judge struck down some of the
provisions of the Alabama law in September 2011, and the Court began
hearings on the Arizona law in the spring of 2012. As a sign of the nation's
increased diversity, Sonia Sotomayor, the first Latina—or even Latino—
justice on the Supreme Court (born in the Bronx to Puerto Rican parents)
asked pointed questions of Arizona's lawyers, specifically expressing
concerns over people being detained based on their race and ethnicity.
Her questions directly related to her own experience, as Sotomayor, who
grew up in a housing project and attended Princeton and Yale on scholar-
ships, has referred before to being discriminated against and the feeling of
being "different" among the people from elite backgrounds.[62]

The Court's ruling on June 25, 2012, on S.B. 1070 was mixed, as the justices issued a ruling that struck down key provisions of the law, including
the provision that made it a crime for illegal immigrants to seek employment. While Obama and some Democrats claimed victory, the law was
not repealed. The Court's 5–3 decision upheld the controversial provision
that allowed police officers to ask about immigration status during stops.
The preservation of this portion, so heavily reviled by Latinos as an
endorsement of racial profiling, meant that Governor Brewer and her allies

could claim victory as well. State and local police can detain an immigrant for being undocumented, but only so that they can report it to the federal authorities who will then make a decision on deportation. Justice Anthony Kennedy said that whatever Arizona's frustrations over illegal immigration, "the State may not pursue policies that undermine federal law." With the supremacy of the federal government in immigration matters clearly spelled out by the Court, this ruling will likely curb the more stringent provisions of the other states' anti-immigration laws as well. But the issue will likely continue, as abuses and racial profiling by local law enforcement as the rest of S.B. 1070 is enforced will no doubt lead to future lawsuits.[63]

The anti-immigration rhetoric also took center stage in the Republican presidential debates and primaries in 2011 and 2012. The candidates largely promised strict enforcement of immigration laws and have endorsed state laws like the Arizona one, which President Barack Obama has opposed. Of the GOP candidates for president, only Newt Gingrich supported even a limited path for citizenship for illegal immigrants, when he indicated that he supported it for immigrants who have lived in the country for decades and have strong ties to their communities.[64]

Former Massachusetts governor Mitt Romney, the Republican nominee for president, embraced a "self-deportation" plan, by which strict enforcement of illegal immigration laws on the state and federal level would drive out illegal immigrants by denying them access to employment and social services. Gingrich mocked the plan and called Romney "the most anti-immigration candidate" in an ad aired over a Spanish-language radio station in advance of the Florida Republican primary. Marco Rubio, the Cuban American senator from Florida, denounced the ad and Gingrich withdrew it. Rubio did recognize that there were major problems with the GOP's anti-immigrant rhetoric and the fear of a backlash by Latino voters against the party in November 2012. He criticized, but did not name, conservative members of his party "who have used rhetoric that is harsh and intolerable, inexcusable" toward immigrants, and that "sometimes we've been too slow in condemning that rhetoric."[65]

Perhaps the most strident shift in anti-immigration rhetoric in recent political history is the use of the term "anchor babies," which refers to immigrants who come to the United States illegally and give birth so that their children can get citizenship under the Fourteenth Amendment, and thus can legally stay as the child's parents. The citizenship clause in Section One of the Amendment says that "all persons born or naturalized in the United States, and subject to the jurisdiction thereof, are citizens of the

United States and of the State wherein they reside." Some conservative politicians and nativist groups have challenged this long-standing part of American law. During her presidential campaign, Representative Michelle Bachmann called for legislation to end "birthright citizenship," declaring to a crowd in Iowa that "we've got to end this anchor-baby program." Bills to end birthright citizenship for immigrants have been presented to Congress. The term "anchor baby" has become a racialized code word referring to Latinas, depicting them as lazy freeloaders giving birth to litters of brown children, much as "welfare queen" in the 1970s and 1980s stereotyped black women the same way. The reality is that a child would have to wait at least 21 years to assist his or her parents this way, and the process could take years after that. Also, many undocumented immigrants fear arrest and deportation if they deliver in hospitals, and some are not even be aware of the specific legal advantages of having a U.S.-born child. Finally, largely due to longstanding legal practice and Supreme Court precedents upholding birthright citizenship, the calls to end it would almost certainly involve amending the U.S. Constitution, a task not easily accomplished.[66]

Ironically, illegal immigration has been declining due to stronger federal enforcement. The number of Border Patrol agents on the U.S.-Mexico border has risen fivefold since 1993, and a third of the border is fenced. Reconnaissance drones, cameras, and sensors add to the enforcement. A weak U.S. economy and falling birthrates in Mexico have also contributed to a decline in new illegal immigrants. In El Paso, Texas, agents picked up 12,251 illegal immigrants in 2010, a 96 percent decline from 1993. In fact, the very ethnic nature of immigration is changing from the stereotype of the Mexican migrant fruit picker or landscaper. In 2012, Asian immigration—most of it legal and consisting of highly skilled workers from China, India, and South Korea—surpassed Latino immigration for the first time.[67] Of course, reality matters little in politics, and the perception of an immigrant "invasion" resonates strongly with white voters in the GOP primaries and Tea Parties.

Romney's anti-immigration rhetoric carried risks for the GOP in 2012. The appeal to white conservative votes in the primaries led Romney to eagerly criticize Texas governor Rick Perry for signing into law a bill that allowed undocumented students to pay the same rates as other state residents at public universities. But unique states like Florida, with its large Cuban American (and Republican) voting bloc, as well as a significant group of Puerto Rican voters, led Romney to address Latino audiences about immigration reform and enhanced trade with Latin America. And in the general election, with independents and Latino voters to appeal to, strong nativist appeals can be alienating. With Latinos at 16 percent of the population nationally but over 20 percent in key states like Colorado, Florida, Nevada, and New Mexico, Latino voters are still a potential swing vote in those states despite their underregistration. In Arizona, anger over the immigration law in a state with a 30 percent Latino population had some Democrats hoping to flip the state into Obama's camp this year, although that did not materialize. All of these factors fueled speculation that Romney was going to pick a running mate like Rubio or Susana Martinez, the governor of New Mexico.[68]

Another factor that acts as a check on anti-immigration sentiment is the corporate base of the GOP, which sometimes conflicts with nativist extremes in the party. The Republican reluctance to go after employers who hire illegal labor goes back to at least Reagan and continues today. That was seen vividly in Texas in the summer of 2011 when Rick Perry, likely seeking to increase his conservative credentials before his ill-fated presidential campaign, pushed a "sanctuary cities" bill aimed at punishing municipalities that did not arrest and deport illegal immigrants. As one Texas political observer noted, the bill was "political theater," since Perry could not name a single such city in the state. The Texas Tea Party strongly supported the bill, but two of Perry's biggest contributors, homebuilder Bob Perry and H.E.B. grocery chain head Charles Butt came out against it, fearing the economic impact of the potential loss of immigrant labor. Their opposition led Republicans in the Texas legislature to kill the bill.[69]

The rise of nativist rhetoric in the GOP does not mean that the Democrats lack problems regarding immigration. While most Latino voters supported Obama in 2008, he did little on immigration reform in his first term. He publicly supported the DREAM Act, a piece of legislation that would allow undocumented immigrant students a path to citizenship, a call he renewed to woo Latino voters in the 2012 election. However, the DREAM Act failed to pass Congress even when the Democrats controlled both houses after the 2008 election, as the president made issues like health care and financial regulation bigger priorities. In fact, deportations rose sharply during the Obama administration to about 400,000 people in 2010, higher than the Bush years. Audits of companies who hired undocumented workers quadrupled after Obama took office. The continued reliance of a Democratic administration on punitive measures led some immigration advocacy groups to ask Obama to stop giving lip service to the DREAM Act and campaigning on it as long as mass deportations of undocumented workers and students continue. Although the Democrats hope to capitalize on Latino fears of anti-immigration Republicans, it is clear that taking these voters for granted—like the party frequently does with its African American base—and not passing immigration reform will not mobilize them in large numbers on Election Day. And as long as Congress remains divided as it is currently between a House of Representatives dominated by anti-immigration Republicans and a Democratic Senate that places immigration reform on the back burner, any real reform in a second Obama term is unlikely.[70]

Yet being an incumbent president in an election year does have its advantages, especially when it comes to bypassing congressional opposition. With the DREAM Act blocked in Congress, Obama took action in the summer of 2012 to appease Latino voters disgruntled over his lack of action on immigration issues. On June 15, he issued an executive order that he called a "temporary stopgap measure" to halt deportations of illegal immigrants who had arrived before age 16, had lived in the United States for at least five years, and were either enrolled in school, had graduated from high school, or were military veterans in good standing. The immigrants also had to be under age 30 with no criminal records. The order would affect an estimated 800,000 immigrants and was warmly received by immigration activists.[71]

The question for the 2012 election regarding immigration was would it become a wedge issue like how Lee Atwater used the Willie Horton case in 1988. That did not happen, largely because unlike black voters, Latino voters do not support the Democrats in overwhelming numbers. GOP efforts at Latino marketing and outreach will no doubt continue after the 2012 election, and Mitt Romney's campaigning from the center tried to lure Latino voters to his standard. Romney already gave some indication of his move to the center when he rejected xenophobic rhetoric in his response to the president's June 15 executive order. He carefully tailored his opposition to the order based on the president's circumvention of Congress with a temporary measure that would make it "more difficult to reach a long-term solution," but he did not criticize the immigrant children who had arrived in the United States "through no fault of their own."[72]

Immigration did become a wedge issue in 2012, but not for the Democrats. The anti-immigration rhetoric from the GOP primaries combined with the successful outreach of the Democrats proved fatal for Romney's campaign. Exit polls conducted by CNN estimated 71 percent Latino support for Obama, but the actual numbers showed that this was likely an underestimation. In the key swing state of Colorado, Latinos favored Obama by 87 percent, while in Ohio, the number was 82 percent. Key Latino-populated states like Nevada and New Mexico also went for Obama. Overall, Latinos gave Obama 5.4 percent of his margin of victory, greater numbers than his overall popular vote, so Latino voters can credibly claim to have been the decisive factor in re-electing the president. Part of this was apparently the failure of the GOP to convince Latino voters that they cared only about *illegal* immigration. Since 60 percent of Latinos know someone in the country illegally, illegal immigration is not an abstract issue for them but a personal one, as Gary Segura, a Stanford University professor who examines Latino voting noted. Perhaps this issue of GOP trouble with the Latino vote will be the one that will motivate House Republicans to break with the nativist wing of their party and champion immigration reform as a way to woo back Latino voters. If the GOP wishes to remain viable in key states—and thus elect Republican presidents—they need a return to the bipartisanship of the Reagan years on immigration reform. There are some signs this may happen, as Republican House Speaker John Boehner said after the election that he was "confident" both parties could reach a deal on immigration. But the Democrats now have to deliver as well, as leaders of immigrant rights and Latino groups told Obama that the price of their support for his reelection is comprehensive immigration reform. As one Latino union officer said, "[t]o both sides we say: 'No more excuses.'"[73] The next four years will see if concrete reform or partisan rhetoric wins the day.

Chapter 5

Access to Voting: Voter ID Cards, Polling Locations, and Places Like Florida

Darrell Kenyatta Evers, a black man from Mississippi, once told his mother Myrlie that he did not see the point of voting. As mother and son argued about the merits of the franchise, she produced a bloodied piece of paper. It was the poll-tax receipt that her husband, National Association for the Advancement of Colored People (NAACP) Mississippi field secretary Medgar Evers, had been carrying when he was shot and killed by a white supremacist outside the couple's Jackson home in 1963. Darrell, chastised by the reminder of his father's ultimate sacrifice, immediately conceded the argument.[1]

Few stories about the right to vote are as poignant as that one, but the tale illustrates the price paid by many for that right of citizenship. Today, in an age of universal suffrage, many Americans imagine that all barriers to voting have been removed and that any citizen who wants to vote can do so with ease. Yet even in the Age of Obama, the right to the franchise is not universal and remains contested, with mechanisms like voter identification (ID) laws and felony disfranchisement serving to depress minority voting. These devices remain superficially nonracial, which allows opponents of minority voting to champion them while fulfilling their actual goal of disfranchisement. The effect is that in a supposed "postracial" America, the race and class of a potential voter can still affect his or her registration and exercise of the franchise.

The history of suppressing minority voting predates even the end of slavery in the United States. In most of the northern and all of the southern states before the Civil War, black men and women were legally free but had few to no political rights. As white workingmen gained the right to vote with the abolition of property-holding requirements in the early nineteenth century, rights for free blacks contracted. States like New Jersey, Maryland, and Connecticut had initially granted free blacks the right to vote during the first years of the nation's independence; but by 1820, they had limited the franchise to white men only. New York kept property-holding require-ments in place for black men as they were abolished for white men, effec-tively denying all but a handful the right to vote. Pennsylvania and North Carolina added the word "white" to their constitutional voting require-ments in the 1830s, and *every* state that entered the union after 1819 denied blacks the right to vote. By 1855, only five states—Massachusetts, Rhode Island, Vermont, New Hampshire, and Maine—allowed black men the vote, but only 4 percent of the nation's free black population lived in these states. The federal government sanctioned this inequality by forbidding black men from voting in the territories it controlled, and the Supreme Court infamously denied that blacks were even citizens in the *Dred Scott v. Sanford* decision of 1857.[2]

The first major shift in attitudes toward black voting came with the Civil War and the abolition of slavery, which raised questions about the political future of the ex-slaves. The immense sacrifices of black soldiers during the war prompted skeptics of black equality like Abraham Lincoln to eventu-ally support suffrage for educated black men and black military veterans. Federal support for black voting came in 1867 when Radical Republicans in Congress pushed through the Reconstruction Act, which divided the defeated Confederacy into five military districts and legalized black male voting in those areas. This military rule would end only when voters in the occupied states ratified the Fourteenth Amendment, which granted citizenship to the freed people and approved universal male suffrage. Ironi-cally, the Reconstruction Act protected black male suffrage in the South while black men still were denied the right to vote in many northern states, a denial of rights that continued as Democrats won state and local elections in the 1867 voting, and referenda to extend the right to vote to black men lost in several northern states.[3]

This situation changed only with the ratification of the Fifteenth Amendment in 1870, which extended the right to vote to all men in the country for the first time, and along with the Fourteenth Amendment added the words "right to vote" to the Constitution. Voting had even expanded in less-noticed areas like absentee balloting, such as when 19 states during the Civil War granted the right to vote to soldiers in the field. By 1870, with black voters sending black men to office in the former Con-federacy and creating biracial Republican coalitions, it seemed as if

Reconstruction were creating a biracial society and moving the country toward racial equality.[4]

Such dreams were obviously premature. White violence against both white and black Republicans and black voters in the South, combined with growing northern indifference to Reconstruction and the vigorous enforcement of civil rights, led to the decline of this biracial politics by the mid-1870s. The "redemption" of the white South by ex-Confederates through threats and violence led to the overthrow of state Republican governments and a drop in black office-holding. With the Compromise of 1877 leading to the removal of federal troops from the South and the Supreme Court weakening the enforcement power of Congress regarding the Fourteenth and Fifteenth Amendments, the federal government largely washed its hands of its experiment with black suffrage and paved the way for the eventual disfranchisement of black voters.[5]

As mentioned in an earlier chapter, with the failure in 1890 of the Federal Elections Bill—or what opponents called the Force Bill—Congress joined the executive and judicial branches in their indifference to black voting and acquiesced in the enactment of the Jim Crow laws of the 1890s and first years of the twentieth century, which created public segregation and denied the right to vote to black men through poll taxes, literacy tests, and other ostensibly nonracial means. Backed up by the mob violence of lynching, black political activity in the South largely ceased to exist by the outbreak of World War I.[6]

By the time of the Progressive Era of the early twentieth century—when black men saw their rights of suffrage slipping away—many of the modern practices and mechanisms of voting came into law in the United States. Voter registration, the Australian (or secret) ballot, residency requirements, and other factors that would create the modern electoral machinery came into effect, with many of these having detrimental effects on non-English-speaking voters and the uneducated. Literacy tests for immigrants were enacted in 1917, largely out of concern over lack off assimilation and assumptions that immigrants would not be informed voters. Many northern and western states also adopted literacy tests similar to the ones used in the South to disfranchise African American voters.[7]

With barriers up that blocked African American voting in the South and limited immigrant voting elsewhere, activists who favored broadening the franchise targeted poll taxes, which had the effect of denying the vote to poor whites as well as blacks. Most southern states had adopted the so-called white primary, which restricted who could vote in the Democratic state primaries. In the one-party Democratic South, this effectively shut African American voters out of any meaningful influence even if they met other voting qualifications. The white primary worked in favor of arguments to abolish the poll tax, since (white) opponents of the poll tax could argue that black voting would not increase if the tax were abolished; instead, it would drop a class barrier and allow more white men and women to vote. As a result of these campaigns, three states—North Carolina, Louisiana, and Florida—abolished their poll taxes by the 1930s. By contrast, no poll taxes existed outside the South by 1940, so support for the taxes became rooted in class biases against poor whites and in fears that abolition would lead to the fall of other barriers to black voting.[8]

Such concerns were valid, since even though white opponents of the poll tax did not challenge other barriers to voting, black opponents did. Civil rights activists and southern liberals began to press for federal action against the poll tax in the 1940s. At the same time, Lonnie Smith, a black dentist in Houston, filed a lawsuit with the help of the NAACP challenging his exclusion from Texas's white primary. The Court dismissed the state of Texas's argument that the Democratic Party had the right to set its own rules of membership—and thus what voters it accepted—when it came to the primaries, and overturned the all-white primary. By 1947, the number of southern blacks who were registered to vote had quadrupled, reaching 12 percent.[9]

National factors, namely the growing black vote in the northern states due to wartime migrations of African Americans, also pushed the Democratic Party toward civil rights, and liberal and moderate Republicans added their support as well. While President Harry S. Truman endorsed stronger voting rights measures, little action on the federal level occurred due to a coalition of southern Democrats and conservative Republicans who blocked any attempts by Truman to expand the New Deal, including in the area of civil rights legislation. Federal action on voting rights did not occur until Congress passed the Civil Rights Act of 1957, adopted in the wake of the *Brown* decision and the massive resistance of southern whites to school desegregation. Believing that the best way to help southern blacks was to restore their right to vote, congressional supporters of the bill, with President Dwight Eisenhower's support, focused on voting rights. Senate Majority Leader Lyndon Johnson ushered through the compromise bill, which won over some southern Democrats and made it to the president's desk.[10]

The act was a modest one that focused on the Justice Department filing civil suits in voting rights cases. Civil rights activists criticized the law's weak enforcement powers and it did little to break down voting barriers, but it was symbolically important as the most important piece of civil rights legislation passed since Reconstruction, indeed the *only* one passed in 80 years. Only 200,000 blacks were registered under the bill, which led to an additional—but still modest—civil rights act, this time passed in 1960. John F. Kennedy continued this go-slow litigious approach to the frustration of African Americans like Martin Luther King, Jr., who organized civil disobedience campaigns to pressure the federal government on civil rights.[11]

It would be Kennedy's successor, Lyndon Johnson, who would pass the most important piece of voting rights legislation in U.S. history. After securing passage of the Civil Rights Act of 1964, which struck down segregation in public education and accommodations, Johnson then pushed for strong legislation on voting rights. King's nonviolent civil rights march from Selma to Montgomery, Alabama, which was attacked by Alabama police during the widely televised "Bloody Sunday" in March 1965, gave additional weight to Johnson's efforts. The Voting Rights Act of 1965 suspended for five years literacy tests and other disfranchising mechanisms in the affected southern states, areas where fewer than 50 percent of all adults had gone to the polls in 1964. It also authorized the attorney general to send federal examiners into the South to enroll black applicants and observe registration practices. New electoral laws were subject to section five preclearance, which meant they had to be approved by the Justice Department or a federal court to determine their effect on minority voting. The act went into effect that summer of 1965, and federal registrars soon entered the Deep South to enroll African Americans. The percentage of blacks registered to vote in the Deep South doubled in one year and reached 60.7 percent of the total black population of the Deep South by 1969. While this still lagged behind the 83.5 percent of white voter registration, it represented a remarkable increase.[12]

The final enforcement of the Fifteenth Amendment's right to vote— 95 years after the passage of that amendment—also created the first body of black elected officials in the South since Reconstruction. By 1982, more than 2,500 black southerners held some form of public office. While many of these were local offices and not state or federal ones, it still marked a major shift in black political power from the days of Jim Crow. These numbers grew as they did because of continuous renewal and enforcement of the act. In subsequent renewals, the act was even broadened and strengthened. In 1970, despite reluctance by the Nixon administration, the act was renewed for five more years, and the suspension of literacy tests extended nationwide. In 1975, the act was extended for seven more years, and it added "language minorities" to its coverage, extending protection to Spanish-speaking and other immigrant groups, as well as American Indians. This expansion mandated foreign-language ballots and translators when necessary at the polls.[13]

The biggest expansion came in 1982, however. Despite the hostility of the Reagan administration to civil rights, the act was extended again for 25 years. Most significantly, the act was newly strengthened by section two of the law, which voided election laws with discriminatory effect, not just intent. Now a law that was passed without the *intent* to discriminate against minorities but still had the *effect* of doing so could be voided. This would end up having a major effect on redistricting and political minority representation. Reagan signed the act into law, as he did not want to be seen as vetoing an effective piece of civil rights legislation that had widespread bipartisan support. As a sign of how the political climate had shifted since the 1960s, longtime southern senators like John Stennis and Strom Thurmond, who had once opposed civil rights, voted for the final bill.[14]

This extension meant that by 2007, key parts of section five would expire, and in the conservative climate of the George W. Bush administration, some African Americans and civil rights activists worried that the act would not be renewed. The Republican majority in the House of Representatives, resulting from the 1994 elections and lasting until the 2006 mid-term losses that put the Democrats back in power, added to their fears. The number of southern Republicans had grown since 1982, and some were openly hostile to section five preclearance, feeling that it placed an undue burden on the South for the sins of previous generations. The addition of the language minorities provisions in 1975 raised the ire of some anti-immigration Republicans, and even some supporters of the act suggested it needed to be altered to fit circumstances in the twenty-first century.[15]

Despite these concerns, the House and Senate voted to reauthorize the act with overwhelming (unanimous in the Senate) support. Reauthorization even occurred a year early, with legislators from both parties meeting in 2005 to negotiate the framework of the extension. In a sign of rising nativism and concern about illegal immigration, most Republicans objected to the language-assistance provisions rather than the act itself.

The Grand Old Party (GOP) leadership, not wanting a stalled act to become an issue mobilizing minority—and largely Democratic—voters, pushed a reauthorization for another 25 years through in 2006 before the mid-term elections, when President Bush then signed it into law.[16]

The act had been passed with bipartisan support in 1965 and signed into law by a Democratic president, but each renewal—in 1970, 1975, 1982, and 2006—saw a Republican president sign into law a renewal that, with 2006 being the only exception, had been passed by a Congress that had one or both chambers controlled by the Democrats. Frank Parker, a lawyer in numerous Mississippi civil rights cases, called this bipartisan acceptance "the national consensus on voting rights." He argued that unlike busing or affirmative action, voting is not viewed with the same reservations or hostility by whites, in part because voting is seen as a fundamental right in a democracy, and partly because it lacks the emotional impact of those aforementioned racial issues.[17]

Even the Supreme Court with its sharp ideological divide has accepted this argument. Eight days after Bush signed the reauthorized Voting Rights Act in 2006, a Texas utility district filed suit to remove itself, or "bail out," from the section five preclearance. The lawyers for the case, *Northwest Austin Municipal Utility District v. Gonzales* (later shortened to *NAMUDNO v. Holder* when the Obama administration took office), argued that the extension of section five was unconstitutional given the changes in race relations since 1965. A three-judge district court, and then later the Supreme Court, disagreed. In 2009, the Court in an 8–1 decision rejected the utility district's claim on the constitutionality of section five, and instead simply ruled that the district could apply for an exemption under the act. Ironically, the only black justice on the Court, Clarence Thomas (whose opposition to affirmative action is well known), was the sole justice to argue that section five was unconstitutional.[18]

With the enforcement of the Voting Rights Act and the ratification of the Twenty-Sixth Amendment, which lowering the voting age to 18, the last major barriers to voting—it seemed—had been removed. Yet exceptions remained. Residents of Washington, D.C., still have no ability to elect federal representatives, and did not even have the right to elect a mayor and city council until 1973. Conservative Republicans, fearing that the liberal, Democratic—and largely black—electorate of the city would add extra Democrats to Congress, have blocked efforts at either congressional representation or D.C. statehood.[19]

A bigger problem concerned voter registration. State registration laws still placed the burden on citizens to register to vote, which meant physically coming to the courthouse or city hall and filling out an application. While some states eased their voter registration practices in the 1970s and 1980s, others resisted. Mississippi, for example, still maintained dual registration in the 1980s, which required voters to register separately for municipal and county elections. Even then, white employers in heavily black areas like the Mississippi Delta routinely intimidated black workers, scheduled overtime, and canceled lunch breaks to prevent them from finding the time to register to vote. State roadblocks like these along with low voter turnout led to efforts beginning in the 1970s to create a national program of voter registration. Some states, like Michigan, had adopted voter registration at libraries, motor vehicle bureaus, and other public offices. This law, adopted by the state in 1977, led to a 10 percent increase in voter turnout.[20]

The United States stood largely alone in placing the burden of registration solely on the potential voter. To remedy this, by the late 1980s, proposals in Congress for registration by mail and at motor vehicle bureaus ("motor voter" registration) appeared but were opposed by Republicans who argued that the laws would lead to fraud and unnecessary costs, as well as infringe on a traditional prerogative of the states. One such motor voter bill passed in 1992, but President George Herbert Walker Bush vetoed it. Yet a year later, President Bill Clinton signed such a bill into law, the National Voter Registration Act of 1993. It authorized states to allow registration by mail, when applying for a driver's license, and at designated public agencies like welfare offices. After the bill took effect in 1995, nine million new voters registered over the next two years. While these voters were disproportionately young, black, and high school educated, the law did not mean a major spike in Democratic gains. In 1996, voter turnout did not break 50 percent, the lowest turnout for a presidential election since 1924. Easier registration did not always mean higher turnout, but as the twentieth century ended, registering to vote was easier than it had ever been in the United States.[21]

The enforcement of the Voting Rights Act and its extensions has also shifted the focus away from minority access to voting—which has become easier due to the act—to minority *representation* through voting. Specifically, the courts have wrestled with the question of whether minorities have the right to a reasonable chance to elect candidates of their choosing (black or Latino candidates) and what constitutes "reasonable." This has led to another continuation of race in electoral politics, the drawing of majority-black or -Latino electoral districts and arguments over whether these districts represent a form of affirmative action or are a logical and constitutional extension of minority access to the ballot.

Race-based redistricting, or racial gerrymandering, arose due to shifts by state and local governments after the Voting Rights Act went into effect in 1965. The enforcement of the act led state and local authorities to grudgingly accept the reality of black voting, but it did not mean they gave up resistance. State and local governments began to devise various schemes to dilute minority voting strength. This included splitting up heavily minority districts ("cracking") and merging the fragments into heavily white districts ("stacking"), or concentrating minorities in one district to minimize their influence in other districts ("packing"). Other methods included cities and counties switching from ward or district elections to at-large elections for their representatives and the use of multimember legislative districts, where two or more representatives were elected at-large from a larger (typically stacked or packed) district, with the goal of preventing minority candidates from winning office.[22]

Not surprisingly, civil rights activists and minority voters challenged these vote dilution mechanisms in court as violations of the Voting Rights Act. In one case in 1960, *Gomillion v. Lightfoot*, black plaintiffs won a victory when the Court ruled that the city of Tuskegee, Alabama, could not redraw its boundaries to specifically exclude black voters, which the justices said was a violation of the Fifteenth Amendment. But even before the Voting Rights Act went into effect, court-ordered redistricting was already well underway due to two important Supreme Court decisions in the early 1960s. Both had to do with the apportionment of electoral districts and the question of unequal representation. The first case, *Baker v. Carr* (1962), involved plaintiffs from urban areas in Tennessee who sued when the legislature refused to reapportion itself, as required by its state constitution. The Court ruled that the malapportionment—which gave unequal voting strength and representation to sparsely populated rural districts—violated the Equal Protection Clause of the Fourteenth Amendment. *Baker* was followed by *Reynolds v. Sims* in 1964, an Alabama case that extended the Court's rulings on reapportionment further, stating that state legislative districts had to be roughly equal in population, a principle that was known popularly as "one man, one vote." While these cases did not directly deal with race, the impact on black voting strength was not lost on the plaintiffs, because racial gerrymandering by white-dominated legislatures could render black voting power meaningless. Yet fears of weakening white supremacy did not deter white southern plaintiffs and their supporters in their pursuit of equal voting strength, and some even thought that appealing to the pro–civil rights sentiments of the Warren Court would aid their case.[23]

After the Voting Rights Act went on the books in 1965, redistricting cases tended to be directly related to race and voting. The first major ruling on voting and the scope of section five preclearance occurred in 1969. The Court heard voting rights cases from Mississippi and Virginia concerning submitting electoral changes like candidate qualifications, switching from single-member to multimember districts, and other such changes for preclearance. The Court reversed lower court rulings that the states and counties did not have to submit these changes for preclearance, instead arguing that the changes limited black political power. This broad interpretation of section five, where the "totality of circumstances" on an electoral change had to be considered, expanded the scope of the Justice Department to enforce the act's provisions on a wide array of electoral changes, not just access to voting.[24]

The use of multimember districts, where more than one representative was elected from a geographic unit, quickly declined due to their use in diluting the black vote. In 1971, the Court ruled in *Whitcomb v. Chavis* that multimember districts were not unconstitutional per se, but were suspect if the state had a history of voter discrimination. Two years later, the Court went further in *White v. Regester*, declaring that multimember districts in Texas were unconstitutional due to their effects on black and Latino voters. The Fifth Circuit Court of Appeals ruled that same year in *Zimmer v. McKeithen* that the totality of circumstances included any electoral change that "enhanced" the effects of past discrimination, however benign or nonracial it seemed when passed. This in effect banned multimember districts throughout the South, although Mississippi managed to hold onto them until 1979.[25]

These rulings and enforcement boosted black electoral gains but began to raise questions about how much representation minority groups should have—specifically, were these groups entitled to representation in proportion to their population? What made that question even more complicated was *which* groups were recognized as having suffered enough discrimination to be entitled to such representation. This issue, fraught with racial and ethnic dynamite, came to the Court from Brooklyn in 1977. It involved 30,000 Hasidic Jews who sued when they found their neighborhood split by a state apportionment plan that made them minorities in two nonwhite districts. They claimed that they in turn had their Fourteenth and Fifteenth

Amendment rights violated by their own inability to elect someone from their own community. The Court, in *United Jewish Organizations of Williamsburgh, Inc. v. Carey*, rejected the petition and said that the Hasidic Jews were "white" and enjoyed adequate representation, and that race could be used as a consideration in redistricting.[26] More cynically, the Court said that an ethnic or religious minority did not have the same coverage under the Voting Rights Act as a racial or language minority.

The Court's message on proportional representation was conflicting, however. In 1975, the justices approved the annexation of white neighborhoods to Richmond, Virginia, in the case of *City of Richmond v. United States*. Justice Byron White, in the majority opinion, said that a potential for reduced black representation in the city government was permissible, and to rule otherwise would sanction proportional representation. The next year, in *Beer v. United States*, the Court issued a similar ruling when it approved a redistricting plan for New Orleans that critics said decreased the potential of black voters to elect their own to the city council.[27]

The Court ended the ambiguity over proportional representation and section five preclearance in 1980 in its *City of Mobile v. Bolden* ruling. The justices, in a fragmented ruling that saw six separate opinions, upheld Mobile's at-large elections for its city commission, which had since its creation in 1911 prevented any black commissioners from being elected. The Court ruled that there was no Fourteenth Amendment right to proportional representation, and four of the justices argued that the Fifteenth Amendment applied only to voting, not to vote dilution or redistricting.[28]

Mobile did not last long, however. Alarm over the ruling prompted civil rights advocates to press for a strengthened Voting Rights Act that led to a strengthened section two in the 1982 renewal of the act. This new section, the so-called result test, meant that civil rights advocates had to prove only racist effect, not intent, when arguing that electoral changes disfranchised black voters. This meant that a law passed without any stated intent to limit the power of minority voters could still be illegal if it depressed minority political power. This brought a new wave of lawsuits on the state and local level in the affected states, and resulted in an even greater increase in minority representation. For example, Mississippi's number of black county supervisors doubled after court-ordered redistricting, the capital city of Jackson abandoned its at-large elections, and the second congressional district was redrawn to help elect a black representative to Congress. Nationally, the number of vote dilution lawsuits rose from 150 annually to 225, and plaintiffs were successful three-quarters of the time.[29]

Of course, the expanded definition of the act and its preservation of the totality of circumstances created a new round of litigation, and the debate over proportional representation did not end. In 1986, the Court heard a redistricting case from North Carolina, *Thornburg v. Gingles*. In that case, the Court set specific criteria for vote dilution, including a ruling that racially polarized voting could be used as a factor when reviewing a redistricting plan. This became known as the Gingles test, and it assumed, using statistical evidence, that white voters would generally not support black candidates. The ruling boosted further the number of minority elected officials in the South to 3,300 African American officials in the seven states covered by the Voting Rights Act, and the number of Latino elected officials reached 3,600 by 1990 in the Southwest. Both these totals together were still only 14 percent of all elected officials in the country, however.[30]

Gingles did not end ambiguity over vote dilution and racial gerrymandering, but it did encourage the creation of "majority-minority" districts in areas that had histories of racially polarized voting. North Carolina again became the test case for a follow up—and sharp departure from—*Gingles* in the case of *Shaw v. Reno* in 1993. The Court ruled in a narrow 5–4 decision that an oddly shaped black-majority district in the state, which was drawn with the sole purpose of electing a black representative, was—in the words of Justice Sandra Day O'Conner—"so bizarre on its face that it is unexplainable on grounds other than race" and that a redrawn minority district "demands the same close scrutiny, regardless of the motivations underlying its adoption." If a minority district strayed too far from geographic compactness, then—according to the Court—it was as harmful as a white district drawn to dilute black votes. The Court broadened this ruling in 1995 in *Miller v. Johnson*, when it struck down an elongated majority-minority congressional district in Georgia, saying it was a "geographic monstrosity." The Court's conservative turn against vote dilution cases in the 1990s was reinforced in *Holder v. Hall*, in which the justices refused to support black plaintiffs in Georgia who were seeking to gain representation in their county government. Clarence Thomas, a black conservative and one of the Court's most conservative jurists, even called for abandoning the totality of circumstances and judicial review of vote dilution cases altogether.[31]

The alarm among civil rights activists over *Shaw v. Reno* led some to worry that the electoral gains of the civil rights movement would be undone. J. Morgan Kousser, an academic expert in voting rights and redistricting as well as an expert witness in 19 federal voting rights cases, argued that the majority opinion in the case was a radical reading of the Fourteenth Amendment and pointed out that electoral laws across the country disfranchised minorities for almost all of U.S. history until recently. For example, in Los Angeles—an area well outside the South— local authorities had gerrymandered districts since the nineteenth century to prevent the election of Latinos to the county government. Now when black and Latino voters finally made gains in public office, the Court cited "reverse discrimination" and limited those gains with no apparent concern about remedying the past. Kousser pointed out that race has always been used to negatively impact minorities in redistricting, and now when it was finally used in a positive matter it became recast as a social ill. Even worse, the Court was arbitrary in its decision making on redistricting, as seen in *Bush v. Vera*, a 1996 case in which District 30, a 50 percent black district in Dallas, was struck down due to its odd shape, but District 6, an equally odd-shaped (and overwhelmingly white and Republican) district in neighboring Fort Worth was upheld. To Kousser, *Shaw* fit the same category as *Dred Scott v. Sandford* (1857) and *Plessy v. Ferguson* (1896), two of the most infamous decisions on race in U.S. history. Unlike Frank Parker, who optimistically predicted the continuance of the consensus on voting rights (and who wrote about that consensus before the *Shaw* ruling), Kousser worried for the future of the Second Reconstruction—the restoration of black political rights in the 1960s—and its gains.[32]

The Court has proved fickle, and the recent partisan breakdown of the Court—which has produced many 5–4 rulings, as well as occasionally erratic and surprising shifts like that of Chief Justice John Roberts on the Affordable Care Act—means that the Voting Rights Act and redistricting is still here for the time being. Aside from the ruling in *NAMUDNO v. Holder*, the Court upheld an alternative to majority-minority districts in 2003 in *Georgia v. Ashcroft*, a state redistricting plan. The case showed how convoluted voting rights had become in the twenty-first century. A Republican attorney general opposed a redistricting plan adopted by the state of Georgia that had passed with the support of nearly all the state's black legislators but without a single Republican vote. The plan deviated from the majority-minority districts by reducing the number of black-majority senate districts and creating "high-impact" districts where coalitions of black and white voters could elect candidates. The reason for the shift by the state Democrats was that the majority-black districts were draining Democratic votes from other districts, and creating a division of white Republican and black Democrats in power. Even though the black

legislators supported the plan, the attorney general argued that it was unconstitutional because it reduced the number of black districts. The Court, split
5–4, upheld the plan, and the conservative majority said that a variety of
"relevant circumstances" should be considered in such cases. As a further
example of the changes in the South since the 1960s, black congressional
representative and civil rights veteran John Lewis endorsed the creation of
these coalition districts. However, fears of the retrogression of minority
gains won out and in 2006, Congress effectively nullified the Court ruling
by modifying section five in the renewal of the Voting Rights Act.[33]

The consensus may still be holding, but it is still being challenged as well.
In 2011, plaintiffs in Alabama and North Carolina filed another challenge
to section five preclearance, since the Court dodged constitutional review
in *NAMUDNO v. Holder*. With the deeply partisan divide on the Court, it
is not impossible that section five could be declared unconstitutional, especially with Chief Justice Roberts writing in 2009 that "due to the success of
that legislation [the Voting Rights Act], we are now a very different
nation."[34]

That sentiment is the core of the argument of political scientist Abigail
Thernstrom, a leading critic of the implementation of the Voting Rights
Act. Thernstrom argues that moving the interpretation of the Voting
Rights Act from access to voting to vote dilution has created proportional
representation for minorities. In short, the interpretation of the Court back
in 1969 in *Allen* has perverted the act's original intent, and created "an
instrument for affirmative action in the electoral sphere." She is especially
critical of the strengthened section two in the 1982 renewal of the act,
which she says has given black and Latino voters "unprecedented power
to insist on methods of power that will facilitate minority officeholding."
She calls for a "new consensus" on the act, which includes scaling back
the scope of section five preclearance so that there is greater respect for
federalism and localism. She also criticized the singular focus on
majority-minority seats, instead endorsing plans like what Georgia would
eventually adopt that created heavily (but not majority) black districts
where blacks would have influence instead of proportional representation
through "safe" black-majority districts. Instead of political balkanization,
she says that such plans would promote interracial political coalitions and
reduce racially polarized voting. She also points out that the focus on
majority-minority districts benefits white Republicans, as black Democratic
votes are drained out of high-impact districts, a rationale that helps explain
the Bush administration's opposition to Georgia's redistricting plan.[35]

Liberal civil rights activists have assailed Thernstrom's views. Frank Parker, whose book *Black Votes Count* was a direct response to Thernstrom's work *Whose Votes Count?* argued that Congress and the federal courts have upheld the strengthened section five in the renewals of the act, and thus the act it its present form of enforcement is not a perversion of the original intent of the legislation. He also took issue with her claims that redistricting to fight vote dilution has become proportional representation, pointing out that Mississippi in 1989 had a 35 percent black population, but blacks held only 13 percent of the state's elective offices. J. Morgan Kousser also raps Thernstrom's views rather sharply, comparing her to Clarence Thomas and criticizing their negative views of *Allen*, accusing both of them of being "stronger on rhetoric than on research." He charges both of them with ignoring evidence, and like Parker points to congressional authorization of the *Allen* standards in the renewals of the act, calling their opposition to that and Supreme Court precedents a "radical disregard for institutions."[36]

Such arguments among scholars on the right and left will likely continue, and Americans can expect a new round of redistricting-based lawsuits after each census as legislatures redraw districts for partisan reasons, which with the overwhelming black support for Democrats means that race will always enter the picture. In heavily Latino states, this includes drawing districts that have to consider Latino voting strength as well, especially in a state like Texas, which is entirely covered by the Voting Rights Act.[37]

This continuing litigation over redistricting and race has led some to propose a shift from the concept of "one man, one vote." The legal scholar best identified with this is Lani Guinier, a Harvard law professor whose nomination to be Assistant Attorney General in 1993 was famously torpedoed by congressional conservatives. Guinier proposed replacing winner take-all elections in single-member districts with multimember districts (ironically largely voided by earlier court rulings) that used proportional representation. This bore some resemblance to parliamentary plans in Western Europe that allotted representation if a party reached a certain percentage of the vote, but Guinier went further and proposed *cumulative voting*, in which a voter would have several votes (each voter would have the same number of votes, however), which he or she then could use to vote for candidates of his or her choice, concentrating or distributing them as he or she saw fit. This voting system has been used by corporations to ensure minority representation on corporate boards of directors and has been adopted in one Alabama county for its school board and county commission. The latter case involved an "exclusion threshold" of one-eighth, meaning that if a candidate got one-eighth of the vote, he or she would get a seat on the electoral body. This is opposed to the exclusion threshold of 50 percent, which is the case in winner-take-all elections. The process creates proportional representation but bypasses the assumption that all minorities have the same interests (what is known as essentialism), it does not define minorities in merely racial terms, and it eliminates gerrymandering by ending the creation of safe seats for candidates. Guinier argues that this plan allows voters to self-select identities based on their interests and would promote cross-racial coalition building. Perhaps just as revolutionary, her plan would promote viable third parties and independent candidacies. This theory—innovative and a radical departure from the present two-party system—is unlikely to ever be adopted widely wholly or in part due to the threat it would pose to the power of the Democrats and Republicans.[38]

One common refrain heard from critics of the Voting Rights Act is that the South is "not the same" as it was in 1965, meaning that racism has (because of the very federal legislation that white southerners opposed) dwindled. But the election of 2000 indicates that questions about the nature of redistricting aside, simple access to the ballot may still not be as universal as most Americans assume. That lack of access burst forth on the national scene in November 2000 during the hotly contested presidential election. The race became a virtual tie in the Electoral College between George W. Bush and Al Gore. Attention quickly focused on Florida, where Bush led by 2,000 votes, a lead that shrank to a few hundred votes as a state-mandated recount was completed by November 10. With such a close margin, the question quickly turned to the thousands of ballots not counted because of ambiguous markings, as well as absentee ballots from servicemen and -women that lacked the proper postmarks required by law.[39]

The media scrutiny highlighted the lack of a federally protected right to vote—a right not mentioned in the Bill of Rights—and on the patchwork of state and local voting laws that influenced the presidential election. Florida also at the time barred ex-felons from voting for life, and with most of those imprisoned being black or Latino, this raised questions of racial disfranchisement. The racial nature became clearer when stories surfaced that law-abiding residents were turned away from the polls because they were misidentified as ex-felons. One black minister in Tallahassee was denied a ballot due to the similarity of his name to a convicted felon. After the election, it was revealed that Republican officials in Florida purchased lists of convicted felons from private corporations and then tried to match those lists to the names of registered voters. The lists lacked social security numbers or other reliable identifiers, and resulted in thousands of individuals being struck from the voting rolls, which many only learned when they tried to vote on Election Day and were told they were no longer registered. The fact that the chief Florida elections official, Secretary of State Katherine Harris, also served as cochair of Bush's state campaign added to the partisan nature of the Florida debacle and lent credence to the conspiracy theories about the GOP deliberately stealing the election. Even more disturbing, the Supreme Court, which halted the Florida recount and gave Bush the presidency in its *Bush v. Gore* (2000) decision, even declared that an individual citizen "has no federal constitutional right to vote for electors for the President of the United States unless and until the state legislature chooses a statewide election as the means to implement its power to appoint members of the Electoral College." Justice Antonin Scalia even declared that there is "no suffrage right" under article 2, section 1 of the Constitution. In short, voters can have a direct vote for president only if their legislatures deem them worthy of that privilege—and it would be a privilege, as it could be rescinded by the legislature at a later date.[40]

Much of the confusion in Florida also stemmed from less-reliable technologies like punch-card ballots, which had a high rate of error, and the "butterfly ballot," a ballot that displayed the names of candidates and issues on both sides and caused voter confusion, such as some Gore voters accidentally voting for Pat Buchanan, the conservative Reform Party nominee. In the wake of the election, increased scrutiny revealed that thousands of votes had not been counted, with many regarded as "spoiled" (unreadable or damaged) and thus discarded. The number of discarded ballots ranged from 3 to 5 percent of the vote in most counties, but predominantly black Gadsden County had 12 percent of its votes rejected. In some black precincts, the rate of rejection approached 30 percent. In Duvall County, 27,000 votes were rejected, and over 12,000 of those came from four districts that were 90 percent black. Adding to the specter of racial disfranchisement was the heavy use of less-reliable voting technologies in poor and minority communities. When Bush was declared the victor after *Bush v. Gore* by less than 500 votes statewide, these rejections fueled allegations—unfounded but understandable given the partisan nature of the vote count and GOP roll-purging —that a GOP conspiracy stole the election from Gore. Some black political leaders alleged that roadblocks and Florida Highway patrol officers were dispatched to black communities to intimidate voters away from the polls.[41]

Much of this was not unique to Florida, however. Most other states used error-prone technologies as well, with underfunded and poorly trained election departments and poll workers. Nationwide, one estimate predicted that 2 million votes did not get counted in the 2000 election. These problems prompted a flurry of proposals for electoral reform to avoid another Florida debacle. The more far-reaching proposals, like instant runoff voting and abolishing the Electoral College, made little headway; eventually, however, in October 2002, President Bush signed into law a bipartisan bill, the Help America Vote Act (HAVA). It provided funds to states to improve election administration and purchase new voting technology, and the states had specific deadlines to comply with the changes.[42]

Little had improved by the time of the 2004 presidential election, however. The new electronic voting machines that optimists hoped would end voting irregularities proved to have plenty of faults of their own, many of them miscounting or undercounting vote totals. Florida continued to experience problems in the primaries and general election with undercounting. Computerized, touch-screen voting proved no more reliable in other states, and skeptics worried about the lack of a physical ballot in the event of a computer crash or malfunction. The companies that manufactured the machines refused to open their software codes to independent experts, and some specialists examined a leaked code from one of the machines and found that it contained flaws. The partisan issue was raised when the chief executive of Diebold Election Systems, one of the manufacturers, raised funds for the GOP and publically said he would "deliver" Ohio's votes to Bush in 2004. In fact, a computer error during that election gave Bush an extra 3,900 votes in a precinct that had only 800 registered voters. Criticism of the technology grew in subsequent elections, but as of the 2008 elections, the technology was still used by a third of all voters.[43]

The 2004 presidential election between Bush and Senator John Kerry came down to Ohio, not Florida, and there many of the same problems of the 2000 election reemerged. Civil rights groups estimated that 92,000 unprocessed votes were cast in the state, mostly from minority precincts. Reports surfaced of state Republicans aggressively challenging black voter registrations and sending inadequate numbers of voting machines to Democratic districts. In Cleveland, local officials voided nearly one-third of all provisional ballots. Hamilton County, which includes Cincinnati, saw a 23 percent voidance rate. Ironically, much of this campaign against minority voters was directed by Secretary of State J. Kenneth Blackwell, a black Republican, who cracked down on provisional ballots and violated the law in some cases. Kerry rapidly conceded the loss of Ohio to Bush, but suspicions over election chicanery continued. Still, postelection reports indicated that the GOP campaign likely cost the Democrats thousands of votes. The 2008 election largely avoided these problems not through any improvements in the voting process, but merely because the election was not close, with Obama winning easily over McCain in several states.[44]

Since the 2000 election, the issue of voter identification has become as contentious as allegations of stolen elections, and one enmeshed in broader concerns about voter fraud. Much of the divide has to do with the differing definitions of voter fraud held by both parties. Whereas Democrats are worried about fraud from rigged voting machines and shady voter-purging by GOP officials, Republicans rail against alleged fraud by Democratic activist groups and labor unions, and the use of falsified voter registrations. For the GOP in recent years, the solution has been to aggressively push voter ID laws. Identification requirements vary from state to state, and only a handful require photo ID. Most allowed documents like utility bills and bank statements as ID, or permitted voters to sign affidavits. Republicans on the state level began to charge that this state of affairs invited voter fraud, and in state legislatures, they pushed bills requiring voters to show ID at the polls. These efforts intensified after the 2004 elections, with Arizona, Georgia, Indiana, and Missouri adopting strict voter ID laws.[45]

Not surprisingly, these laws invited lawsuits alleging they placed undue burdens on voters and disproportionately affected young people, older adults, and racial minorities, all of whom were less likely to own government-issued IDs. Nationally, around 11 percent of registered voters lack government-issued photo IDs, and these laws place burdens on states since they cannot charge for IDs required to vote. In states under the Voting Rights Act, the additional hurdle of preclearance had to be overcome. The response of the courts and federal government has been mixed, as the state Supreme Court in Missouri voided that voter ID law, but the Supreme Court allowed Arizona's, and the Justice Department under Bush approved Georgia's photo ID requirement. The Supreme Court ruled definitely on Indiana's voter ID law in 2008 in *Crawford v. Marion County Election Board*. The Indiana law was approved purely along party lines, with no Republicans opposing and no Democrats supporting it. The law required showing an unexpired government-issued ID at the polls, and lack of an ID meant a voter could cast a provisional ballot but had to report with an ID to the county clerk's office within 10 days of the election. This law was passed and upheld by an appellate court even though the state of Indiana admitted there had been no recent instances of voter impersonation fraud. In April 2008, the Court upheld the law in a 6–3 decision, with Justice John Paul Stevens declaring that the ID requirement was an "inconvenience" but not "excessively burdensome." Justice David Souter dissented strongly and insisted that since the state could not prove any known cases of voter impersonation, the law was unnecessary.[46]

The debate over voter ID did not end there. Today, more than two dozen states have some form of voter ID requirement for voting, and of those regulations, 11 were passed from 2010 on by Republicans who claimed that voter fraud needed to be stopped. These rules were pushed by GOP governors and legislatures who won office in the 2010 elections, in which the Tea Party played a prominent role in mobilizing conservative voters. States that have adopted voter ID laws since 2010 include Wisconsin, where it was part of Governor Scott Walker's broader conservative agenda that included antiunion legislation and spending cuts. After hearing testimony from the NAACP about the problems 40 qualified voters experienced under the Wisconsin law, a county judge blocked its enforcement, declaring that it was more restrictive than other laws that survived court scrutiny.[47]

Although the Bush administration's Justice Department approved Georgia's restrictive law, the Obama administration has not been as accommodating. Attorney General Eric Holder has moved against voter ID laws in the states covered under the Voting Rights Act. Unlike Indiana, these states then have to go through section five preclearance and prove that ID laws do not disproportionately impact minorities. South Carolina and Texas, both states covered by the act, adopted voter ID laws in their Republican-controlled statehouses. In South Carolina alone, more than 178,000 registered voters lack the required identification. In Texas, the number affected is almost 800,000. The Texas law, in an obvious attempt to suppress young voters more likely to vote Democratic, allows a concealed handgun license as an acceptable form of photo ID but not ID cards from universities and colleges. Tennessee's voter ID law drew unwanted attention—and a fundraising boost for state Democrats—when Dorothy Cooper, a 96-year-old black woman from Chattanooga, was denied a photo ID at a driver's license station because she did not have her marriage certificate, even though she had her birth certificate, voter registration card, and other documents, and had been a registered voter since the 1930s.[48]

The Justice Department, while not able to stop a law like Indiana's due to judicial approval of the law, has acted against ID laws in states covered by the Voting Rights Act. Attorney General Eric Holder blocked South Carolina's voter ID law in December 2011, citing its effect on minority voters, who are 20 percent more likely than white voters to lack the required photo ID. As in other voter ID cases, Holder also pointed out that the state did not submit "any evidence or instance" of "in-person voter impersonation," the kind of fraud targeted by the law. Although these recent actions by Holder focus on the South, ID laws outside the scope of section five—such as new voter ID laws in Kansas, Rhode Island, and Tennessee—can still be challenged in court by the Justice Department.[49]

Not surprisingly, South Carolina and Texas have taken the Justice Department to court, and in the summer of 2012, hearings on the Texas law began. Texas attorney general Greg Abbott contradicted evidence from the National Conference of State Legislatures when he told the media that "voter fraud is real," citing 50 election fraud convictions in Texas, a number that he seems to think would create a massive shift in the solidly Republican state and hurt "integrity in the electoral system." The ID cases go well beyond the scope of ID laws, as Texas hopes to strike down completely section five of the Voting Rights Act, something Alabama tried unsuccessfully in May 2012. A federal court blocked enforcement of the voter ID act in Texas on racial grounds before the November 2012 election, and at any rate it had little impact given that Texas went easily for Romney.[50]

Proof of voter fraud, as the Indiana case showed, is largely nonexistent. The Republican National Lawyers Association (RNLA) published a report on voter fraud to boost support for state voter ID laws and reported 400 cases of voter fraud prosecution that had occurred over 10 years, which works out to not even one per state per year. In many of those cases, the law involved falsifying voter registration forms or buying votes, which means a requirement to show an ID at the polls would not have stopped the crime. The GOP secretary of state in Tennessee said that he did not know of a single case of anyone committing voting fraud but still supported the voter ID law proposed by Republicans in the legislature. None of that matters to voter ID supporters like Michael Thielen of the RNLA, who claims that most voter ID fraud goes "unreported and unprosecuted," which raises the question of just how exactly he knows it is so widespread if it is so hard to detect. The states have to cover the costs of issuing the IDs if they are acquired for voting purposes, but fiscal concerns do not seem to deter supposedly budget-minded Republicans.[51]

Occasionally, the partisan nature of voter ID supporters shows itself. A Republican leader in Pennsylvania, speaking about the voter ID law that adopted for that state for the 2012 general election, said that the law would allow GOP presidential nominee Mitt Romney to win the state over President Obama. The law was reviewed by the state Supreme Court in September 2012, and the court told the state judge who initially upheld the plan to determine whether the state was doing enough to provide voters with the necessary IDs. If the state was not, the justices said, the law would not be allowed to take effect. That is exactly what happened on October 2, when the judge who originally upheld the law then voided it for the 2012 election, in line with the state supreme court's directions. Adding to the controversy—and irony—over voter ID was that Indiana secretary of state Charlie White, a Republican, was convicted in 2012 of lying about his address on voter registration forms in his 2010 election. This mean that the most high-profile case of voter fraud in the state came from the very party that railed against it. Republicans in turn have cited the Justice Department's use of Catalist, a firm with Democratic connections, in their analysis of the Texas voter ID law, but independent groups like the National Conference of State Legislatures have also demonstrated that in-person voter fraud at the polls is almost nonexistent.[52]

These laws have even affected Republicans. In Indiana, an elderly couple in their 80s who did not have a government-issued ID was barred from voting in the GOP primary. Indiana and Georgia, two of the states with the strictest voter ID laws, rejected more than 1,200 votes in the 2008 general election. In those two states and Tennessee, hundreds of ballots were blocked in the 2012 primaries. All of this suggests that in the name of fighting fraud, hundreds of legitimate voters are losing their right to vote.[53] Of course, the future of voter ID laws will rest with the Supreme Court, and these ID cases can reach far beyond their initial focus if the justices strike down section five of the Voting Rights Act, which would impact redistricting and minority office-holding as well. With Obama's reelection, the possibility of any new conservative jurists on the Supreme Court is effectively dead for the next four years, but the current conservative tilt of the court does not mean that a striking down of all or part of the Voting Rights Act is out of the question.

For the 2012 election, voter ID laws had a minimal impact. With judges blocking them in key states like Pennsylvania and Wisconsin, GOP hopes of turning those states from blue to red evaporated. In conservative states like Texas and South Carolina, the suspending of voter ID laws by the Justice Department did not flip those states to the Democratic fold, as they were already strongly Republican. One of the states that judges did allow a voter ID law to be upheld, Tennessee, was another Republican-leaning state that was unlikely to go for Obama and did not give Romney any advantage in his decisive loss in the Electoral College. The court there watered down the law as well, allowing library cards to be used as acceptable photo ID.[54] Whether all these ID laws will survive legal scrutiny in the coming years and affect future elections remains to be seen.

Although not as widely publicized as voter ID laws, another area where denial of voting occurs involves some of the least noticed and regarded people in society, that is, ex-convicts. Felony disfranchisement has received growing attention from civil rights activists and academics in recent years as scholars speak of the growth of the "prison-industrial complex" and the "carcereal state." The numbers tell some of that story. Between 1970 and 2010, the United States embarked on a period of mass incarceration unprecedented in its history. In 2006, there were 7.3 million Americans who had fallen afoul of the criminal justice system, and one out of every 31 U.S. residents was under correctional supervision, from incarceration to probation to parole. African American men experienced this supervision most acutely, with an imprisonment rate 6.5 times the rate of white males and 2.5 times that of Hispanic males. By In 1989, twenty-three percent of African American males were either in prison or jail, or on probation or parole. By 2006, these numbers had risen to one out of every 15 black men over the age of 18 was behind bars, as was one in nine black men in the 20 to 34 age range. For African American women, the imprisonment rate was almost double that of Hispanic women and three times that of white women.[55]

Much of the new focus on enforcement and incarceration in urban areas came from the "war on drugs." While this phenomenon is best remembered for its association with crack cocaine in the 1980s, it actually began with New York and the Rockefeller Drug Laws of 1973. Governor Nelson Rockefeller, a moderate Republican, embraced a tough-on-crime approach to appease party conservatives. While he demonstrated this most vividly in his violent crushing of the Attica prison rebellion in 1971, he also signed into law legislation enacting lengthy prison terms for selling narcotics. This led to a soaring of the state's prison population with new inmates from urban areas, and by the end of the 1990s, of all inmates in New York, 32.2 percent were imprisoned for drug offenses. These laws were adopted in other states, and the incarceration of inner-city residents rose significantly.[56]

The arrival of crack cocaine in the 1980s, the extant of which was exaggerated and whipped up by the media, was a major factor in the increase in mass incarceration as thousands of nonviolent drug offenders were arrested and warehoused with violent criminals. Punitive drug laws that included mandatory prison sentencing became part of the drug war, with laws passed by a Democratic Congress and signed into law by Republican presidents Ronald Reagan and George Herbert Walker Bush. These laws included harsher penalties for possession of crack cocaine, a drug associated with inner-city gang violence, than for powder cocaine, the preferred drug of affluent whites. Even the Democrat Bill Clinton continued this mass incarceration with his 1994 anticrime legislation, which included a federal version of the "three strikes and you're out" law that mandated a life sentence upon the conviction of a third felony. This law, which mandated $30.2 billion in new spending, included funds for new prison construction, and Clinton's eight years as president saw the nation's prison population increase by 700,000.[57]

These incarceration rates are correlated to cuts in other domestic programs, part of the overall retreat of policymakers from the welfare state since 1970. Cuts in social expenditures have generally accompanied increased state and federal expenditures on law enforcement and prisons. The antidrug legislation of 1986, for example, had a price tag of $1.7 billion while in the same era, the Reagan administration cut social welfare spending, especially for the inner cities. Overall, the United States spent $185 billion for police protection, detention, judicial, and legal activities in 2003, a tripling of expenditures since 1982, after adjusting for inflation. This system employed 2.4 million people, creating a powerful lobby of prison guards, police, and other related personnel. No such increase in spending occurred for inner-city schools. The incarceration of young black men has then meant that fewer and fewer would finish high school and go to college, creating a gender disparity in African American enrollment. As of 2005, black women made up 63.6 percent of black undergraduate enrollment. In 2005, black men received only one-third of all bachelor's degrees and less than 40 percent of all doctorates awarded to African Americans. While these numbers speak well of black women and their educational achievements, the overall number of black degrees is negatively impacted by eliminating a large pool of black men from consideration. The result is fewer black doctors, teachers, lawyers, corporate officials, and other higher-paying professionals.[58]

Politically, mass incarceration has also depressed black political rights and voting power. Only two states, Maine and Vermont, allow inmates to vote while incarcerated. Most states withhold prisoners' right to vote when they are paroled, and some states continue to deny the right to vote after punishment has ended for anywhere from several years to life. In the context of world history, the United States stands apart from other industrialized countries in this area, just as it does regarding health care, the death penalty, and other domestic issues. Most of Western Europe allows prisoners to vote while incarcerated, and most European countries do not restrict voting once the inmate is released. Many of the felons denied the right to vote are, due to mandatory sentencing laws, nonviolent drug offenders. The number of people disfranchised is considerable. In Florida alone, 600,000 former felons disfranchised for life who had completed their sentences were not allowed to vote in the 2000 presidential election, a number that could have easily decided the hotly contested election in the state.[59]

Historically, felon disfranchisement has built on the laws of the Jin Crow era; black men at the turn of the century would be disqualified from voting if they were convicted of crimes, often petty or property-related crimes rather than violent ones. The prototype for disfranchisement, the Mississippi Constitution of 1890, relied in part on disqualifying from the ballot black men convicted of bigamy, arson, petty theft, and fraud. Many African American felons, especially in the South, still do not register to vote even if they have the right to due to their fear of local authorities, a situation reminiscent of the fear black men and women in the South had of trying to vote in the 1950s and 1960s.[60]

On the question of felon disfranchisement, the United States has, like the states have with voter ID, sometimes gone against its historical trend of expanding voting rights. That was seen vividly in Massachusetts, which through a popular referendum in 2000 repealed prisoners' right to vote. This was the first time the state had narrowed its franchise, a particular irony in the cradle of the American Revolution and abolitionism. While most states were working to loosen voting laws, states like Massachusetts, as well as Utah in 1998 and Kansas in 2002, went in the opposite direction.[61]

While more than a dozen states liberalized their laws on felon exclusion between 2000 and 2008, the fact that many of the felons were African American, and thus likely voters for the Democratic Party, has meant that many Republicans have opposed liberalization. Moreover, the liberalization trend has not reduced the total numbers of African Americans disfranchised, who continue to grow in number, as the rate of mass incarceration has not slowed down. As of 2008, with one out of every 15 African American men in jail or prison, 5.3 million Americans were barred from

voting due to their criminal records, a number so great that it has drawn
condemnation from the UN Committee on the Elimination of Racial
Discrimination. This continues even though these laws defeat the purpose
of assimilating former criminals back into society by branding them long-
term or permanently as political nonpersons.[62]

Florida, which has the highest rate of incarceration of felons in the
United States, has received significant attention for its harsh felony disfranchisement laws, scrutiny that has been heightened by the critical role the
state has played in presidential elections. Florida, along with Iowa, Virginia,
and Kentucky, withholds all voting rights from felons even after they serve
their sentences and are off parole. In 2007, Florida governor Charlie Crist, a
Republican, fulfilled a campaign promise and reversed the course of his
predecessor, Jeb Bush, who opposed franchise restoration. Crist enacted a
change with the Clemency Board that authorized an almost automatic
restoration of voting rights for felons who had served their time for nonviolent offenses. This move led 115,000 men and women to regain their voting
rights by the spring of 2008. In Iowa, Democratic governor Tom Vilsack
also issued an executive order that restored voting rights for felons.[63]

The governors who succeeded Crist and Vilsack have taken steps to
reverse these gains, a move likely spurred by a majority of voters in Florida
and Iowa voting for Barack Obama in 2008. In 2011, Rick Scott, the
Republican governor of Florida, rolled back Crist's reforms by proposing
a five-year waiting period for restoration of voting rights, and the
Clemency Board adopted it in 2012. Terry Brandstad, the Republican
governor of Iowa, did the same and reversed Vilsack's executive order,
making it so that ex-felons now must reapply for voting rights, a process
that includes a detailed 31-question form and a review process that takes
as long as six months. Former president Bill Clinton sharply criticized
Scott's rollback as racist in effect and aimed at minorities who would likely
vote Democratic. This action by Crist was part of a larger effort to limit voting in his state. This included a voter ID law and a law that put severe
restrictions on voter registration groups, even nonpartisan ones like the
League of Women Voters. A federal judge tossed out the registration
restrictions in September 2012, but the law had already been in effect
for a year and left groups scrambling to make up for the sharp drop in
registration caused by the law. Scott and the GOP-dominated legislature
also reduced the number of early voting days from 8 to 14, including eliminating voting the Sunday before the election, when many black church
congregations typically voted. And although much of the impact of voter

ID laws has focused on the potential effect they would have on black voters, Latino voters are potentially affected as well. One civil rights group predicted that as many as 10 million Latino voters could be affected by new voter laws, especially voter ID and proof-of-citizenship laws. Obama led among Latino voters by 70 percent versus Romney's 30 percent, but with the race close in Nevada, Colorado, and Florida, high or low Hispanic voter turnout could have made the difference for either candidate. New Mexico and Colorado also adopted measures similar to Florida that restrict the ability of third-party groups to register voters. Ultimately these voter ID laws, as mentioned earlier, had little impact. While the election was close in Florida, Obama's decisive victory rested on high Latino turnout, and Colorado and New Mexico went to the Democratic column, just as they had in 2008.[64]

There are some positive signs. In 2004, hip-hop mogul and millionaire Russell Simmons and others lobbied the New York state legislature to reform the Rockefeller Drug Laws. While they were unable to get them repealed, they were effective in their efforts to end indeterminate sentencing. They also were successful in lobbying for reduced sentences for nonviolent felons and sentencing that encouraged treatment for drug offenders. And not every politician has embraced disfranchisement. Chris Christie, the GOP governor of New Jersey, publicly supported a bill in his state's legislature that established mandatory drug treatment instead of incarceration for first-time drug offenders. He declared that "addiction is a disease and that we need to give people a chance to overcome that disease and restore dignity and meaning to their lives." However, as scholar Michelle Alexander has noted, the combined effects of the retreat from the liberal welfare state since 1970 and the shift to the punitive state is so deeply rooted it will take more than simply a few laws to repeal it. Meanwhile, the detrimental political fallout from mass incarceration continues to erode the gains of the civil rights era, to say nothing of negative social and economic effects. Combining mass incarceration with voter ID laws and the Court's renewed hostility to racial redistricting, black and Latino gains since the 1960s appear to be under a sustained attack thinly disguised by the rhetoric of "voter fraud" and other nonracial terminology. Little wonder then, in this age of Obama and an imagined postracial society, Alexander calls this an era of a "new Jim Crow."[65]

Chapter 6

Race and Racism in the Obama Campaign, Election, and Presidency

In 1998, Toni Morrison, the Nobel Prize–winning author, famously defended scandal-ridden President Bill Clinton in a piece in the *New Yorker* by labeling him the "first black president." She meant this in reference to his rural southern upbringing and the way the partisan attacks on him mirrored attacks on African American men.[1] While perhaps understandable in this context, the quote seems ludicrous in hindsight since the United States has now actually elected a black president. Yet in 1998, despite the gains of the civil rights movement, few people thought a black person would rise to the nation's highest office, given the historic reluctance of whites to support black candidates.

What a difference a decade can make. The meteoric rise of Barack Obama to the most powerful office in the world symbolically broke one of the last racial barriers in U.S. politics. In the wake of his election, optimism abounded as political pundits predicted that the United States was entering a postracial America, a belief famously and awkwardly expressed by MSNBC commentator Chris Matthews on Election Day 2008, when he said, "I forgot he [Obama] was black tonight for an hour."[2]

Perhaps Matthews was more prescient than he realized. The fact that Obama won and did not lose to a much-predicted "Bradley effect" seemed to indicate that white people could put aside any racial feelings and vote for a black candidate for the presidency.[3] Obama's election represented more than breaking a racial barrier, however. He also symbolized the nation's long history of immigration through his Kenyan father, and his father's marriage to his Caucasian mother also seemed to embody U.S. history related to assimilation and a transcendence of racial barriers. To many observers this universal, unifying politics, bound up in his optimistic campaign, put him on a much higher level than the traditional liberal identity politics and racial polarization that marked the campaigns of Jesse Jackson and most recently Al Sharpton in 2004.

Yet the belief that the United States has entered a postracial era did not hold true in 2008 and still is not the case today. Racially polarized voting existed and intensified in 2008 in both the Democratic presidential primaries and the general election, and in the wake of Obama's victory, white racial conservatives have mobilized racial opposition to Obama coated in a (at times rather thin) veneer of color-blind language. The election of Barack Obama, while undeniably a groundbreaking and historical moment, has not led to a decline in racism in the United States and in fact has sparked an upsurge as a sort of counterrevolution to the events of 2008.

Barack Hussein Obama's story begins in with his birth and youth in Hawaii in the 1960s. His father, also named Barack Obama, was a black man from Kenya of the Luo tribe, whose father, Hussein Onyaango Obama, had been a medicine man and prominent farmer and tribal elder. Obama's father was the first African student at the University of Hawai'i, and there he met Obama's mother, Stanley Ann Dunham, an 18-year old white student. They married but stayed together only briefly, as the senior Obama then won a prestigious PhD admission to Harvard University but lacked the funds to take his new family to Massachusetts. The future president and child of that marriage saw his father only once again after that, in 1971, before the elder Obama died in a motor vehicle crash in Kenya in 1982.[4]

Obama's childhood in Hawaii gave him an experience unlike other black children throughout the United States, as the state was a racial melting pot of whites, Asians, and native Hawaiians. This diversity did not mean that the future president did not experience racial prejudice and isolation at school—quite the contrary, since he was one of the few black students there. After his parents divorced, his mother married a man named Lolo, an Indonesian student she also met at the University of Hawai'i. This marriage prompted a move to Indonesia in 1967, since Lolo had been conscripted into the army after General Suharto seized power in a coup. There Obama spent two years attending a Muslim school and two more in a Catholic school before his mother sent him back to Hawaii to live with his grandparents in 1971.[5]

Obama's youth was hardly typical of any American, black or white, since he had been born and raised in racial diversity, been educated in a variety of religious experiences, and traveled and lived overseas. His life experience—which his political opponents would use against him later—meant he gained a worldly and multicultural experience unlike many other African American politicians (or white ones either). Racially he may be African American but culturally he was not in his youth.

Obama's birth in 1961 and childhood outside of the mainland United States meant that he had little exposure to the events of the civil rights movement, but as a college student, he was briefly involved in the divestment campaign against the apartheid regime of South Africa. After graduating in 1983, he worked as a community organizer in Chicago. This came after a brief stint working for a financial consulting firm, in which it looked like he would follow the path of corporate assimilation into the growing black middle class, and was even discouraged by other black Chicagoans from going into a community organizing, since it carried the taint of politics. He worked as an organizer in Altged Gardens, a low-income and largely black housing project. While he was there, he advocated for improvements like a job training center and dealt firsthand with the frustrations of local residents and the problems in the community, especially in the Chicago Housing Authority and public school system. While there, he also experienced black nationalists like the Nation of Islam and first met the Reverend Jeremiah Wright, the pastor of Trinity United Church of Christ, who was deeply influenced by black liberation theology.[6]

Obama left Chicago to go to Harvard Law School, and there he became the first black president of the *Harvard Law Review*, which gave him the opportunity to publish his first book, *Dreams from My Father*, a memoir of growing up and exploring the history of his absent father. After graduation, he returned to work as a civil rights lawyer in Chicago, running a voter registration project and teaching constitutional law at the University of Chicago. He and his wife Michelle resided in Hyde Park, a racially mixed neighborhood in the city's South Side. At age 35, four years out of law school, he made his first run for political office in the Illinois state legislature and won a seat. He soon moved to higher office and in 2000, made an ill-fated run for a U.S. House seat. He lost badly to the sitting Democratic incumbent, Bobby Rush, a four-time representative and civil rights veteran. Rush attacked his challenger's roots and at least indirectly his blackness when he told a newspaper that Obama "went to Harvard and became an educated fool . . . Barack is a person who read about the civil-rights protests and thinks he knows all about it." Obama lost the primary by 30 points.[7]

Obama's political prospects were kept alive by his supporters in Hyde Park, including a corps of black businesspeople who advised him. His next break came in 2004, when he ran for the U.S. Senate. Although there were no black men or women in the U.S. Senate then, his campaign was not without hope. Illinois had a history of electing black candidates to statewide office, and Carol Mosley-Braun, an African American woman from Illinois, had already served one term in the U.S. Senate. He won his seat that fall, and during his campaign, he became famous nationally for addressing the Democratic National Convention. In the wake of this publicity, he began to plan a presidential run and published the best-selling political work *The Audacity of Hope*, in which he outlined his views on American politics and society, including the subject of race.[8]

On racial issues, Senator Obama began to walk a racial tightrope that would preserve black support while at the same time building coalitions with whites and Hispanics. Having already done that on a state level, he was now seeking to do it nationally. In *The Audacity of Hope*, he endorsed the legal gains of the civil rights movement, a safe (and wise) choice for any politician with national aspirations. On affirmative action, he offered a traditional liberal defense of the practice and criticized lax enforcement of civil rights laws by Republican administrations. On the topic of welfare, however, he accepted conservative critiques and cannily linked himself to the bipartisan consensus on the issue, declaring that "conservatives—and Bill Clinton—were right about welfare as previously structured . . . [t]he old AFDC program sapped people of their initiative and eroded their self-respect."[9]

Obama also presented some of this doublespeak when discussing the wider effects of race. He discussed his personal experiences with race, presenting much of the problems of racism as the attitudes of racist individuals, not the overall society—police harassment, white condescension, and other slights—but also cited statistics on racial disparities and said that "to suggest that our racial attitudes play no part in these disparities is to turn a blind eye to both our history and our experience—and to relive ourselves of the responsibility to make things right." But what that responsibility is, Obama does not make clear. He counsels minorities to be conscious of how whites view them so as to combat stereotypes, but nowhere does he discuss controversial solutions like reparations for slavery. When he discussed Hurricane Katrina and meeting displaced black residents of New Orleans in the Houston Astrodome, he publicly insisted on the news shows that the federal government's incompetence was color-blind and not a product of racism. He instead used class terms, indicating that the Bush administration did not "take into account the plight of poor communities." He used the same unifying, race-neutral comments in 2004 at the Democratic Convention, arguing that "there is not a black America and a white America and Latino America and Asian America—there's the United States of America." He also included the requisite deference and praise of civil rights veterans like Rosa Parks, whose funeral he attended.[10] This rhetoric—acknowledging racial problems while downplaying or even denying institutional racism—represented a careful strategy to not alienate whites. Combined with Obama's youth and lack of association with the civil rights movement, he could avoid the taint of black radicalism or "angry black man" syndrome associated with the presidential runs of Jesse Jackson and Al Sharpton.

Of course, Barack Obama was still black, and no black candidate had won the presidential nomination of a major party. Senator Obama announced he was seeking the Democratic nomination for president on February 10, 2007, in a speech at the Illinois State Capitol. At that time, his stature had risen even higher in the Democratic Party as he campaigned for congressional Democrats in the 2006 mid-term elections and was even featured on the cover of *Time*. However, political observers considered him still a long-shot candidate against the potential front-runner, former first lady and New York senator Hillary Rodham Clinton.[11]

Long-shot or not, he was a credible candidate who also happened to be black, and that meant death threats. His office received hate mail and calls, and while that is not unusual for a high-profile politician, the threats were deemed disturbing enough by the Department of Homeland Security and a congressional advisory board to approve Secret Service protection for the Illinois senator in May 2007. This protection was granted at Obama's request. He was not the first black presidential candidate to receive Secret Service protection, as Jesse Jackson had a detail in 1988. But at nine months before the first primaries, the protective detail was the earliest ever granted for a presidential candidate. By contrast, John Kerry and John Edwards did not receive protection until February 2004, after the first primaries. Although the Department of Homeland Security denied any specific threats against Obama, fellow Illinois Senator Dick Durbin confirmed that there were racial threats involved.[12]

Initially, it seemed that Obama would not have the Secret Service protection for long. A month before the New Hampshire primary, he trailed Hillary Clinton by 20 percent. But as the month passed, Obama's momentum built, and he scored a surprise win in the Iowa caucuses. Final polling showed that he had a lead of 30 to 38 percent going into New Hampshire, but then Clinton upset that lead by taking the primary with a 2.6 percent lead. Once again, political commentators cited the influence of the Bradley effect, or the phenomenon of a black candidate seeing his or her lead shrink as whites told pollsters once thing and voted another way. Studies after the fact indicated that like in other cases, the Bradley effect had little outcome on the primary race and other factors, including a possible late shift of women voters toward Clinton, had a greater effect.[13]

New Hampshire lacked a large number of black voters, so the issue of race did not really come into sharp view until South Carolina, the second Democratic primary state, where black voters comprised more than half of the primary electorate. By that time, people were wondering whether black voters would cast their votes for the black candidate or Hillary Clinton, the wife of the "first black president." This raised questions about Obama's "blackness," like Bobby Rush had raised in Chicago, that is, could a man who was racially but not culturally African American—or more fairly, a product of an African American experience that differed from most African Americans—win over black voters from a political couple who enjoyed extraordinary popularity with African Americans? Obama's high polling numbers going into South Carolina seemed to indicate the former. In response, the Clintons, in a highly controversial move, upped the racial rhetoric to counter Obama's downplaying of race and blunt any momentum he would gain from a win in the Palmetto State. Hillary Clinton compared Obama to Martin Luther King, Jr., and herself to Lyndon Johnson, a comparison that Senator Edward Kennedy thought was a subtle attempt to highlight racial difference. Subtlety did not concern Bill Clinton, who credited Obama's campaign skills but suggested South Carolina was not important because Jesse Jackson had won the state in 1984 and 1988, and still had not gotten the nomination. This comment—a direct attempt to link the centrist Obama to the liberal, controversial Jackson as well as a perceived insult to the political relevance of black South Carolinians—triggered an angry phone conversation between Kennedy and the former president. The question of whom black voters would back seemed settled after South Carolina, as the voters gave the Illinois senator a 28 percent win over Clinton, and even white voters supported him in higher-than-expected numbers.[14]

The Clintons' attacks on Obama prompted Edward Kennedy to endorse Obama after South Carolina, largely because he was concerned that the

Clintons were trying to pigeonhole Obama as an angry black man like Jackson. Caroline Kennedy, daughter of John F. Kennedy, also lent her endorsement. This support from the Kennedy political dynasty, so heavily identified with the civil rights movement, gave Obama even more postracial and coalition-building credibility, and cut further into Hillary Clinton's support. Even more civil rights credibility came Obama's way when he won the support of John Lewis, the Democratic representative from Georgia and veteran of the civil rights movement. Lewis switched his support from Clinton to Obama in mid-February, concluding that "something is happening in America, and people are prepared and ready to make that great leap." Obama then drew even with Clinton in a series of primaries and caucuses on Super Tuesday, and began to lead her in national polls. Still, Clinton supporters played the race card. Geraldine Ferraro, who had broken gender barriers in 1984 when she was named Walter Mondale's running mate, said that Obama had come as far as he had in the primaries only because he was black; then when she was criticized for the comment, she—without a hint of irony—said that she was being targeted because she was white and dared to criticize a black candidate.[15]

Then the runner stumbled. Obama lost the March 3 Ohio and Texas primaries, and 10 days later, ABC News ran a story on his association with the Reverend Jeremiah Wright, which thrust race back into the headlines. The report included clips from Wright's sermons, which criticized U.S. foreign policy and the historical treatment of minorities by the U.S. government. Most famously, ABC focused on footage of Wright declaring in a 2003 sermon that "[t]he government gives them the drugs, builds bigger prisons, passes a three-strike law and then wants us to sing 'God Bless America.' No, no, no, God damn America, that's in the Bible for killing innocent people. God damn America for treating our citizens as less than human." Shortly after the attacks, Wright referenced 9/11 in another sermon, arguing that "[w]e bombed Hiroshima, we bombed Nagasaki, and we nuked far more than the thousands in New York and the Pentagon, and we never batted an eye." Since Obama had a 20-year association with Wright at his church, the story quickly became a question of whether the senator endorsed the reverend's views.[16]

The Wright story became the most reported story of the primary season, receiving three to eight times more coverage than the next most reported topic between January 1 and May 4, 2008. The fact that the story dealt with race and black anger against white America ensured such disproportionate coverage, as seen in Republican front-runner John McCain's endorsements from controversial far-right pastors like John Hagee and Pat Robertson, who also possessed extreme viewpoints. The *New York Times* and *Washington Post*, papers that conservatives have long denounced as liberal, published 12 times as many articles on the Wright controversy as they did articles on Hagee and McCain, and the ratio of editorials and op-eds on the two topics was 15 to one. Much of the coverage of Wright's comments was taken out of context or distorted by the media. For example, Wright, despite the claims of ABC and other media outlets, never said the U.S. government caused the September 11 attacks; he merely said that they should not have been a surprise considering how the U.S. treated foreign countries and waged wars abroad.[17]

Many white Americans did not like hearing a black man complain about white America, however historically true some of the statements were. As academic Tiffany Ruby Patterson points out, Wright was continuing the long "jeremiad" tradition of both black and white preaching, pointing out U.S. sins and hoping the country would redeem itself. His own sermons were not significantly different from the famous 1852 Rochester antislavery speech given by black abolitionist Frederick Douglass, "What to the Slave Is the Fourth of July?" But the controversial statements clearly cast Wright as the angry black man, and Obama suffered by association. At first, Obama claimed not to have heard the sermons, but few believed him. The growing controversy prompted Obama to deliver his famous "More Perfect Union" speech on March 18, 2008 in Philadelphia. In the speech, he commented on black anger as well as white racism and privilege, but he refused to disown Wright, saying that he could "no more disown him than I could my white grandmother . . . , who has on more than one occasion uttered racial and ethnic stereotypes that made me cringe." But he did repudiate Wright's remarks, declaring that "[t]he profound mistake of Reverend Wright's sermons is not that he spoke about racism in our society. It's that he spoke as if our society was static; as if no progress has been made; as if this country . . . is still irrevocably bound to a tragic past." This was Obama's reclaiming of the postracial mantle—acknowledging racial injustice but appeasing whites by insisting that such things were fading, by again denying or downplaying institutional racism. Obama offered no hard talk of reparations or of a fundamental realigning of the economy or political power to address racism in society. That is likely why the speech was well received and defused the Wright controversy. The speech showed Obama's skill as a politician and his willingness to jettison controversial supporters, no matter how long they had supported him. His stand is in marked contrast to the earlier trailblazing candidacy of Shirley Chisholm, the first African American to run for office on a major party ticket. Chisholm received the endorsement of the Black Panthers during her 1972 run and rejected her moderate supporters' suggestions that she disavow the endorsement. Obama's wins continued and eventually Clinton, under pressure to spare the Democratic convention a nasty fight, suspended her campaign on June 8, 2008.[18]

The divisive nomination battle between Clinton and Obama exposed racial wounds and stirred resentments in the party. It also threatened its unity going into the summer and fall general election season. If Obama counted race as a major factor for his support (despite his efforts to be postracial), then Hillary Clinton's base rested heavily on gender (white women) and class (the white working class). Sean Wilentz, a historian at Princeton University and a Clinton supporter, accused Obama's followers of snubbing the white working class, which he identified as the base of the Democratic Party going back to 1828. Wilentz, conveniently ignoring the racist roots of the formation of the Democratic Party—as a party resting on white working-class identity and support for slavery, and later segregation until the 1960s—painted Obama as an elitist and branded his strategy to mobilize younger voters and independents as "a virtual reprise of the Democratic doomed strategy from the 1972 McGovern campaign that the party revamped in 1988." He gave only lip service to the decline of the white working class in America and assumed that the Democratic Party could win only by ignoring demographic trends and in effect assuming that the base of the party had remained rigid and unchanging since the antebellum era. Wilentz also denied any serious racial motivation on the party of white Democratic voters. However, other academics have disputed Wilentz's partisan defense and pointed out that Clinton remained the choice of racial conservatives in the primaries and that racial resentment toward Obama played a role in the peaking of her favorability ratings in March 2008 at the height of the Wright controversy.[19]

Academics like Wilentz were hardly the only ones to make overt appeals to the white working class to support Clinton against the perceived elitist black intellectual. Clinton herself made such racial appeals when she said that Obama's support "among working, hard-working Americans, white Americans, is weakening again." Black Americans, then, were apparently not "hard working," a deliberate play to welfare stereotypes of lazy African American "welfare queens." As her nomination hopes faded and she sought to win the election through the votes of the super delegates in the

Democratic Party, who had the power to override the popular vote, she said that "whites in both states [Indiana and North Carolina, two of the later primaries] who had not completed college degrees were supporting me. There is a pattern emerging here." She also stated, in line with Wilentz, that the Democrats could not win unless they appeased this historical constituency.[20]

With Obama now facing off against Arizona senator John McCain in the general election, that support Clinton enjoyed could now shift to McCain, as race would expectedly trump party loyalty, much as it had for white voters in earlier elections like that of Harold Washington in Chicago in 1983. Gender added to the electoral volatility, as the Grand Old Party (GOP) sought to exploit women voters' resentment over perceived sexist treatment of Hillary Clinton into votes by picking little-known Alaska governor Sarah Palin as his running mate. Her selection guaranteed that gender would remain a prominent issue in the campaign, even if it did not materialize into a hoped-for gender gap in November.[21]

But gender meshed with race during the primaries and general election for another figure—Michelle Obama. As media scrutiny of the wife of the Democratic nominee grew during the election, the fact that she was the first black woman to potentially become first lady unearthed an unpleasant media depiction of her own life and how it did not adhere to white expectations of what a black women should be. In one sense, Michelle Obama as first lady would be even more racially significant than her husband's presidency, since she was descended from African American slaves.[22] Early in the presidential race, bloggers and critics drew on offensive stereotypes of black women to criticize her in ways no white first lady ever experienced. Pro-Hillary Clinton bloggers, while not part of her mainstream defenders, posted comments insulting Michelle Obama's fashion choices and physical appearance, attacking her alleged lack of "class" and dubbing her "Michelle Antoinette," which likened her to Marie Antoinette, the unpopular and extravagant queen who was overthrown during the French Revolution. Other critics painted her as an angry black woman just as they tried to caricature her husband as an "angry black man." Her comments about racism in the United States prompted suggestions that she was ungrateful, and even her 1985 senior thesis from Princeton University was excerpted to portray her as a black separatist. The conservative journal *National Review* put her on its June 2008 cover, labeling her "Mrs. Grievance" and calling her "America's angriest would-be First Lady." Pro-Clinton bloggers and later conservative media outlets and talk radio reported on a nonexistent video of Michelle Obama "railing about whitey" at a Chicago forum. No evidence of this event ever surfaced, but it became another part of the lore about Michelle Obama being presented (and famously parodied in a *New Yorker* cover) as a twenty-first-century Angela Davis, a controversial 1970s black revolutionary. The media scrutiny subsided only later in the election season when a new female target—Sarah Palin—emerged to attract the media's attention.[23]

Of course, in the general election, race did not fade as an issue. Much of it continued with the perception of Obama as the "other"—or more directly, as Barack *Hussein* Obama. Persistent rumors of him being a secret Muslim existed alongside contradictory rumors about him belonging to a black separatist Christian church due to his association with Reverend Wright. His middle name, inescapably identified in the minds of Americans with the recently deposed and executed Iraqi dictator Saddam Hussein, perhaps made this inevitable. His own childhood, including the two years spent at a Muslim school in Indonesia, added to these rumors. This perception was widespread among anti-Obama voters during the campaign. Most famously, it occurred when a Minnesota woman who supported John McCain said to him, "I can't trust Obama. I read about him and he's . . . an Arab," to which the Arizona senator replied that "[he]e's not," and that "[h]e's a decent family man citizen that I just happen to have some disagreements with on fundamental issues." This belief, what some academics have labeled the "mistaken-identity hypothesis," meshed with antiblack sentiment and has arguably became a cover for racism in a "color-blind" America. Polls during the 2008 election showed that consistently 10 to 20 percent of Americans thought Obama was a practicing or former Muslim. However, these numbers did not translate into a Bradley effect for him on Election Day, since the voters who held these views were ideologically conservative and thus already highly unlikely to vote for Obama. These rumors, along with the widespread belief that he was not born in the United States and lacked a proper birth certificate, persisted after the election and among his domestic opponents.[24]

The less overt appeals to race included McCain and Palin's populist appeals to working-class whites who might have favored Hillary Clinton, just as the selection of Palin was engineered to exploit gender resentment with white women who supported Clinton. Palin in particular portrayed herself as an everyday American and called herself a "hockey mom." She said that she and McCain represented rural, small-town America, the "real America." Her stumbles in the media hurt her in the polls, and a much-publicized designer clothing spending spree tarnished her populist image. McCain's last populist appeal to the white working class came during the third and final presidential debate on October 15, when McCain invoked "Joe the Plumber," an Ohio resident named Samuel Werzelbacher who had an exchange with Obama over his tax proposals for small businesses. Werzelbacher claimed he was going to buy a business with an income over $250,000 and that Obama's tax proposals would negatively affect him. This tactic fizzled as well, as Joe the Plumber, aside from not being named Joe, was not a licensed plumber, had not paid his taxes, and did not have the funds or credit to purchase the business.[25]

Obama was able to trump an expected Bradley effect due to the economic downturn late in the campaign season and the onset of recession. McCain's now-infamous statement that "the fundamentals of the economy are sound" came back to haunt him. Obama won easily, with 53 percent of the vote, and even carried former Confederate states like Virginia and North Carolina, long thought to be unreachable for a Democrat. Among families with annual incomes less than $50,000, Obama won by 60 percent. Economic issues triumphed over cultural and racial ones, and despite GOP appeals to the white working class, low-income whites have primarily and consistently voted Democratic over the past half-century. The irony of this reality is that Obama was no economic populist and even muted his rhetoric during the campaign. Of course, much of the reason for his lack of economic populism is that like the GOP, the Democrats enjoy support from big business. Obama received 46 percent of his money from corporations, which would explain the limited and procorporate scope of his reforms like the Patient Protection and Affordable Care Act (PPACA).[26] Little if any attention was paid to his cozy corporate relationships as Obama broke a major racial barrier with his election, but becoming the first black president essentially meant copying all of the characteristics and positions of a white one.

A brief period followed as President-Elect Obama was mentioned in the same breath with words like "postracial" and "color-blind." Observers predicted he would focus on economic issues and racial ones would be downplayed or put on the back burner. Obama's election in particular triggered an upsurge in optimism for black Americans. For white people, perhaps Chris Matthews's election night gaffe summed up how many felt, namely that race (or namely black people talking about race) would cease to be an issue with a black president.[27]

A black president did not mean racial issues faded. Instead, it meant that attention became even more focused on race, since some of his opposition was racial in nature. In his first two years in office, race surfaced a number of times to attract controversy and detract from his legislative agenda. Some of these controversies came from critics, while others were the president's own doing. When Obama began to push for an overhaul of the nation's health care system, a vocal grassroots opposition of conservatives opposed to this and other domestic spending arose in opposition and coalesced into the Tea Party movement. While the Tea Party denied any racist motivations, it remained an overwhelmingly white political movement identified with conservatism and the Republican Party, and some demonstrators waved racist signs at Tea Party rallies. While this may not be surprising, occasionally the president's own comments contributed to racial controversy. In July 2009, Obama offered his opinion that Cambridge, Massachusetts, police had acted "stupidly" when they arrested Henry Louis Gates, Jr., a prominent African American professor and intellectual, for a disorderly conduct charge at his home. The arrest stemmed from a heated conflict between the academic and the white officer who arrested him. After considerable criticism, Obama said he regretted the comments.[28]

In other cases, the Obama administration, likely out of fear of being perceived as overly sympathetic to African Americans, has acted hastily on racial issues and has further fueled tensions. This famously occurred in July 2010 during the Shirley Sherrod affair, when Sherrod, an official in the U.S. Department of Agriculture (USDA), gave a speech that a conservative blogger edited out of context. Selectively edited videos from the blogger on the Internet made Sherrod appear to hold racist attitudes toward whites, and the subsequent media attention led the National Association for the Advancement of Colored People (NAACP) to prematurely condemn her and Agriculture Secretary Tom Vilsack to force her resignation. As the true story surfaced, the Obama administration in particular was embarrassed by its hasty denunciation of Sherrod, apologized, and offered Sherrod a new job, which she refused.[29] Obama's desire to avoid any perception of favoring minorities meant that the media and his critics were allowed to frame the rules of debate, distorting and slandering innocent people in the process.

Despite Obama's missteps, his right-wing critics have been quick to play the race card while accusing Obama himself or his associates of being racist. Andrew Breibart, the blogger who created the Sherrod affair, also made it a racial attack on the Obama administration by selectively editing the videotaped speech she gave to make her appear to hold antiwhite sentiments. Glen Beck, the former Fox News commentator and a Tea Party favorite, accused the president of holding a "deep seated hatred" of white people and white culture. He contradicted himself, arguing that he "was not saying he [Obama] didn't like white people. He has a problem. This guy is, I believe, a racist." Beck made his comments in the wake of the Gates affair. Beck and other conservative pundits began to publish a cottage industry of diatribes against the president, and they were not shy about accusing the first black president of having an antiwhite bias. David Limbaugh, brother of conservative talk radio host Rush Limbaugh, wrote one such book, *Crimes against Liberty: An Indictment of President Barack Obama*. Limbaugh focuses much of his attack on policy items like the PPACA and foreign policy, but also delves into race. He cites Attorney General Eric Holder's decision not to pursue voter intimidation charges against the New Black Panther Party (NBPP) as an example of reverse discrimination. The George W. Bush Justice Department had filed suit against the NBPP for alleged voter intimidation at a Philadelphia polling station. When Holder ordered the case dropped in 2009, Christian Adams, a Bush-era trial attorney with the Justice Department, resigned in protest. However, no less a conservative scholar of the civil rights movement than Abigail Thernstrom pointed out the evidence of voter intimidation was weak and that the case was "very small potatoes." Limbaugh also blasted Obama for other racial matters, such as his comments regarding the Gates arrest, accusing the president of exhibiting "knee-jerk racism." To Limbaugh, these comments and other actions by Obama, such as his perceived lack of support for Israel, are proof positive that the president "shares Reverend Wright's basic worldview" of black liberation theology and "racist, anti-capitalist, anti-Semitic, and anti-American screeds."[30]

Jerome Corsi, another conservative author who first rose to prominence in 2004 with a book attacking John Kerry's military service and questioning his fitness to be president, published his anti-Obama tome even before the president was elected. Corsi devotes an entire chapter to the links between Wright and Obama, discussing Wright's adherence to black liberation theology. In doing this, Corsi attempts to link Obama to 1960s radicalism, specifically black power figures like Malcolm X and the anticolonial scholar Franz Fanon. Any criticism of white society then becomes painted as white-hating black radicalism. Corsi says that "as a product of the radical politics of the 1960s and as a son of a Kenyan seeking to advance independence in Africa, Obama was intellectually and emotionally prepared to encounter and accept black-liberation theology." According to Corsi,

Fanon "clearly taught a revolutionary socialist doctrine" and he quoted Fanon's declaration that "the colonized man finds his freedom in and through violence." One could easily say that the American patriots in 1776 followed the same philosophy, but Corsi apparently thinks that black desires for freedom are fundamentally less important than white ones and inherently radical. Corsi puts Obama, through his attendance at Wright's church and his exposure to a father he met only once in his life, in the same category as Louis Farrakhan, thus painting every black Democratic politician, no matter how centrist, as a white-hating radical. Even David Freddoso in his book *Gangster Government*, which focuses more on Obama's roots as a Chicago politician, delves into the coded language of race by calling the first black president's administration a "thugocracy."[31]

These right-wing publications and invectives against Obama, in reality thinly disguised racial attacks, have largely obscured the fact that some African Americans are dissatisfied so far with the lack of attention by the president to African American issues. The other side of Obama being portrayed as a postracial candidate who bridges racial gaps is that he has been reluctant to do anything that would specifically help the black community for fear of alienating whites. Black unemployment was 11.9 percent in 2008, with the unemployment rate for black males ages 16 to 19 at 32.8 percent. By comparison, white employment was 5.8 percent. By 2009 relevant unemployment numbers had increased to 8 percent for whites, but 15.0 percent for blacks and 11.3 percent for Latinos. The median household incomes of blacks and Latinos in 2009 were $38,269 and $40,000 respectively, compared to $61,280 for whites. Black and Latino poverty rates are 24 percent and 21 percent respectively, compared to 10 percent for whites. People of color are 24.5 percent more likely to be poor and 54 percent more likely to remain poor. The typical African American family possesses 10 percent of the net worth of the average white family, with almost 30 percent of black families having zero or negative net worth.[32] These economic numbers also need to be considered alongside other aspects of institutional racism discussed in earlier chapters that negatively affect African Americans, such as the prison-industrial complex and mass incarceration. These numbers perhaps most starkly indicate that for all the publicity surrounding the election of a black president, black and Latino poverty and inequality remain alive and well in this country.

Obama largely avoided racial issues in his first term (aside from rhetorical gaffes like the Gates affair), unless they were ones that directly affected his reelection chances, like voter ID laws.[33] He has said little on the subject of mass incarceration and its effect on African Americans and has continued the "war on drugs," even cracking down on medical marijuana. On another crime and punishment issue that affects minorities disproportionately, the death penalty, Obama has also been silent. He has been criticized by some academics for supporting the death penalty. His lack of concern became apparent in 2011 in the Troy Davis case, which involved a black man accused of murder in Georgia. Evidence in the Davis case, such as recanted witness statements, suggested he may have been wrongly convicted, and groups like the NAACP, Amnesty International, and other human-rights groups urged clemency. Despite calls from Davis supporters for intervention or even a public statement on his behalf by Obama, the president refused to order a federal investigation into the case or even publically comment as Davis's appeals for a new trial and clemency were rejected by the courts and the state and he was executed. Obama's press secretary simply said a statement was "not appropriate."[34]

In general, Obama has continued his postracial approach by advocating legislation that would focus on poor and working Americans, such as the PPACA. This "rising tide lifts all boats" approach has not won over all in the black community. Maxine Waters, a black representative from California and head of the Congressional Black Caucus's (CBC) jobs initiative, has become increasingly critical of the administration's lack of attention to black unemployment. This criticism has surfaced when black Democratic representatives like Waters have met with their constituents and other African Americans around the country. The increase in criticism has worried some black leaders who fear depressed black turnout in 2012. Some, like the Reverend Al Sharpton, have called on black elected officials to mute their criticism during the election year, fearing that if Obama does make an overt racial appeal, it will foster a white backlash. Others, like Representative Charlie Rangel of New York have said that it is fine for the black community to complain and that discontent over the president's lack of attention to black issues did not mean they should not support Obama in 2012.[35]

Obama addressed these concerns in 2011 when he spoke to the CBC, at a time when his "strongly favorable" ratings with black Americans had dropped from 83 to 58 percent in a five-month period. In his speech, the president addressed the economic problems of the black community and proposed a jobs creation bill to address these issues, even though such legislation stood little chance of passing the GOP-controlled House of Representatives. He ended his speech by declaring his expectations that the CBC—and by implication black Americans—supports him for re-election, stating that he did "expect all of you to march with me and press on . . . Stop complaining, stop grumbling, stop crying. We are going to press on. We've got work to do, CBC." While the speech received applause, not everyone welcomed it. Maxine Waters questioned his blunt language and said she did not know who he was addressing in the speech, calling his remarks "a bit curious." Other prominent African American critics included Princeton professor Cornel West and talk-show host Tavis Smiley, both of whom objected to his criticism. Smiley asked, "[h]ow does he get away with saying this to black folk?"[36]

Of course, he gets away with it *because* he is the first black president, just as the first Jewish president will no doubt be given a pass if he or she pressures Israel on Palestine, to use a hypothetical example. Obama's criticism of the black community brought to mind comedian Bill Cosby's 2004 remarks criticizing black men and low-income black parents. Such comments and a public rift with more liberal members of the black community certainly could not hurt Obama with white voters. But his base of black voters is critical as well, and with U.S. Census data from 2009 showing that black net worth fell 83 percent from 2007 to 2009—versus a 24 percent drop in that same time period for whites, and white net worth reaching on average 20 times that of blacks—low black voter turnout threatened his reelection. This turned out to be wishful thinking on the part of the Republicans, for despite lower overall voter turnout compared to 2008, black voters came out in levels close to Obama's first presidential victory. When adding overwhelming Latino support, as well as support from young voters and women, Obama held his 2008 coalition together despite the sluggish economy. Black turnout increased in key states like Virginia, where it rose from 18 percent in 2008 to 20 percent in 2012. With unemployment at 7.9 percent on Election Day, this meant that Obama was the first president to win reelection with unemployment about 7.2 percent since Franklin Delano Roosevelt won in 1936. It also means that like Roosevelt in that historic election, Obama appears to have crafted a coalition for the twenty-first century Democratic Party similar to the legendary New Deal coalition that Roosevelt set up with his victory—although a far more modest coalition in its numbers politically for Obama and modern Democrats than FDR's 1936 landslide was in creating the Democratic coalition that drove American politics until the 1960s.[37] Whether this coalition can hold together under future Democratic candidates will determine the long-term staying power of the party.[38]

Chapter 7

The Tea Party: Racists in Disguise?

"Congress = Slaveowner, Taxpayer = Niggar [sic]." That sign appeared at a February 27, 2009, Tea Party rally in Houston and was carried by Dale Robertson, a Tea Party activist who operates the website TeaParty.org. A photograph of the sign and Robertson, a middle-aged white man, circulated over the Internet and surfaced to hamper later Tea Party events he tried to organize. The Houston Tea Party Society moved against Robertson and expelled him from the event for displaying the sign.[1]

Spelling errors aside, the expulsion of Robertson indicates one of the continuing legacies of the civil rights movement, namely that overt expressions of racism are no longer tolerated in U.S. political discourse. But the presence of these and other racist signs has given the Tea Party political movement a problem as it has risen to prominence in the wake of the election of President Obama in 2008. The overwhelmingly white composition of the Tea Party, and the occasional forays of its members into crude racist outbursts—despite the best efforts of its leaders—has fueled perceptions that it is little more than racial backlash against the nation's first black president, instead of a grassroots revolt of taxpayers. The extent of this racism in the movement, and the role of race in the 2010 mid-term elections and the Republican primaries of the 2012 presidential election are major questions that continue to shape and influence U.S. politics today.

One must begin by first understanding what the Tea Party exactly is and how it started. Since the Tea Party is not a formal political party like the Republicans or Democrats, its genesis is harder to pinpoint. The "legendary"—if that word may be applied to a movement less than four years old—beginning of the movement was on February 19, 2009, on the floor of the Chicago Mercantile Exchange when Rick Santelli, a financial news commentator, said on CNBC that Barack Obama's proposed mortgage assistance plan "promoted bad behavior" and punished those who had played by the rules. Santelli then invited others who felt that way to join him for a "Chicago Tea Party in July." The video received widespread coverage on the Internet and news media, and helped stimulate other rallies across the country.[2]

The reality is less clear-cut, as the Tea Party did not emerge solely from one video clip, however influential the Internet has become today. The first Tea Party meeting had already taken place three days earlier in Seattle, organized by a half-Mexican 29-year-old woman named Keli Carender, not exactly representative of the later rank-and-file of the movement. She organized the gathering in response to Obama's $787-billion economic stimulus plan, and used a blog and local media to organize the modest turnout. But these modest beginnings soon changed as conservative talk radio and Fox News began to give extensive coverage to the movement in the spring of 2009, with thousands rallying on April 15, Tax Day, against taxes and government spending. These local affiliates enjoyed support from conservative talk-show hosts like Rush Limbaugh and Glen Beck, and sent vocal activists to confront congressional representatives at town hall meetings that summer. Politically, the Tea Partiers organized in Republican circles and with the help of party operatives, becoming effectively a conservative advocacy group within the Republican Party.[3]

But if one person can be linked to the origins of the Tea Party—and given its large number of grassroots activists, there is no one definable creator—it is Texas Grand Old Party (GOP) representative Ron Paul. The libertarian congressional representative's failed 2008 presidential bid spawned Campaign for Liberty, a spin-off group of his supporters. Paul's views put him out of much of the mainstream Republican Party, as his opposition to big government and spending as well as his adherence to a strict interpretation of the Constitution clashed with the procorporate wing of the party. Even more heretically, his opposition to overseas military action and defense spending put him at odds with Republicans who couched their generous support for defense with patriotic appeals. His followers, on average younger and better educated than other members of the Tea Party movement, represented the libertarian, small-government outlook of the Tea Party, which meant opposition to government spending and deficits created by both parties. Paul's influence on the grassroots led commentators like Fox News correspondent Juan Williams to call him the major ideological and organizing influence of the Tea Party.[4]

Events in 2009 and 2010 largely saw a co-opting of the grassroots organizing of the Tea Party. Some of this was due to the influence that media celebrities like Sean Hannity, Glen Beck, and Rush Limbaugh gained by publicizing Tea Party events and rallies. This accompanied the influx of Republican money into the Tea Party. Political action committees peddling corporate dollars eagerly passed themselves off as grassroots organizations, such as the Tea Party Express (TPE), which spent $2.7 million on congressional candidates in 2010, mostly to defeat moderate Republicans in GOP primaries and elect them that fall. The TPE arose from the actions of Sal Russo, a partner in a GOP consulting firm that launched the Our Country political action committee (PAC), which ran factually incorrect anti-Obama ads in the 2008 election. TPE money has sponsored bus tours and rallies, effectively becoming a top-down stimulator of political action rather than a bottom-up grassroots organization. Another group, FreedomWorks, an organization that advocates lower taxes and less government regulation, has also become a major Tea Party organizer. FreedomWorks arose from Citizens for a Sound Economy, a group founded in 1984 and funded by the Koch brothers, two arch-conservative billionaires who made their fortunes in petrochemicals.[5]

The other faction from the GOP that diverted the Tea Party from its libertarian origins is the social conservative wing of the GOP, better known as the religious right. Religious conservatives were an important force in the GOP that, beginning in the 1970s, helped shift the party toward conservative positions on abortion, school prayer, and gay rights. One 2010 study by the Pew Forum identified Tea Party supporters as more likely to oppose same-sex marriage and abortion, and white evangelical Protestants were rated as the religious denomination most likely to support the movement. Sixty-nine percent of those who supported the religious right supported the Tea Party, as 42 percent of Tea Party supporters supported the religious right. The growth of social conservatives in the Tea Party has led to sharp splits with libertarians over abortion and gay rights as well as other issues dear to libertarians like drug legalization. Many local Tea Parties have become dominated by social conservatives, which has led to less religious and more libertarian activists being pushed to the periphery, and less of a focus on purely fiscal issues in policy debates in the organization. Still, the Tea Party has managed to blend social and fiscal conservatism, rather than focusing almost exclusively on social issues like the old Moral Majority of Jerry Falwell once did.[6]

The Tea Party represents a long line of right-leaning populist movements in U.S. history. From the anti-immigrant Know-Nothings of the 1850s to the nationwide revival of the Ku Klux Klan of the 1920s, many of these populist movements have been associated with racism or nativism. More recently, the backlash against the civil rights movement, especially the presidential candidacy of Alabama governor George Wallace, represented the political expression of whites, especially working-class whites, against school integration and civil rights enforcement. This also occurred in northern cities, most famously in Boston in the 1970s. The historian Richard Hofstadter describes the rationale of these movements, specifically the resurgent conservatism that came in the wake of Barry Goldwater's failed 1964 presidential bid, as a "paranoid style" of politics. This style included a strong anti-intellectual component, which Hofstadter cited in movements like McCarthyism that heavily influenced his analysis.[7]

The Tea Party as a conservative movement shares many of these characteristics. Its supporters are disproportionately older whites from middle-class backgrounds, including many senior citizens. They are overwhelmingly conservative Republicans and heavily influenced by evangelical Protestant Christianity. Within the Tea Parties, the libertarian Tea Partiers are more likely to have postgraduate educations and higher incomes; they also tend to be far less religious than social conservatives.[8]

It would be facile to say that based on these characteristics, the Tea Party is automatically racist, even if black Tea Partiers are almost nonexistent. But clearly race and religion affect how one views or identifies with the Tea Party. Black Protestants, the religiously unaffiliated, and Jews all disproportionately view the Tea Party negatively. Of black Protestants, only 7 percent agreed with the Tea Party, even though many black churchgoers share the party's general opposition to abortion and same-sex marriage. On immigration, Tea Partiers support stronger border security and oppose citizenship for undocumented immigrants by much wider margins than the average voter.[9] This latter issue hinders Tea Party support among Latinos, and the perceptions of blacks and Jews, two traditionally Democratic constituencies, reinforce the partisan if not racial composition of the Tea Party.

What has helped fuel these perceptions has been a number of racist comments and demonstrations by members of the Tea Party. Examples include the demonstration by Dale Robertson mentioned at the beginning of this chapter as well as other racist signs seen at Tea Party rallies. Aside from racial epitaphs and slurs like the one mentioned earlier in this chapter, some Tea Partiers have waved signs declaring that Obama wants "white slavery." Another highly publicized charge came from John Lewis, the black Georgia representative and civil rights veteran, who said that some Tea Partiers called him a "nigger" as he was leaving the Cannon

House Office Building in Washington. No video or audio of the incident surfaced, so many Tea Partiers refuse to believe it ever occurred. Other expressions have been milder, but still racial, such as signs at rallies that said "[d]on't tax me, bro"—something not seem when previous (white) Democratic presidents (or Republicans for that matter) raised taxes. These expressions tend to be confined to public demonstrations, however. Scholars and journalists who have conducted private interviews with Tea Party members have noted that the respondents did not express such views in private. Also, Tea Party leaders have acted quickly to quell racist individual expressions, like in the case of Robertson. Some leaders have also worried that outsiders might infiltrate meetings with racist signs to depict the movement negatively.[10]

Still, racism has been a significant problem in the movement. Even journalists who have written defenses of the Tea Party have admitted that the movement needs to do more to address racism in its ranks. Scott Rasmussen and Douglas Schoen, authors of the pro–Tea Party book *Mad as Hell*, said that they interviewed individuals who held anti-Semitic and racist viewpoints, but insisted that "these individuals were the exception, not the norm." Still, they admitted that the Tea Party movement "must deal with the small faction of right-wing populists who hold radical and offensive views and thus threaten to discredit or derail the movement." In addition, Islamophobia pervades many rank-and-file Tea Partiers. While individual Tea Partiers have not expressed racist sentiments in their interviews, they have had little compunction about declaring their anti-Muslim sentiments, even about U.S. citizens who are Muslims.[11]

This latter sentiment also plays into another sentiment that has circulated widely among Tea Party supporters, the belief that Obama is a Muslim and lacks a legitimate birth certificate. As mentioned in the previous chapter, this belief circulated during the 2008 election and continued to remain prevalent even during Obama's first term, despite the lack of evidence to support the claim and the release of the president's long-form birth certificate in 2011, which followed up on his short-form birth certificate release in 2008. Those that believe that Obama is foreign-born and thus unable to serve as president under the Constitution are known as birthers and have remained a persistent but vocal minority peddling the conspiracy. Obama's "otherness"—black, with a foreign-born father and Muslim name—to the largely white birther movement only fuels their belief in his illegitimacy.[12]

Ironically, the birther movement began with supporters of Hillary Clinton and surfaced as anonymous e-mails from them in April 2008 as her campaign faltered against Obama's in the Democratic primaries. Conservative opponents of Obama, like author Jerome Corsi, picked up these theories and alternately claimed that the president was born in Kenya, held multiple citizenships, was not eligible to become a citizen due to his mother's young age, or lost it when he visited Pakistan in the early 1980s. These claims hold no truth, and the last two are based on incorrect readings of immigration law and a supposed ban on U.S. passport holders traveling to Pakistan (a ban that never existed). The linkage of these theories to radical fringe elements and conspiracy theorists was reinforced by the involvement of Phil Berg, a former Pennsylvania deputy attorney general who garnered publicity in earlier years for alleging that George W. Bush helped to arrange the 9/11 attacks. Berg filed a complaint in federal district court in August 2008 that Obama held multiple citizenships and was ineligible to serve as president. This and other citizenship suits were dismissed, but still the allegations continued and were spread by the Internet. Birthers jeered as a forgery Obama's release of his short-form birth certificate in 2008, although FactCheck.org, a nonpartisan website, viewed the original and declared it authentic, backing up the state of Hawaii's declaration that it was real. Facts have meant little to birthers, many of whom are active in Tea Party groups, if the facts conflict with their anti-Obama values. Tom Grimes, a stockbroker and active Tea Party member, told a reporter that "you can have all the facts, but if you don't trust the mind-set [sic] or the value system of the people involved, you can't even look at the facts anymore." Some Tea Partiers have even made openly racist statements about the birth certificate issue, such as when Marilyn Davenport, an elected member of the Los Angeles–area Orange County, California, Republican Party's central committee, sent out an e-mail depicting Obama as a baby chimpanzee held by his parents with the caption "Now you know why—No birth certificate!" After a media leak of the e-mail and heavy criticism, including from members of her own party, she apologized but refused to resign.[13]

Republican leaders have largely rejected these claims. Mitt Romney and Tim Pawlenty both dismissed these notions in the GOP presidential primaries. Conservative websites like Redstate.org have purged birthers from their sites, and conservative talk-show host Michael Medved has said that the birther movement "makes us [Republicans] look crazy." But when one-fourth of Americans, according to one 2010 poll, harbor doubts about

Obama's citizenship, some Republican officials give lip service to the movement. Nathan Deal, a Georgia representative who later became governor, was the first member of Congress to request Obama's birth certificate. Senator David Vitter of Louisiana publicly supported legal organizations that brought suits over the issue. The most prominent proponent of the birther controversy has been Donald Trump, who sent investigators at his own expense to Hawaii to investigate the birth certificate, all part of a publicity stunt linked with his flirtations with a presidential campaign. Even in the 2012 election campaign, GOP presidential nominee Mitt Romney made a widely criticized joke about the whole affair, commenting in his home state of Michigan that "[n]o one's ever asked to see my birth certificate."[14]

The likely reason Romney made this reference to the controversy is that despite his claims that he believes Obama to be legitimate, he needed the paranoid anti-Obama base to mobilize in high numbers to vote for him in November 2012. Therefore he—just like southern Republicans who make appeals to the memory and imagery of the Confederacy to win white racist votes—felt the need to stir the issue a bit. Polls have shown that a majority of Republicans believe Obama was not born in the United States or that they are unsure. One poll in Utah found that middle-aged, lower-income, Republican-leaning individuals without a college education were the most likely people to believe that Obama lacks U.S. citizenship.[15] With these views widespread among the GOP rank-and-file and the Tea Party (two groups that have become largely indistinguishable), it will likely be a continuing annoyance in his second term, but also one that the GOP will have to overcome as it tries to reach independent and moderate voters in future elections.

The birther issue and Obama-is-a-Muslim rumors are part of portraying him as an "other," foreign, Orientalized individual living part of his youth in a foreign, Islamic country (Indonesia) and the rest in Hawaii, the last state admitted to the United States, one that votes consistently Democratic, and one that has large numbers of Asians and native Hawaiians, another part of that racial other.[16] Much of this diverse background of Obama's is a stand-in for his blackness, a cover, since direct attacks on his race would be unpalatable in the rhetoric of the post–civil rights era. But even among mainstream elected Republicans, there has been a lack of respect shown to Obama even as he holds the office of president. Of course, so-called "mainstream" Republicans have moved largely to the right as a result of the rise of social conservatives and the Tea Party, so sharp anti-Obama viewpoints have become increasingly the norm in the GOP's political discourse. During the last days of the 2012 election, GOP vice-presidential running mate Paul Ryan told evangelical Christians in a conference call that Obama through his policies sought to "compromise those values, those Judeo-Christian, Western civilization values that made us such a great and exceptional nation in the first place." This rather unsubtle reference that Obama was hostile to Judaism and Christianity—and by extension presumably coddling Islamic extremists—represented a marginally softer version of painting Obama as the "other." Another famous example was at the State of the Union address in 2009 during which Representative Joe Wilson of South Carolina interrupted the president. When Obama mentioned that illegal immigrants would not receive health insurance coverage in pending bills in the House and Senate, Wilson shouted, "You Lie!" His outburst prompted a rebuke from the Democratic-controlled House, and while Wilson said he apologized privately to the president, he refused to do so publically. Another example was the encounter Obama had with Governor Jan Brewer of Arizona when he arrived at the Phoenix-Mesa Gateway Airport in January 2012. Brewer handed him a letter about immigration, a point of contention between them since the Obama administration had challenged Arizona's strict anti-immigrant bill. The two got into a heated exchange, and Brewer was photographed wagging her finger at the president. Phoenix mayor Greg Stanton, a Democrat, criticized her for engaging in a debate on the airport tarmac when she should have been "an ambassador for your community."[17]

Former president Jimmy Carter called incidents such as the Wilson outburst racism on the part of whites who cannot accept a black president, calling it "an abominable circumstance."[18] While not explicitly racist, the treatment of Obama in this fashion demonstrates the continuance of subtle, covert racial treatment. Bill Clinton had his detractors and was a target of vitriol from the political right, and this coalesced into his impeachment when he gave Republicans an opportunity because of his affair with Monica Lewinsky. But during the Clinton presidency, the president was not subjected to outbursts from Republican representatives during his State of the Union addresses, and he did not experience disrespectful treatment from Republican governors during visits. George W. Bush attracted hateful comments from the political left for waging the Iraq War but never casual disrespect from Democratic politicians. A black president appears to be held to a double standard, as it is difficult to believe that a white president would experience the kind of disrespect from elected officials of the opposition party that President Obama has received from some Republican officeholders today.

Of course, the Tea Party denies any prevalence of racism in its ranks, and one cover they use is their support for certain black conservatives. One of the biggest stars of the Tea Party is Alan West, a black representative and former military officer from Florida who has famously expressed anti-Muslim sentiments, such as when he called fellow representative Keith Ellison, a Muslim Democrat from Minnesota, the "antithesis of the principles upon which this country was established." He has also said that the United States' war against Islamic terrorism and invasions of Islamic countries are in the same historical tradition as the Battles of Tours and Thermopylae in defense of so-called "Western" civilization and famously told Democratic leaders to "get the hell out of the United States of America." Another black favorite of the Tea Party is Representative Tim Scott of South Carolina, who was elected with West in the Tea Party–backed House elections in 2010. Scott, unlike West, refused to join the Congressional Black Caucus, claiming that his "campaign was never about race."[19]

White Tea Party support for black conservatives, just like earlier white conservative support for Clarence Thomas, is a variation on the "some of my best friends are black" defense. This idea is commonly cited by many whites as proof of their alleged color-blindness, usually followed by a complaint about how something like affirmative action or the welfare system discriminates against whites or makes minorities lazy. The fact that many of these black conservatives are out of the mainstream of the black electorate does not matter to them and in fact validates that there are other minorities who think like them and share their values. Support for the black conservative Republican acts as a shield to charges of racism, just as Latino Tea Party favorites like Senator Marco Rubio of Florida and senatorial candidate Ted Cruz in Texas are held up as covers for the Tea Party's anti-immigrant rhetoric.[20]

The Tea Party scored impressive victories in the 2010 mid-term elections, winning control of the House Representatives. Tea Party mobilization helped Republicans gain six seats in the Senate and six new governorships, as well as 700 new state legislative seats. However, some Tea Party–backed Senate candidates were too conservative for the electorate, which cost the GOP control of the Senate when Tea Party favorites in Colorado, Nevada, and Delaware lost their general elections.[21]

Despite the claims of the Tea Party that it focuses on fiscal conservatism and cutting spending, social issues have dominated in many of these Tea Party–backed legislatures. Abortion emerged as a major issue, with Tea

Party–elected legislatures introducing bills that implemented new restrictions, from mandatory ultrasounds to new clinic regulations to personhood amendments that would grant legal rights to fertilized eggs. On the issue of race, voter ID laws designed to combat fraud but disproportionately affecting the poor, elderly, and minorities proliferated in the same legislatures. Some Tea Party–backed officials have stepped into racial controversies, such as Maine governor Paul LePage, who refused to take part in Martin Luther King, Jr. Day ceremonies despite it being a national and state holiday. When the National Association for the Advancement of Colored People (NAACP) criticized him for turning down invitations to the events, he told them to "kiss my butt." These racial battles have carried over to education, where some Tea Partiers have tried to mandate rewriting history curriculum in public schools to downplay slavery. In Tennessee, members of the Tea Party demanded that state legislators pick history textbooks that exclude what one local leader called "an awful lot of made-up criticism about, for instance the founders intruding on the Indians or having slaves or being hypocrites in one way or another." This denial of history—since the ownership of slaves by most of the Founding Fathers has been well documented—was deemed enough of an issue by the parties that it made a list of the five priorities for Nashville legislators to consider in the 2011 session.[22]

Still, the influence that Tea Party activists, now backed by corporate money and other arms of the GOP establishment, could exert in the GOP presidential primaries meant that the parties would have an effect in 2011 and 2012. The result was a rightward tilt by GOP presidential candidates in late 2011 and early 2012 as they sought the support of Tea Party activists and social conservatives in the quest for the Republican nomination. Republicans like Minnesota representative Michelle Bachmann were Tea Party favorites early on, while establishment Republicans like former Minnesota governor Tim Pawlenty openly sought the group's support. Fringe undeclared candidates like Donald Trump also courted the Tea Parties. More mainstream candidates like former Massachusetts governor Mitt Romney were more wary of the Tea Party, since an overly extreme position in the primaries carried the risk of alienating centrist voters in the general election. This feeling was mutual, as FreedomWorks, one of the Tea Party lobbying organizations, called the field of candidates "a little frustrating." Much Tea Party dissatisfaction with Romney came from the health care plan he implemented for Massachusetts, which heavily influenced Obama's own PPACA. Still, Romney led in Tea Party voters in some

2011 polls, with 24 percent support, to 13 percent for Ron Paul and 12 percent for Sarah Palin; he hardly had a commanding plurality.[23]

As candidates more conservative than Romney jockeyed for Tea Party support, race occasionally surfaced. Some, like Michelle Bachmann, did not shy away from attacking government programs that specifically benefited black Americans. She criticized the Pigford settlement, a 1999 ruling that paid billions to black farmers who suffered discrimination for decades from the federal government in lending and other federal aid. The renewed criticism came when in 2010, President Obama signed into law authorization of $1.2 billion for farmers covered by Pigford who had missed filing deadlines. Bachmann called it an "inefficient project" and the claims "potentially fraudulent." Representative Peter King of Iowa, a Tea Party supporter, went further, calling the settlement "modern-day reparations" for African Americans. This claim of fraud in a financial settlement for black Americans played to familiar rhetoric about undeserving welfare recipients, a coded racialized image that has a long history in American political rhetoric.[24]

Welfare surfaced more directly in the primaries in comments made by former Pennsylvania senator Rick Santorum and former house speaker Newt Gingrich. Welfare, a favorite conservative target, came under attack by both candidates. Santorum said that he did not "want to make black people's lives better by giving them somebody else's money," a comment that played to white stereotypes about undeserving blacks receiving the earnings of hard-working (white) taxpayers. This overshadowed the message in the second part of his statement, which was that he wanted "to give them the opportunity to go out and earn the money and provide for themselves and their families." His stumbling in subsequent interviews, during which he said he did not recall the "context of the question," did not help defuse the media attention. Newt Gingrich made similar remarks at a town hall meeting in New Hampshire, saying he would go before the NAACP and ask "why the African-American community should demand paychecks and not be satisfied with food stamps." He was already on record calling Obama the "best food stamp president in American history." Marc Morial, the president of the National Urban League, called Gingrich's comments appeals to racist elements in the GOP, since most people on food stamps were white, not black. Like Santorum, the comment about creating opportunities for unemployed African Americans was overshadowed by the racial connotations, although it is unclear if the racialism was intentional on the part of the candidates. Gingrich's own past history of comments denigrating "welfare Americans" who "quit their jobs" and "start cheating on their rent" did not help his denials of racial pandering.[25]

Gingrich's racial comments on President Obama were more explicit when he told a reporter from *National Review* that the president followed a "Kenyan, anti-colonial worldview," citing a *Forbes* article written by conservative author Dinesh D'Souza. This reference to Obama's father's political activism in colonial Kenya and critique of an anticolonial position is curious, given that Gingrich's own doctorate dissertation from Tulane University was on education policy in the Belgian Congo, where he blamed much of the postindependence chaos in the African state on failures of Belgian colonial administrators. More pointedly, the comment—especially the reference to Kenya—was more likely a phrase tossed off to win birther support by calling attention to the foreign origins of the president's father.[26]

Gingrich cited D'Souza's article, which was related to his book, *The Roots of Obama's Rage*. In this book, D'Souza alleges that Obama is continuing the anticolonial behavior of his dead father, a "rage" that is making him reduce America's role in the world, weaken longtime allies like Israel, and in general hold and enact anti-American attitudes—all from the White House. This Manchurian Candidate–style thesis of D'Souza's avoids calling Obama a Muslim but does paint him as a modern-day Franz Fanon, the anticolonial psychiatrist from Martinique who defended 1960s Algerian revolutionaries in his book *The Wretched of the Earth*. To D'Souza, Obama's multiculturalism is part and parcel of his strangeness, his otherness. This thesis is dubious when one considers that Obama met his father once in his life, at age 10, yet supposedly he exerted such a pervasive control over his son's ideology. Adding to this was Obama's education, during which he studied books that detailed the mistreatment of American Indians and the internment of the Japanese Americans during World War II. D'Souza mocks this as Oppression Studies, rather than acknowledging historical realities about America's past. When it comes to race, he separates Obama from the African American experience due to his growing up in multicultural Hawaii. D'Souza's views on race are equally ignorant, both in his historical knowledge and the actual experience of race. He says that the "one drop" rule of blackness in America came from segregation and not slavery, a position that is completely at odds with scholars like Winthrop Jordan and that ignores the enslavement of mixed-race people. D'Souza also says that Obama "recognized from early adolescence on that he needed to be black." This assumes that white people, and black people for that matter, were not looking at him and considering him black due to his skin color. Such an assertion suspends disbelief to the point of improbability.[27]

D'Souza then developed this thesis into a movie, *Obama's America 2016*, which opened in the summer of 2012 during the presidential campaign season. The film became the highest-rossing documentary that year, earning over $20 million by Labor Day. Using interviews, D'Souza repeated much of what he said in his book, and the entire production carried an overt anti-Obama tone throughout its 87 minutes. The Associated Press fact-checked the documentary and found it riddled with inaccuracies about some of the charges made against Obama, such as the growth of the national debt. Many of his other assertions, such as Obama's alleged pro-Muslim sympathies, are purely conjecture and questionable when one looks at the president's ordering of the raid that killed Osama bin Laden.[28] The film, like his books, is an attempt by D'Souza to provide a veneer of intellectual sophistication to the claims of Obama's "otherness" and inherent unfitness to be president. His refusal to embrace birther conspiracies will likely be lost on the audience for this film, likely made up of people already holding pronounced anti-Obama viewpoints and seeking further validation for their beliefs.

Mitt Romney, the front-runner and eventual victor in the GOP primaries, had his own difficulties connecting with black voters, although this has more to do with his own background than any effort to win Tea Party votes. Romney, a Mormon and multimillionaire, told a crowd in Prattville, Alabama, that he "could relate to black people very well indeed." The reason was that his "ancestors once owned slaves, and it is in my lineage to work closely with the black community." He added a paternalistic comment that he planned as president to "bring a sense of pride and work ethic back into view for them." Not surprisingly, Romney's support among African American voters was at 0 percent versus 94 percent for Obama in August 2012. He did not help his standing with them in September when he was secretly recorded at a fundraiser dismissing "47 percent" of Americans who are Obama's supporters as "dependent upon government, who believe that they are victims, who believe the government has a responsibility to care for them." Even many Republicans distanced themselves from his remarks, and the dependency comment echoed earlier coded statements about ungrateful, lazy (black) welfare recipients. Some of Romney's own supporters have also made racial stumbles. Days before the election, former secretary of state and Republican Colin Powell endorsed Obama for reelection, a repeat of the endorsement he gave in

2008. John Sununu, a top aide of Romney's whose past political history included serving as governor of New Hampshire and then as George H. W. Bush's chief of staff, said the endorsement was not about policy but instead due to both Powell and Obama being black. Sununu said on CNN's *Piers Morgan Tonight* that Powell supported Obama because it was a case of "when you have somebody of your own race that you're proud of being President of the United States." After experiencing criticism for the comment, Sununu retracted the comment a few hours later.[29]

Race in the Republican presidential primaries has also affected the primaries of less-prominent candidates. As mentioned before, Texas representative Ron Paul is the politician linked to the origins of the Tea Party. As leader of its libertarian wing, however, he saw an inability to gain traction in the primaries as he ran up against the procorporate, prodefense, and socially conservative factions of the GOP base. Yet Paul's own views on devolution—the restriction of federal powers and reserving of them for the states under the Tenth Amendment—has exposed him to charges of insensitivity to race, and the actions of some his supporters have crossed into outright racism and embarrassed his candidacy.

The center of Paul's campaign is his opposition to the Federal Reserve, or Fed. He embraces the Austrian school of economics and a return to the gold standard, and as part of that belief he wants an audit—and eventual abolition—of the Fed, which he says has unconstitutionally manipulated the economy and debased the U.S. dollar. He even outlined these ideas in a book, *Ending the Fed*, written after the 2008 financial collapse. But his views on landmark legislation like the Civil Rights Act of 1964 created significant controversy, as seen in 2004 on the fortieth anniversary of the act when he spoke against House Resolution 676, a congressional commemoration of the law. He said that while he favored "racial harmony and individual liberty," the act was a "massive violation of the rights of private property and contract." He opposed the use of the interstate commerce clause to enforce nondiscrimination in employment and said that the end result of this was the creation of racial quotas for private employers by federal bureaucrats and judges. This stance is shared by his son Rand, who during his successful Senate race in Kentucky in 2010 created a controversy when he said on the *Rachel Maddow Show* said that for the same reasons that his father believed, he did not support the provision of the act covering private business and nondiscrimination. When he faced criticism that he supported repealing this landmark legislation, Rand Paul responded by saying that he "unequivocally . . . will not support any efforts to repeal the Civil Rights Act of 1964." Neither Ron Paul nor his son embraced a racist defense of segregated businesses, and both embraced the intent of the legislation but opposed or had reservations about federal intervention to achieve those ends. The elder Paul, a better libertarian, did not engage in the backtracking of his more establishment-oriented son and did tell MSNBC host Chris Matthews that due to the property rights issue, he would have voted against the act had he been in Congress in 1964 and said that the free market would have ended Jim Crow laws. However questionable that outcome, it is consistent with libertarian ideas that the free market and desire for profits will trump racial biases.[30]

Unfortunately for Representative Paul, not all of his supporters are as ideologically opposed to civil rights enforcement on property rights grounds. As the *Economist* noted, "Mr. Paul's obsession with the Fed is an anti-government conspiracy theory. And in America, anti-government conspiracy theorists attract a lot of wingnuts." A lot of these "wingnuts" are out-and-out racists, and this caused significant problems for Paul's already long-shot campaign for the presidency. Some of these racial controversies had the official stamp of his campaign on it, such as some racist newsletters published under his name in the 1990s that contained anti-black, homophobic, and anti-Semitic statements. Paul disavowed the newsletters and said that they do not reflect his opinions, but that did not stop candidates like Newt Gingrich from using them against the representative in the GOP presidential debates. Gingrich demanded that Paul explain the newsletters and tried to get him to defend the language that Paul repudiated. Another one of the GOP candidates, former Utah governor Jon Huntsman, ran an anti-Paul ad for the New Hampshire primary that included Paul's criticism of Lincoln's waging the Civil War. Paul's supporters from an independent group responded by running an ad showing Hunstman, who once served as ambassador to China, talking to his daughter in Chinese, and implied that his contact with China made him "weak on China" and lacking "American values." The ad also made an issue of Huntsmen's adopted Chinese and Indian daughters as part of this lack of "values." Paul disavowed the ad. Even worse for Paul, a Paul supporter and failed political candidate for city council in Carson, California, called Obama a "monkey" in a Facebook post and followed it with another post declaring "[a]ssassinate the fucken [sic] nigger and his monkey children."[31]

Even though Paul cannot and should not be held accountable for every supporter's statements, and certainly supporters of Democratic candidates have made embarrassing and hyperbolic comments as well, Paul's disavowals rang a bit hollow since in 2007 he received a $500 donation from Don Black, a self-described "white patriot" who runs a racist website called Stormfront. A Paul spokesman said the candidate did not agree with Black's white supremacist views but refused to return the money, arguing that "that's $500 less that this guy has to do whatever it is he does." While it was unlikely and not surprising that Paul did poorly in the primaries given that his stands alienated much of the GOP's key constituencies, the racist associations and links, no matter how much he disavowed them, gave his opponents ammunition to weaken him further.[32]

Not surprisingly, Democrats, especially black Democrats, have responded with their own highly charged rhetoric against the rise of the Tea Party and the perception of widespread racism in its ranks. Representative Andre Carson of Indiana, the chief vote counter of the Congressional Black Caucus, said at an event in Miami in 2011 that the Tea Party wanted "to see you and me . . . hanging on a tree." Representative Maxine Waters of California simply told the Tea Party to "go straight to hell." In a less inflammatory fashion, the NAACP passed a resolution in 2010 condemning racist elements in the Tea Party—but not the entire movement—and called on Tea Party leaders to repudiate racists in their ranks. Black celebrities have also joined in the criticism. Morgan Freeman, appearing on *Piers Morgan Tonight*, called the movement "a racist thing" for their anti-Obama efforts, arguing that their objective is "to get this black man outta here." Samuel L. Jackson agreed with his fellow film star and said that "it all boils down pretty much to race." Vice President Joe Biden likely set the record for overheated rhetoric when in August 2012, he told a mostly black audience in Danville, Virginia, that the Republicans would "put y'all back in chains" through the proposed deregulation of Wall Street in the House GOP budget. Biden said his comments were a reference to a statement by Representative Paul Ryan, Romney's running mate, that the GOP would "unshackle" the economy. Biden's comment brought the expected Republican cry of outrage, but the racial connotation of "chains" before a black audience is obvious to even the densest of observers.[33] Comments like Biden's and Carson's are born of the overheated rhetoric of Washington politics, the vice president's in particular of the presidential campaign season. Still, whatever the racial feelings of some rank-and-file Tea Partiers, to suggest they wish to return to the days of slavery and lynching is a gross exaggeration and one that does not help diffuse racially charged discourse in the country. The other comments, however angry in tone, do represent a legitimate frustration and feeling among many African

Americans that the Tea Party coddles racists and is reluctant to hurt its efforts by confronting its own white privilege.

With all the charges and denials of racism concerning the Tea Party, a black presidential candidate who enjoyed Tea Party support briefly shook up the GOP presidential race. Herman Cain, a successful corporate executive, briefly challenged Mitt Romney for front-runner status in late 2011. Unlike Obama, Cain's experience as an African American was more typical of the black American experience. He was born in Memphis in 1945, and his parents soon moved to Atlanta, where he was raised. Like many black women, his mother worked as a maid while his father had managed to find employment during World War II in a tire-manufacturing plant. Cain grew up in segregated Atlanta in the 1950s and 1960s, where his father worked three jobs to support the family. He attended Morehouse College, one of the elite black universities of the nation, where worked to put himself through school. He graduated in 1967 with a degree in mathematics and received numerous job offers, which he admitted made him "a beneficiary of the civil rights movement." He then entered management at Coca-Cola (where his father had worked) and then moved on to Pillsbury. He then led the buyout of Godfather's Pizza, a Pillsbury subsidiary, and became famous as the head of that company. His stints in government service included serving on and eventually chairing the board of the Federal Reserve in Kansas City. He ran for the presidency in 2000 and for the U.S. Senate from Georgia in 2004 but has never held elective office.[34]

Cain's entry into the race came from the enthusiasm he stirred up with conservative audiences on the lecture circuit, and when he entered the race, he drew attention for his 9-9-9 economic program, named after the tax rates he wanted on personal, corporate, and sales taxes. This simple plan appealed to voters offset by Romney's cumbersome 59-point economic plan, and Cain's charisma also contrasted to the woodenness of the Massachusetts governor.[35]

Cain differed from other famous black conservatives like Clarence Thomas in that he avoided criticizing civil rights enforcement and in fact openly talked about his youth in the segregated South, acknowledging the debt he owed to civil rights leaders like Benjamin Mays, the longtime president of Morehouse College. Yet he also appealed to white voters by declaring that Obama supporters were too frequently playing the race card when the president received criticism. This charge also related to his comment that when he was in high school, his father had encouraged him to focus on his studies rather than participating in the civil rights movement, a statement that drew criticism from black liberals.[36]

It was of course easier for a black conservative to criticize Obama on race than a white one, and Cain did not hesitate to do so. He said that the president has "never been a part of the black experience in America," a jab both at Obama's blackness as well as his foreign parentage. Cain highlighted his African American roots by pointing to his own descent from slaves in Georgia and Tennessee. These comments built on earlier ones in which he said that the president was not a "strong black man" in the same mold as Martin Luther King, Jr. Cain also showed that he would not use race in a purely partisan manner as he criticized Texas governor Rick Perry for "insensitivity" when he attending a hunting camp leased by his family that had a rock at the entrance painted with the word "Niggerhead."[37] Cain's invoking civil rights heroes and criticizing Obama's blackness—as well as the racial missteps of his fellow Republicans—showed he was not afraid to discuss race and made the kind of charges of "Uncle Tomism" that critics frequently used against black conservatives like Thomas harder to use credibly against him.

Cain also appeared to suffer racist threats himself as he campaigned. He requested Secret Service protection in November 2011 and was granted it due to death threats he received. While the nature of the threats was not released, he was the earliest GOP candidate in the 2012 election to receive such protection, a characteristic he shared with Obama, who received unprecedented early protection when he announced his run for the presidency before the 2008 primaries. The fact that Cain was the only black GOP contender suggests that the threats may have been racially motivated. However, the protection did not last long, as Cain's campaign was already rocked by that time by allegations of sexual harassment and an extramarital affair by the candidate, and he suspended his bid in December 2011. As his campaign unraveled, his defenders, from Rush Limbaugh to conservative bloggers, showed that they could be just as quick to play the race card as any liberal when they accused the media of racial bias against Cain in their reporting of the sexual allegations.[38]

A final analysis of Cain's campaign and race indicates that for all his invoking of the memory of Martin Luther King, Jr., his positions on many issues showed an explicit rejection of the multicultural and egalitarian view celebrated by King, such as the civil rights leader did in his interracial Poor People's Campaign in 1968. King died while leading this movement when he stopped in Memphis to lend aid to a sanitation workers' strike. Cain, on the other hand, openly expressed antiunion sentiments in his writings and statements, and he opposed the expansive welfare state that King sought to combat poverty. On the issue of immigration, Cain backed Arizona's harsh anti-immigration law and opposed amnesty for illegal immigrants. He also criticized fellow Republicans for being too soft on illegal immigration. Cain even told jokes about building electrified fences on the border with Mexico.[39]

Cain's sharpest break with the King tradition came in his hostility to Islam. He expressed concern that a doctor treating him for cancer was a Muslim, telling a conservative Christian audience that he thought the doctor, whose name was Abdallah, sounded "too foreign." Cain indicated he was relieved when he found out the doctor was Christian. He also said in an interview that he believed the majority of Muslims held "extremist views." Most tellingly, he waded into the controversy over opposition to a planned mosque in Murfreesboro, Tennessee, declaring that the mosque was "not an innocent mosque" but was "another way to try to gradually sneak Sharia law into our laws." Local communities, he said, had a right to ban such houses of worship.[40] This fundamental violation of the First Amendment struck at the heart of the ecumenical vision of the civil rights movement, and one wonders if Cain would have felt the same way about a synagogue or black church being opposed in the same manner by local white supremacists. In a sense, Cain was running as a postracial black man by embracing many of the same prejudices against Latino immigrants and Muslims that his white Tea Party supporters shared.

As the 2012 presidential election drew closer, it was clear that the Tea Party would continue to exert an influence in the election, as conservative candidates in Texas and Indiana won GOP primaries with Tea Party support. The Tea Party had by that point become effectively indistinguishable from the GOP as the GOP moved increasingly rightward and the movement, backed by corporate dollars, came to represent the most conservative ideological wing of the Republican base. The November election delivered a sharp rebuke to the Tea Party and may prove critical to the movement's future. Tea Party–backed U.S. Senate candidates in Montana, Missouri, and Indiana lost their races. The last two states saw the losses of Representatives Todd Akin and Richard Mourdock, respectively, as these two seats— easily expected to go Republican in states that Romney carried handily— stayed or went Democratic as both men made controversial comments about rape as they explained their opposition to abortion. As in 2010, Tea Party demands for far-right ideological purity in GOP candidates cost the

Republicans an opportunity to gain control of the Senate. In the House Tea Party Caucus, while most of the Republicans held onto their seats in 2012, Alan West lost his bid for reelection and Michelle Bachman, the caucus chairwoman, barely fended off a Democratic challenger.[41] With Barack Obama's reelection the GOP could move away from Tea Party extremism and try to attract a broader coalition, especially Latino voters, or possibly experience the counter effect, with the party's racist elements gaining even more attention as they mobilize against Obama's second term. It is likely the Tea Party's long-term cohesion and influence will fade in Obama's second term as GOP leaders try to rebound from the losses of 2012 and the party will be regarded historically as an expression of anti-Obama sentiment, not exclusively but undeniably tied to white racial sentiments.

Epilogue: The Continuing Significance of Race in U.S. Politics

With the 2012 presidential election over as this book goes to print, no other major racial controversies surfaced in the last days of the campaign. While a Willie Horton–style attack on the president was always unlikely, it was not impossible due to the role of so-called super PACs that have prolifer-ated and increased the amount of corporate money in politics since the Supreme Court's *Citizens United* ruling in 2010.[1] Other factors, such as voter ID laws, did not have the anticipated effect since ones in key states like Wisconsin and Pennsylvania were suspended by the courts. Obama's high turnout with blacks, Latinos, women, gays and lesbians, and young voters, while not reaching the total popular vote he enjoyed in 2008, allowed him to hold together a center-progressive coalition, but one lacking the coattails to give the Democrats back control of the House. Obama's expected problem with white voters did not materialize, either. He won 39 percent of the white vote, which was down from the 43 percent he won in 2008. But he won larger majorities in critical states like Ohio and Wisconsin, and his minority coalition added to the white votes gave him victory. His share of the white vote nationally also exceeded the percentages that George McGovern received in 1972, Jimmy Carter in 1980, and Walter Mondale in 1984—putting to rest the argument that a white Democrat was the only path to two terms in the White House.[2]

What was deeply ironic about Obama's victory was that he won by employing the same basic tactics honed by Lee Atwater and Karl Rove—drive up your opponent's negatives to make him unelectable. Unlike Atwater's appeals to white racial fears or Rove's mobilization of evangelical voters over same-sex marriage, Obama and his advisors used social class to undermine Romney, or "class warfare" as the Republicans labeled it. The

Democrats portrayed Romney in early attack ads as an out-of-touch super-rich corporate executive who exported jobs overseas, an image taken from his work with Bain Capital. This undercut Romney's argument that his business experience best suited him to combat high unemployment and revive the economy, and defined him negatively in the minds of the voters as a man who would favor the rich, an image not helped by his tax-cutting proposals. As Karl Rove put it, the Democrats "effectively denigrated Mitt Romney's character, business acumen, business experience and made him unworthy."[3] This approach lacked the kind of divisiveness and intolerance that would have characterized a Democratic attack on Romney's Mormon faith, another potential weakness of the former governor. Perhaps this is the greatest statement of a "postracial" American politics—a black president defeating a wealthy white male challenger with targeted attack ads that exploited class resentment.

The country will see 2013 open with the nation's first black president sworn into a second term (and thus becoming the first black person to do so). The question that remains for the future is whether Obama's victory makes it easier for future black chief executives. His reelection and a successful second term may well do so, but a disastrous second term could also have the opposite effect. For the Republican Party, the way forward appears grim from the vantage point of early 2013. With white voters making up 72 percent of the electorate—a decline of 4 percent from 2008—and black voters remaining at 13 percent while Latinos have grown from 9 to 10 percent, the Republican Party must diversify its base beyond older white voters and Christian evangelicals.[4] Simply put, a GOP base of the old Confederacy combined with Mormons in Utah and Idaho is not enough to gain the presidency in the future, as America has become too multicultural for a party to win solely with the white, largely male and older vote. Obama held onto Virginia and Florida, proving that his inroads into the edges of the South were not a fluke of 2008. The most obvious thing the GOP could do to broaden its base is to reach out to Latinos by dropping their opposition to immigration reform and pass a bipartisan bill (like what Reagan did in 1986) that includes a path to citizenship, but this will mean standing up to the Tea Party elements bitterly opposed to immigration. Other elements, such as softening opposition to abortion and gay rights to attract younger and moderate voters also present opportunities to rebuild a broader GOP coalition, but the continued influence of religious evangelicals makes this approach questionable. Ending attempts at voter suppression through voter ID laws and other means would at least have the effect of not stimulating a high (and very angry) black voter turnout in response, especially when one considers that the impact of these laws has been marginal to nonexistent due to judicial review. Some or all of these approaches need to be taken if the GOP is to have a viable chance at winning the White House in 2016.

The obstacles that a black man has faced in running for the presidency and governing will likely resurface with a woman as a nominee—an entirely possible situation in 2016, since Hillary Clinton will likely be a major Democratic frontrunner. With Democratic representative Tammy Baldwin, an out lesbian, winning an open Senate seat in Wisconsin and becoming the first openly gay U.S. senator, and growing public acceptance of same-sex marriage—seen vividly through the legalization by popular referendum of same-sex marriage in three states in 2012—it now seems plausible that America will in the future see a credible run for the presidency by a gay candidate.[5] Such a candidate will likely face veiled homophobic attack ads much like the racial "dirty tricks" that hurt both white and black candidates during earlier elections. After winning a party nomination, a Jewish presidential candidate may face questions as well on everything from separation of church and state to suspicions that he or she may be more loyal to Israel than the United States. A Latino presidential candidate may face similar questions about illegal immigration and self-identification as an American. And in the highly charged anti-Muslim rhetoric of the era, one can only imagine the vitriol that would be unleashed against a Muslim candidate for president or vice president. Mitt Romney himself experienced a far more muted version of that religious bias with questions about his Mormon faith raised by both Republicans and Democrats. What is clear is that even with the decline of overt, legalized racism, the racist notion of treating other Americans as a "them" against a white "us," as George Frederickson noted, still persists in U.S. politics and society today.[6]

In elections from federal to local, institutionalized racism will play a bigger part in America's unfinished transition to a full democratic society. Despite a few glimmers of hope, the United States shows little appetite for reversing its preference for mass incarceration as a means to combat nonviolent crime and health issues like drug addiction. The results of this prison-industrial complex and its effects on minority communities and voting will continue to act as permanent check on the gains of the civil rights movement and inhibit full political integration of minorities into politics. For all the talk of Obama breaking racial barriers, blacks and

Latinos remain seriously unrepresented in politics and overrepresented in crime and poverty statistics. To many white voters and politicians, these issues are invisible or of no consequence and thus unlikely to be addressed. These factors depressing full participation in the electoral process by the poorest members of society, combined with white voters' continuing racial antagonism and susceptibility to coded racial messages, are ultimately more important than the skin color or surname of the president as factors keeping racial issues and racism alive in U.S. politics today and for the foreseeable future.

Notes

Introduction

1. George M. Frederickson, *Racism: A Short History* (Princeton, NJ: Princeton University Press, 2002), 9.

2. Ibid., 8–9.

3. Earl Black and Merle Black, *The Rise of Southern Republicans* (Cambridge, Mass.: Harvard University Press, 2002), 4.

4. Matthew D. Lassiter, *The Silent Majority: Suburban Politics in the Sunbelt South* (Princeton, NJ: Princeton University Press, 2006), 14. For more on color-blind racism, see Eduardo Bonilla-Silva, *Racism without Racists: Color-Blind Racism and Racial Inequality in Contemporary America*, 3rd ed. (Lanham, MD: Rowman & Littlefield, 2010).

Chapter 1

1. David T. Courtwright, *No Right Turn: Conservative Politics in a Liberal America* (Cambridge, MA: Harvard University Press, 2010), 85.

2. For biographies of Wallace and Eastland, see Dan T. Carter, *The Politics of Rage: George Wallace, The Origins of the New Conservatism, and the Transformation of American Politics* (Baton Rouge and London: Louisiana State University Press, 1995) and Chris Myers Asch, *The Senator and the Sharecropper: The Freedom Struggles of James O. Eastland and Fannie Lou Hamer* (New York: New Press, 2008). For the anti-Asian sentiment during Hawaii's statehood vote, see Robert Dallek, *Lone Star Rising: Lyndon Johnson and his Times 1908–1960* (New York and Oxford: Oxford University Press, 1991), 554.

3. The literature on the civil rights movement is vast, but for a general overview centered on Martin Luther King, see Taylor Branch's three-volume series, *Parting the Waters: America in the King Years, 1954–63* (New York: Simon & Schuster, 1988); *Pillar of Fire: America in the King Years, 1963–65* (New York: Simon & Schuster, 1998); and *At Canaan's Edge: America in the King Years, 1965–68* (New York: Simon & Schuster, 2006). For a recent study of Kennedy and civil rights, see Nick Bryant, *The Bystander: John F. Kennedy and the Struggle for Black Equality* (New York: Basic Books, 2006). For an example of a study of a grassroots

civil rights organization, see Clayborne Carson, *In Struggle: SNCC and the Black Awakening of the 1960s* (Cambridge, MA and London: Harvard University Press, 1995). For a survey of interracial marriage and the law culminating in the *Loving* case, see Peter Wallenstein, *Tell the Court I Love My Wife: Race, Marriage, and the Law: An American History* (New York: Palgrave Macmillan, 2002).

4. Robert Dallek, *Flawed Giant: Lyndon Johnson and His Times, 1961–1973* (New York and Oxford: Oxford University Press, 1998), 222; James T. Patterson, *America's Struggle against Poverty, 1900–1994* (Cambridge, MA and London: Harvard University Press, 1994), 141. For King's embrace of Christian democratic socialism, see James A. Colaico, *Martin Luther King, Jr.: Apostle of Militant Nonviolence* (New York: St. Martin's Press, 1993), 186–88.

5. Jill Quadagno, *The Color of Welfare: How Racism Undermined the War on Poverty* (New York and Oxford: Oxford University Press, 1994), 49–52, 91, 101–2; Colaico, 149.

6. Allen J. Matusow, *The Unraveling of America: A History of Liberalism in the 1960s* (New York: Harper & Row, 1984), 194–97; Patterson, *America's Struggle against Poverty*, 178. Moynihan did not lack for condescending or even insulting attitudes toward black Americans. In 1963, he concluded that "the Negro is only an American, and nothing else. He has no values and culture to guard and pro-tect." James T. Patterson, *Grand Expectations: The United States, 1945–1974* (New York: Oxford University Press, 1996), 384.

7. Patterson, *Grand Expectations*, 666, 670–71, 672–73; Jeremy D. Mayer, *Running on Race: Racial Politics in Presidential Campaigns, 1960–2000* (New York: Random House, 2002), 88; *Gideon v. Wainwright*, 372 U.S. 335 (1963); *Miranda v. Arizona*, 384 U.S. 436 (1966); *Shapiro v. Thompson*, 394 U.S. 618 (1969); *Goldberg v. Kelly*, 397 U.S. 254 (1970). For a brief overview of criticism of the Court, see Patterson, *Grand Expectations*, 392–95, 416–17, 640–41.

8. Patterson, *Grand Expectations*, 701–2; Matusow, *Unraveling of America*, 403–4, 422–25; Mayer, *Running on Race*, 87–88.

9. Quadagno, *Color of Welfare*, 19–81; Patterson, *Grand Expectations*, 723–25.

10. Adam Fairclough, *Better Day Coming: Blacks and Equality, 1890–2000* (New York: Viking Penguin, 2001), 324; Quadagno, 80–81; Steve M. Gillon, *"That's Not What We Meant to Do": Reform and Its Unintended Consequences in Twentieth-Century America* (New York and London: W. W. Norton & Co., 2000), 142–45.

11. Civil Rights Act of 1964, sec. 706 g, http://www.ourdocuments.gov/doc.php ?flash=true&doc=97&page=transcript (accessed November 12, 2011); Gillon, *That's Not What We Meant to Do*, 127.

12. Gillon, *That's Not What We Meant to Do* 142–44, 146–47.

13. Patterson, *Grand* Expectations, 724; *Griggs v. Duke Power Co.*, 401 U.S. 424 (1971).

14. Gillon, *That's Not What We Meant to Do* 150–51.

15. Dominic Sandbrook, *Mad as Hell: The Crisis of the 1970s and the Rise of the Populist Right* (New York: Alfred A. Knopf, 2011), 254; Laura Kalman, *Right Star Rising: A New Politics, 1974–1980* (New York and London: W. W. Norton & Co., 2010), 183–84; *DeFunis v. Odegaard*, 416 U.S. 312 (1974).

16. Kalman, *Right Star Rising*, 191–93; Carson, *In Struggle*, 268–69. For a brief overview of Jewish neoconservatism, see H. W. Brands, *The Devil We Knew: Americans and the Cold War* (New York and Oxford: Oxford University Press, 1993), 151–52, 179–80.

17. J. Harvie Wilkinson III, *From Brown to Bakke: The Supreme Court and School Integration, 1954–1978* (New York and Oxford: Oxford University Press, 1979), 254.

18. Ibid., 254–55; Kalman, *Right Star Rising*, 184–86.

19. Kalman, *Right Star Rising*, 187, 193; Wilkinson, *From Brown to Bakke*, 255, 260.

20. Wilkinson, *From Brown to Bakke*, 266–68, 282–84.

21. Manning Marable, *Race, Reform and Rebellion: The Second Reconstruction and Beyond in Black America, 1945–2006*, 3rd ed. (Oxford: University Press of Mississippi, 2007), 167; Kalman, *Right Star Rising*, 193–94, 195–96.

22. *Regents of the University of California v. Bakke*, 438 U.S. 265 (1978); Wilkinson, 298–99, 303; Sandbrook, 255.

23. Kalman, *Right Star Rising*, 199–200; Sandbrook, *Mad as Hell*, 256.

24. *United Steelworkers v. Weber*, 443 U.S. 193 (1979); Sandbrook, 256.

25. Wilkinson, *From Brown to Bakke*, 131–32.

26. Ibid., 116–17, 137–39; Patterson, *Grand Expectations*, 732; *Green v. County School Board of New Kent County*, 391 U.S. 430 (1968); *Swann v. Charlotte-Mecklenburg Board of Education*, 402 U.S. 1 (1971). For a survey of post-*Green* cases, see Wilkinson, *From Brown to Bakke* 118–27.

27. Wilkinson, *From Brown to Bakke*, 135–36; Sandbrook, *Mad as Hell*, 105.

28. Sandbrook, *Mad as Hell*, 108–9, 111–17; Christopher Reed, "Obituary: Louise Day Hicks," October 28, 2003 (http://www.guardian.co.uk/news/2003/oct/29/guardianobituaries.usa (accessed September 11, 2012).

29. Patterson, *Grand Expectations*, 732–34; *Milliken v. Bradley*, 418 U.S. 717 (1974).

30. Steven F. Lawson, *Running for Freedom: Civil Rights and Black Politics in America Since 1941*, 2nd ed. (New York: McGraw-Hill, 1997), 171–72.

31. Ibid., 172–73.

32. Ibid., 173–74.

33. Ibid., 175–77.

34. Ibid., 177–78.

35. Ibid., 163–65. For a detailed study of white flight in Atlanta, see Kevin M. Kruse, *White Flight: Atlanta and the Making of Modern Conservatism* (Princeton, NJ: Princeton University Press, 2005).

36. Lawson, *Running for Freedom*, 165–66; Sandbrook, 252; Marable, 169. The adjustment of salaries for inflation was compiled using the Consumer Price Index (CPI) Inflation Calculator on the U.S. Department of Labor's website, http://www.bls.gov/data/inflation_calculator.htm (accessed 27 October 2012).

37. For redistricting and other vote dilution measures, see Chapter 5.

38. Earl Black and Merle Black, *Politics and Society in the South* (Cambridge, MA and London: Harvard University Press, 1987), 145–48, 150.

39. Lawson, *Running for Freedom*, 140–41, 143.

40. Mayer, *Running on* Race, 152–53, 156, 164–65, 171; Sean Wilentz, *The Age of Reagan: A History, 1974–2008* (New York: HarperCollins Publishers, 2008), 122, 180.

41. Wilentz, *Age of Reagan*, 141; James T. Patterson, *Restless Giant: The United States from Watergate to Bush v. Gore* (New York and Oxford: Oxford University Press, 2005), 157; Marable, 178–80, 206.

42. Marable, *Race, Reform and Rebellion*, 178; Wilentz, 180–82. For a thorough study of Reynolds and his civil rights enforcement, see Raymond Wolters, *Right Turn: William Bradford Reynolds, the Reagan Administration, and Black Civil Rights* (Piscataway, NJ: Transaction Publishers, 1996).

43. Chris Danielson, *After Freedom Summer: How Race Realigned Mississippi Politics, 1965–1986* (Gainesville: University Press of Florida, 2011), 162–63; WIlentz, *Age of Reagan*, 182; *Bob Jones University v. United States*, 461 U.S. 574 (1983). For a detailed study of the private school movement and its relation to the Bob Jones case, see Joseph Crespino, *In Search of Another Country: Mississippi and the Conservative Counterrevolution* (Princeton, NJ and Oxford: Princeton University Press, 2007), 252–66.

44. Wilentz, *Age of Reagan*, 180–81; Steven F. Lawson, *In Pursuit of Power: Southern Blacks and Electoral Politics, 1965–1982* (New York: Columbia University Press, 1985), 276–77; *City of Mobile v. Bolden*, 446 U.S. 55 (1980).

45. Danielson, 196, 198; Lawson, 287.

46. Lawson, *In Pursuit of Power*, 287, 290–92; Alexander Keyssar, *The Right to Vote: The Contested History of Democracy in the United States*, rev. ed. (New York: Basic Books, 2009), 237–38.

47. Frank R. Parker, *Black Votes Count: Political Empowerment in Mississippi after 1965* (Chapel Hill and London: University of North Carolina Press, 1990), 207–9; Keyssar, 238; *Thornburg v. Gingles*, 487 U.S. 30 (1986).

48. Danielson, *After Freedom Summer*, 162–66. Reagan won over 80 percent of white Southern voters in 1984. Ibid., 207.

49. Lawson, *Running for Freedom*, 210–15; Bradford Martin, *The Other Eighties: A Secret History of America in the Age of Reagan* (New York: Hill and Wang, 2011), 123, 125.

50. Lawson, *Running for Freedom* 216.

51. Martin, *The Other Eighties*, 132–33; Lawson, 220–21; Devin Fergus, *Liberalism, Black Power, and the Making of American Politics, 1965–1980* (Athens and London: University of Georgia Press, 2009), 125–28.

52. Martin, *The Other Eighties* 131, 133; Lawson, *Running for Freedom*, 216, 222.

53. Mayer, *Running on Race*, 180–81.

54. Wilentz, 172–73; Martin, *The Other Eighties* 133–34; Mayer, *Running on Race* 184.

55. Martin, *The Other Eighties* 134–35.

56. Mayer, *Running on Race*, 178–79, 187, 191.

57. Wilentz, *Age of Reagan*, 174; Mayer, *Running on Race*, 193–94.

58. Bill Moyers, "Second Thoughts: Reflections on the Great Society," *New Perspectives Quarterly* 4, no. 1 (Winter 1987), http://www.digitalnpq.org/archive/1987_winter/second.html (accessed September 11, 2012); Earle Black and Merle Black, *The Rise of Southern Republicans* (Cambridge, MA and London: Harvard University Press, 2002), 4; Marable, 194.

59. Danielson, *After Freedom Summer*, 208–9, 211.

60. Wilentz, *Age of Reagan*, 184.

61. Wilentz, *Age of Reagan*, 184–85; *Grove City College v. Bell*, 465 U.S. 555 (1984); Mayer, *Running on Race*, 202; Marable, *Race, Reform and Rebellion*, 179.

62. Mayer, *Running on Race*, 204–5.

63. Ibid., 203.

64. Mayer *Running on Race*, 206–7; Martin, *The Other Eighties*, 136.

65. Mayer, *Running on Race*, 210–11; Martin, *The Other Eighties*, 136–37; Wilentz, *Age of Reagan*, 267.

66. Mayer, *Running on Race*, 206, 214–18.

67. Wiletnz, 270–71; Mayer, *Running on Race*, 219.

68. Mayer, *Running on Race*, 218–21. For an extended discussion of the racial politics of the Willie Horton ad, see Chapter 2.

69. Marable, 213; Mayer, *Running on Race*, 222; Wilentz, *Age of Reagan*, 272–73.

70. Raymond Wolters, *The Burden of Brown: Thirty Years of School Desegregation* (Knoxville: University of Tennessee Press, 1984), 3–4, 7–8, 273–74.

71. Charles W. Eagles, "Towards New Histories of the Civil Rights Era," *Journal of Southern History* 66, no. 4 (November 2000): 844–45.

72. Dinesh D'Souza, *The End of Racism: Principles for a Multiracial Society* (New York: Free Press, 1995), viii–ix, xiii. For example, D'Souza said on page 91 in his chapter on U.S. slavery that "the American slave *was* treated like property, which is to say, pretty well." For his discussion of racial redistricting, see 226–29.

73. William Julius Wilson, *The Declining Significance of Race: Blacks and Changing American Institutions* (Chicago and London: University of Chicago Press, 1978), 1–2, 19, 120–21, 143.

74. Marable, *Race, Reform and Rebellion*, 147–49, 151–52, 184.

75. Richard J. Herrnstein and Charles Murray, *The Bell Curve: Intelligence and Class Structure in American Life* (New York: Free Press, 1994), 280–82, 286–95,

312; Charles Murray, *Losing Ground: American Social Policy, 1950-1980* (New York: Basic Books, 1984). For critiques and the debate over *The Bell Curve*, see Russell Jacoby and Naomi Glauberman, eds., *The Bell Curve Debate: History, Documents, Opinions* (New York: Three Rivers Press, 1995) and Steven Fraser, *The Bell Curve Wars: Race, Intelligence, and the Future of America* (New York: Basic Books, 1995).

76. Marable, *Race, Reform and Rebellion* 197–98.

77. Wilentz, *Age of Reagan*, 181–82.

78. Eric Foner, *The Story of American Freedom* (New York and London: W. W. Norton & Co., 1998), 328–29.

79. Malcolm X, "The Ballot or the Bullet," speech delivered at Cory Methodist Church, Cleveland, Ohio, April 3, 1964; reprinted in George Breitman, ed., *Malcolm X Speaks: Selected Speeches and Statements* (New York: Grove Press, 1990), 25.

Chapter 2

1. Annette Gordon-Reed, *The Hemingses of Monticello: An American Family* (New York and London: W. W. Norton & Co., 2008), 554–55, 582–83, 590.

2. Harry L. Watson, *Liberty and Power: The Politics of Jacksonian America* (New York: Hill and Wang, 1990), 92; Lynn H. Parsons, *The Birth of Modern Politics: Andrew Jackson, John Quincy Adams, and the Election of 1828* (New York and Oxford: Oxford University Press, 2009), 142–44.

3. The literature on the subject of race and the sexual double standard is vast, but one of the best recent treatments of the civil rights era is Danielle L. McGuire, *At the Dark End of the Street: Black Women, Rape, and Resistance: A New History of the Civil Rights Movement from Rosa Parks to the Rise of Black Power* (New York: Alfred A. Knopf, 2011). The term the "ruling race" is from James Oakes, *The Ruling Race: A History of American Slaveholders* (New York and London: W. W. Norton & Co, 1998).

4. James McPherson, *Battle Cry of Freedom: The Civil War Era* (New York and Oxford: Oxford University Press, 1988), 125–26, 168.

5. Ibid., 174–75, 182, 184–85; *Dred Scott v. Sandford*, 60 U.S. 393 (1857).

6. McPherson, *Battle Cry of Freedom*, 185–86. For more on Lincoln and his views on black rights, see James Oakes, "Natural Rights, Citizenship Rights, States' Rights, and Black Rights: Another Look at Lincoln and Race," in *Our Lincoln: New Perspectives on Lincoln and his World*, Eric Foner, ed. (New York and London: W. W. Norton & Co., 2008), 109–34.

7. Ibid, 187–88.

8. Ibid, 224–25.

9. Ibid, 609–10; 771–72, 789–90; Manisha Sinha, "Allies for Emancipation?: Lincoln and Black Abolitionists," in Foner, *Our Lincoln*, 186–87.

10. McPherson, *Battle Cry of Freedom*, 776, 805. For an overview of these issues, see Eric Foner, *Reconstruction: America's Unfinished Revolution 1863–1877* (New York: Harper & Row, 1988), notably Chapters 3, 6, and 7, and pp. 446–48.

11. Foner, *Reconstruction*, 267.

12. Ibid., 340–45.

13. Ibid., 512–13, 523–24, 550–53, 558–62, 581–83.

14. Michael Perman, *Struggle for Mastery: Disfranchisement in the South 1888–1908* (Chapel Hill and London: University of North Carolina Press, 2001), 11. For example, in the 1880 presidential election in Mississippi, 66 percent of registered black voters did not vote. Neil R. McMillen, *Dark Journey: Black Mississippians in the Age of Jim Crow* (Urbana and Chicago: University of Illinois Press, 1989), 39.

15. Ibid., 38–41.

16. McMillen, *Dark Journey*, 38–44, 47; Edward L. Ayers, *The Promise of the New South: Life after Reconstruction* (New York and Oxford: Oxford University Press, 1992), 269; *Plessy v. Ferguson*, 163 U.S. 537 (1896); *Williams v. Mississippi*, 170 U.S. 213 (1898). For a state-by-state study of this disfranchisement, see Perman, *Struggle for Mastery*.

17. C. Vann Woodward, *Tom Watson: Agrarian Rebel* (New York and Oxford: Oxford University Press, 1963), 220; Ayers, *Promise of the New South*, 272–73.

18. Ayers, *Promise of the New South*, 155–59; McMillen, 224; W. Fitzhugh Brundage, *Lynching in the New South: Georgia and Virginia, 1880–1930* (Urbana and Chicago: University of Illinois Press, 1993), 198. Between 1889 and 1945, Mississippi alone accounted for 13 percent of the nation's 3,786 recorded lynchings. McMillen, *Dark Journey*, 229.

19. Edmund Morris, *Theodore Rex* (New York: Modern Library, 2001), 203. Roosevelt's most famous action to the detriment of African Americans was his expulsion of 167 black soldiers from the Army after a race riot in Brownsville, Texas. Morris, *Theodore Rex*, 453–55, 462–63, 464–67.

20. Nick Salvatore, *Eugene V. Debs: Citizen and Socialist* (Urbana and Chicago: University of Illinois Press, 1982), 226–27, 264.

21. Arthur S. Link, *Woodrow Wilson and the Progressive Era 1910–1917* (New York: Harper & Row, 1954), 63–66.

22. Robert K. Murray, *The Harding Era: Warren G. Harding and his Administration* (Minneapolis: University of Minnesota Press, 1969), 399–400; Andrew Glass, "President Harding condemns lynching, Oct. 21, 1921," http://www.politico.com/news/stories/1009/28512.html (accessed February 1, 2012). For a state-by-state study of the Klan's political influence in the 1920s, see David M. Chalmers, *Hooded Americanism: The History of the Ku Klux Klan*, 3rd ed. (Durham, NC: Duke University Press, 1987). See Chalmers, 300–3, for the 1928 presidential campaign.

23. William E. Leuchtenburg, *Franklin Roosevelt and the New Deal 1932–1940* (New York: Harper & Row, 1963), 184–87.

24. Ibid., 185–86.

25. David Fairclough, *Better Day Coming: Blacks and Equality, 1890–2000* (New York: Viking Penguin, 2001) 149–57.

26. Ibid., 133–45; Robin D. G. Kelley, *Race Rebels: Culture, Politics, and the Black Working Class* (New York: Free Press, 1996), 127. For an overview of the Scottsboro case, see Dan T. Carter, *Scottsboro: A Tragedy of the American South* (Baton Rouge: Louisiana University Press, 1979).

27. Fairclough, *Better Day Coming*, 88–90; Marable, *Race, Reform, and Rebellion: The Second Reconstruction and Beyond in Black America, 1945–2006*, 3rd ed. (Oxfrod, Miss.: University Press of Mississippi, 2007), 9–10.

28. David McCullough, *Truman* (New York: Simon & Schuster, 1992), 294, 296–97, 311; Marable, *Race, Reform and Rebellion*, 14.

29. Fairclough, *Better Day Coming*, 206–10.

30. Ibid, 209–10; McCullough, *Truman*, 645, 710–11; Jack Bass and W. Scott Poole, *The Palmetto State: The Making of Modern South Carolina* (Columbia: University of South Carolina Press, 2009), 104–5.

31. Fairclough, *Better Day Coming*, 212–14; James Patterson, *Grand Expectations*, 189.

32. Stephen E. Ambrose, *Eisenhower: Soldier and President* (New York: Simon & Schuster, 1990), 440–48; Patterson, *Grand Expectations*, 253, 305, 398.

33. See Chapter 1 for more on this period.

34. Dominic Sandbrook, *Mad as Hell: The Crisis of the 1970s and the Rise of the Populist Right* (New York: Alfred A. Knopf, 2011), 51.

35. Patterson, *Grand Expectations*, 565–67, 640–41; Dennis A. Deslippe, " 'Do Whites Have Rights?': White Detroit Policemen and 'Reverse Discrimination' Protests in the 1970s," *Journal of American History* 91, no. 3 (December 2004), 932–960.

36. Sandbrook, *Mad as Hell*, 50–53, 55–56.

37. David Courtwright, *No Right Turn: Conservative Politics in a Liberal America* (Cambridge: Harvard University Press, 2010), 81–84.

38. Ibid., 161–63; Michelle Alexander, *The New Jim Crow: Mass Incarceration in an Age of Colorblindness* (New York and London: New Press, 2010), 49–52; Erich Goode and Nachman Ben-Yehuda, *Moral Panics: The Social Construction of Deviance*, 2nd ed. (West Sussex, UK: Wiley-Blackwell, 2009), 206. For more on mandatory drug sentencing laws and their effects on black voting, as well as the moral panic that crack cocaine created, see Chapter 5.

39. John Brady, *Bad Boy: The Life and Politics of Lee Atwater* (Reading, MA: Addison Wesley, 1997), 17–18, 19, 21–22, 31–32, 37–38.

40. Ibid., 39, 47–48, 63.

41. Ibid., 70–71.

42. Ibid., 66, 71–73.

43. Ibid., 72–73; James T. Hammond, "Greenville Honors Contribution of Former Mayor Max Heller with Statue on Main St.," *Charleston Regional Business Journal*, May 29, 2009, http://www.charlestonbusiness.com/news/27910 -greenville-honors-contributions-of-former-mayor-max-heller-with-statue-on -main-st (accessed February 8, 2012); Stefan Forbes, *Boogie Man: The Lee Atwater Story*, DVD. Directed by Stefan Forbes (InterPositive Media, 2008).

44. Brady, *Bad Boy*, 82–85; Forbes, *Boogie Man*; Dan T. Carter, *From George Wallace to Newt Gingrich: Race in the Conservative Counterrevolution, 1963–1994* (Baton Rouge: Louisiana State University Press, 1996), 69–70.

45. Brady, *Bad Boy*, 85–86, 90, 92, 111–12.

46. Ibid., 117–18; Carter, *From George Wallace to Newt Gingrich*, 31–34.

47. Brady, *Bad Boy*, 119; Carmina Danini, "No One Told Ford Tamales Needed to Be Unwrapped," *San Antonio Express-News*, December 31, 2006, at http:// www.chron.com/news/houston-texas/article/No-one-told-Ford-tamales-need-to -be-unwrapped-1536700.php (accessed February 12, 2012).

48. Brady, *Bad Boy*, 131–32, 134–35.

49. Ibid., 160–61, 166–68.

50. Ibid., 171–72.

51. Ibid., 173–74.

52. Ibid., 173–76; Jack Germond and Jules Whitcover, *Whose Broad Stripes and Bright Stars? The Trivial Pursuit of the Presidency 1988* (New York: Warner Books, 1989), 12.

53. Mayer, *Running on Race: Racial Politics in Presidential Campaigns, 1960–2000* (New York: Random House, 2002), 212–13, 223; Germond and Whitcover, *Whose Broad Stripes and Bright Stars?*, 11; Forbes, *Boogie Man*, directed by Stefan Forbes, (Interpositive Media, 2008).

54. Brady, *Bad Boy*, 176, 183; Mayer, *Running on Race*, 213–14; Germond and Whitcover, *Whose Broad Stripes and Bright Stars?*, 162–63.

55. Brady, *Bad Boy*, 178; Carter, *From George Wallace to Newt Gingrich*, 73–74.

56. Mayer, *Running on Race*, 218–19; Brady, *Bad Boy*, 178–79; Carter, 74–75; Germond and Whitcover, *Whose Broad Stripes and Bright Stars?*, 159–61.

57. Carter, *From George Wallace to Newt Gingrich*, 71.

58. Alexander P. Lamis, "The Two-Party South: From the 1960s to the 1990s," in *Southern Politics in the 1990s*, Alexander P. Lamis, ed. (Baton Rouge: Louisiana State University Press, 1999), 7–8.

59. Brady, *Bad Boy*, 182; Mayer, *Running on Race*, 220–21. For more on the Jackson campaign in 1988, see Chapter 1.

60. Brady, *Bad Boy*, 180–81, 183.

61. Brady, *Bad Boy*, 190 *Running on Race*, -9; *Boogie Man*.

62. Mayer, *Running on Race*, 219, 221; Brady, 189–90.

63. Mayer, *Running on Race*, 218; Carter, *From George Wallace to Newt Gingrich*, 77; Germond and Whitcover, *Whose Broad Stripes and Bright Stars?*, 422–23.

64. Mayer, *Running on Race*, 220–21; Brady, *Bad Boy*, 192;, *Boogie Man*.

65. Brady, *Bad Boy*, 171–72, 202.

66. Brady, *Bad Boy*, 188; Carter, *From George Wallace to Newt Gingrich*, 72, 78–79; Mayer, *Running on Race*, 223–24.

67. Carter, *From George Wallace to Newt Gingrich*, 76, 78–79.

68. Mayer, *Running on Race*, 223–24; Maureen Dowd, "Bush Says Dukakis's Desperation Prompted Accusations of Racism," *New York Times*, October 25, 1988, http://www.nytimes.com/1988/10/25/us/bush-says-dukakis-s-desperation -prompted-accusations-of-racism.html (accessed January 24, 2012).

69. Mayer, *Running on Race*, 222–23; Brady, *Bad Boy*, 200.

70. Mayer, *Running on Race*, 226–28. For more on Bush and the drug war, see Chapter 5.

71. Brady, *Bad Boy*, 200, 210–13, 221–22.

72. Marable, *Race, Reform and Rebellion*, 200–1; Brady, *Bad Boy*, 236; Carter, *From George Wallace to Newt Gingrich*, 82.

73. Peter Applebome, "Racial Politics in South's Contests: Hot Wind of Hate or a Last Gasp?" *New York Times*, November 5, 1990, http://www.nytimes .com/1990/11/05/us/racial-politics-in-south-s-contests-hot-wind-of-hate-or-a -last-gasp.html (accessed February 18, 2012); Carter, 82–83; Steven Lawson, *In Pursuit of Power*, 291.

74. Brady, *Bad Boy*, 321; Carter, *From George Wallace to Newt Gingrich*, 89–91.

75. Marable, *Race, Reform and Rebellion*, 216–17; Mayer, *Running on Race*, 231, 239–41.

76. David Mills, "Sister Souljah's Call to Arms," *Washington Post*, May 13, 1992, B1; Thomas B. Edsall, "Clinton Stuns Rainbow Coalition," *Washington Post*, June 14, 1992, A1; Mayer, 242.

77. Mayer, *Running on Race*, 246–47.

78. E. J. Dionne, Jr., "Buchanan Heaps Scorn on Democrats," *Washington Post*, August 18, 1992, A18; Mayer 247–48; Madison Gray, "The L.A. Riots: 15 Years After Rodney King," *Time*, http://www.time.com/time/specials/2007/la_riot/ article/0%2C28804%2C1614117_1614084_1614511%2C00.html (accessed February 21, 2012).

79. Mayer, *Running on Race*, 248–50; Sharon LaFraniere, "Governor"s Camp Feels His Record on Crime Can Stand the Heat," *Washington Post*, October 5, 1992, A6; Alexander Nguyen, "Bill Clinton's Death Penalty Waffle," *American Prospect*, December 19, 2001, http://prospect.org/article/bill-clintons-death -penalty-waffle (accessed February 21, 2012).

80. Mayer, *Running on Race*, 250–51; Marable, 218.

81. Marable, *Race, Reform and Rebellion*, 233–34; Suzy Hansen, "Why Blacks Love Bill Clinton," http://www.salon.com/2002/02/21/clinton_88/ (accessed February 21, 2012).

82. Mayer, *Running on Race*, 276–78; Frank Bruni, "Bush and McCain Tiptoe through Dixie Minefield," *New York Times*, January 13, 2000, A26; David Firestone, "McCain Aide's Conservatism Runs Deep," *New York Times*, February 8, 2000, A22.

83. Bass and Poole, *The Palmetto State*, 42–43; Mayer, *Running on Race*, 277–78; Frank Bruni and Nicolas D. Kristof, "Bush Rues Failure to Attack Bigotry in Visit to College," *New York Times*, February 28, 2000, A1.

84. Elisabeth Bumiller, "2 Divergent McCain Moments, Rarely Mentioned," *New York Times*, March 24, 2008, A16; Mark Leibovich and David D. Kirkpatrick, "Serving a Cause and a Desire to Succeed," *New York Times*, September 4, 2008, A1; Jennifer Steinhauler, "Confronting Ghosts of 2000 in South Carolina," *New York Times*, October 19, 2007, http://www.nytimes.com/2007/10/19/us/politics/19mccain.html (accessed February 22, 2012); Frank Rich, "The Terrorist Barack Hussein Obama," *New York Times*, October 12, 2008, WK10; Maureen Dowd, "Mud Pies For 'That One,' " *New York Times*, October 8, 2008, A31; Paul Vitello, "How to Erase That Smea . . . " *New York Times*, August 17, 2008, WK3; Andy Barr, "Karl Rove Denies Role in John McCain Rumor in South Carolina," http://www.politico.com/news/stories/0310/34075.html (accessed February 22, 2012); Richard Gooding, "The Trashing of John McCain," http://www.vanityfair.com/politics/features/2004/11/mccain200411 (accessed February 22, 2012).

85. Mayer, *Running on Race*, 286–90. For more on the 2000 election and voter access, see Chapter 5.

86. Robin Toner, "Democrats' Senate Hopes May Ride on Tennessee," *New York Times*, May 31, 2006, http://www.nytimes.com/2006/05/31/us/31 tennessee.html (accessed February 18, 2012).

87. Ibid.; Germond and Whitcover, *Whose Broad Stripes and Bright Stars?*, 44–45; Michael Barbaro, "Harold Ford, Jr. Weighs Challenge to Gillibrand," *New York Times*, January 5, 2010, http://www.nytimes.com/2010/01/06/nyregion/06 ford.html (accessed February 22, 2012).

88. Toner, "Democrats' Senate Hopes"; Robin Toner, "Ad Seen as Playing to Racial Fears," *New York Times*, October 26, 2006, http://www.nytimes.com/2006/10/26/us/politics/26tennessee.html?pagewanted=all (accessed on February 18, 2012); John Files, "A Playboy Party at the Super Bowl, a Wink and an Invitation," *New York Times*, October 26, 2006, A22.

89. Files, "A Playboy Party," A22; "Compounding a Political Outrage," *New York Times*, October 27, 2006, A18.

90. William D. Mounger and Joseph L. Maxwell III, *Amidst the Fray: My Life in Politics, Culture, and Mississippi* (Brandon, MS: Quail Ridge Press, 2006), 263.

91. Toner, "Ad Seen as Playing to Racial Fears"; Robin Toner, "GOP Pulls Ad versus Black Candidate," *New York Times*, October 26, 2006, http://www.sfgate.com/cgi–bin/article.cgi?f=/c/a/2006/10/26/MNGO5M02E11.DTL (accessed February 17, 2012).

92. Toner, "Ad Seen as Playing to Racial Fears"; "U.S. Senate/Tennesee," http://www.cnn.com/ELECTION/2006/pages/results/states/TN/S/01/index.html (accessed 27 October 2012).

93. Gordon-Reed, *The Hemingses of Monticello*, 583.

94. John M. Coski, *The Confederate Battle Flag: America's Most Embattled Emblem* (Cambridge and London: Harvard University Press, 2005), 1, 99–101, 104–105.

95. Ibid., 133–34, 139–40, 148–49.

96. Chris Danielson, *After Freedom Summer: How Race Realigned Mississippi Politics, 1965-1986* (Gainesville, Fla.: University Press of Florida, 2011), 201, 203.

97. Danielson, *After Freedom Summer*, 221–22. For a summary of the flag referendum and campaign, see Coski, 263–67.

98. Coski, *The Confederate Battle Flag*, 252, 260–63.

Chapter 3

1. Adam Nargourney, Jim Rutenber, and Jeff Zeleny, "Near Flawless Run Is Credited in Victory," *New York Times*, November 5, 2008, http://www.nytimes.com/2008/11/05/us/politics/05recon.html?pagewanted=1&_r=1&hp (accessed February 29, 2012).

2. Eric Foner, *Reconstruction*, 351–54. For a study of black political power in South Carolina, see Thomas Holt, *Black Over White: Negro Political Leadership in South Carolina during Reconstruction* (Urbana and Chicago: University of Illinois Press, 1977).

3. John Henry Cutler, *Ed Brooke: Biography of a Senator* (Indianapolis and New York: The Bobbs-Merrill Company, 1972), 14, 33, 43–44, 54, 60–61, 63, 89.

4. Ibid., 65–66, 72–73, 118–19, 120, 122; Edward W. Brooke, *Bridging the Divide: My Life* (New Brunswick, NJ and London: Rutgers University Press, 2007), 106–107.

5. Cutler, *Ed Brooke*, 123–24, 145; Brooke, *Bridging the Divide*, 108, 140.

6. Cutler, *Ed Brooke*, 146–47, 159, 194; John F. Becker and Eugene E. Heaton, Jr., "The Election of Senator Edward W. Brooke," *Public Opinion Quarterly* 31, no. 3 (Autumn 1967): 352.

7. Cutler, *Ed Brooke*, 162–63, 172, 175–76, 182; Brooke, *Bridging the Divide*, 140–41; Becker and Heaton, "The Election of Senator Edward W. Brooke," 353.

8. Cutler, *Ed Brooke*, 175, 178, 187–88; Brooke, *Bridging the Divide*, 139.

9. Becker and Heaton, "The Election of Senator Edward W. Brooke," 352, 358.

10. Cutler, *Ed Brooke*, 192.

11. Brooke, *Bridging the Divide*, 153, 172–73, 175–76, 200–1, 222.

12. Ibid., 247–52, 255, 257.

13. Ibid., 257–58.

14. Thomas F. Pettigrew and Denise A. Alston, *Tom Bradley's Campaigns for Governor: The Dilemma of Race and Political Strategies* (Washington, D.C.: Joint Center for Political Studies, 1988), vii; Steven F. Lawson, *Running for Freedom: Civil Rights and Black Politics Since 1941* (New York: McGraw Hill, 1997), 178. For a study of Bradley's coalition-building during and after his election, see Raphael J. Sonenshein, *Politics in Black and White: Race and Power in Los Angeles* (Princeton, NJ: Princeton University Press, 1993).

15. Pettigrew and Allison, *Tom Bradley's Campaigns for Governor*, 5–6, 9.

16. Ibid., 7–8, 10–11.

17. Ibid., 11–14.

18. Ibid., 30.

19. Ibid., 32–33.

20. Ibid., 33–35.

21. Ibid., 25–27.

22. Ibid., 27–29; Jack Citrin, Donald Phillip Green, and David O. Sears, "White Reactions to Black Candidates: When Does Race Matter?" *Public Opinion Quarterly* 54, no. 1 (Spring 1990): 92.

23. Pettigrew and Allison, *Tom Bradley's Campaigns for Governor*, 12, 18.

24. Ibid., 18–19.

25. Ibid., 31–32, 59; Sal Russo, "Tom Bradley Didn't Lose because of Race," *Wall Street Journal*, October 20, 2008, http://online.wsj.com/article/SB122446015501248689.html?mod=googlenews_wsj#articleTabs%3Darticle (accessed March 25, 2012); Citrin, Green, and Sears, 93.

26. Citrin, Green, and Sears, "White Reactions to Black Candidates:," 93–94. For more on Washington's election as mayor of Chicago, see Chapter 1.

27. Margaret Edds and Thomas R. Morris, "Virginia: Republicans Surge in the Competitive Dominion," in Alexander P. Lamis, ed., *Southern Politics in the 1990s* (Baton Rouge: Louisiana State University Press, 1999), 137; Margaret Edds, *Claiming the Dream: The Victorious Campaign of Douglas Wilder in Virginia* (Chapel Hill, NC: Algonquin Books of Chapel Hill, 1990), 21, 26, 29–30, 32–33, 36–37.

28. Edds, *Claiming the Dream*, 37–38, 41–43.

29. Edds and Morris, "Virginia," 137.

30. Edds, *Claiming the Dream*, 33; Jeremy D. Mayer, *Running on Race: Racial Politics in Presidential Campaigns, 1960–2000* (New York: Random House, 2002), 236; J. L. Jeffries, *Virginia's Native Son: The Election and Administration of Governor L. Douglas Wilder* (West Lafayette, IN: Perdue University Press, 2000), 24–25.

31. Jeffries, *Virginia's Native Son*, 16–19.

32. Edds, *Claiming the Dream*, 138–39; Jeffries, *Virginia's Native Son*, 53. As an example of this longstanding gentility in Virginia politics, V. O. Key commented in 1949 that Virginia was a "political museum piece" that was controlled by an oligarchy (the Byrd machine of Senator Harry F. Byrd) that "demonstrates a sense of honor, [and] an aversion to open venality." V. O. Key, *Southern Politics in State and Nation* (New York: Alfred A. Knopf, 1949), 19.

33. Manning Marable, *Race, Reform, and Rebellion: The Second Reconstruction and Beyond in Black America, 1945–2006*, 3rd ed. (Oxford, Miss.: University Press of Mississippi, 2007), 214.

34. Edds, *Claiming the Dream*, 146, 147–48; Edds and Morris, "Virginia," 141.

35. Mark J. Rozell, "Local vs. National Press Assessments of Virginia's 1989 Gubernatorial Campaign," *Polity* 24, no. 1 (Autumn 1991): 81–85.

36. Jeffries, *Virginia's Native Son*, 57–58; Alvin J. Schexnider, "The Politics of Pragmatism: An Analysis of the 1989 Gubernatorial Election," *PS: Political Science & Politics* 23, no. 2 (June 1990): 154–56.

37. Jeffries, *Virginia's Native Son*, 58; Michael W. Traugott and Vincent Price, "Exit Polls in the 1989 Virginia Gubernatorial Race: Where Did They Go Wrong?" *Public Opinion Quarterly* 56, no. 2 (Summer 1992): 246, 251–52; Steven E. Finkel, Thomas M. Guterbock, and Marian J. Borg, "Race-of-Interviewer Effects in a Pre-election Poll: Virginia 1989," *Public Opinion Quarterly* 55, no. 3 (Autumn, 1991): 319; Scott Keeter and Nilanthi Samaranayake, "Can You Trust What Polls Say About Obama's Electoral Prospects?," Pew Research Center Publications, February 7, 2007, http://pewresearch.org/pubs/408/can-you-trust-what-polls-say -about-obamas-electoral-prospects (accessed March 30, 2012).

38. Rozell, "Local vs. National Press Assessments of Virginia's 1989 Gubernatorial Campaign," 87–88; Judson L. Jeffries, "Press Coverage of Black Statewide Candidates: The Case of L. Douglas Wilder of Virginia," *Journal of Black Studies* 32, no. 6 (July 2002): 687–88, 691–92.

39. Edds and Morris, "Virginia," 142–43; Marable, *Race, Reform, and Rebellion*, 214–15; Edds, *Claiming the Dream*, 22.

40. Mayer, *Running on Race*, 235–36; Edds and Morris, "Virginia," 142, 144–45.

41. Lawson, *Running for Freedom*, 256–57.

42. Ibid., 258–59; Keeter and Samaranayake, "Can You Trust What Polls Say About Obama's Electoral Prospects?," February 7, 2007.

43. Mylon Winn, "The Election of Norman Rice as Mayor of Seattle," *PS: Political Science and Politics* 23, no. 2 (June 1990): 158–59.

44. See Chris Danielson, *After Freedom Summer: How Race Realigned Mississippi Politics, 1965–1986* (Gainesville, Fla.: University Press of Florida, 2011), Chapter 9, for the creation of the district and the subsequent congressional races.

45. Keeter and Samaranayake, "Can You Trust What Polls Say About Obama's Electoral Prospects?," February 7, 2007; Alex Altman, "The Bradley Effect," *Time*,

October 17, 2008, http://www.time.com/time/magazine/article/0,9171, 1853294,00.html (accessed March 21, 2012). For more on Barack Obama's election and presidency, see Chapter 6.

46. Christina Bejarano, "What Goes Around, Comes Around: Race, Blowback, and the Louisiana Elections of 2002 and 2003," *Political Research Quarterly* 60, no. 2 (June 2007): 328–30, 332, 336–37. Not all nonwhite Republicans have suffered from the Bradley effect. Julius Caesar (J. C.) Watts, an African American congressional representative from Oklahoma, won election in a mostly white House district in 1994. Watts ran as a Christian conservative and was already well known as a Sooners quarterback. Sam Howe Verhovek, "The 1994 Campaign: The Republicans; More Black Candidates Find Places on Republican Ballots," *New York Times*, October 7, 1994, http://www.nytimes.com/1994/10/07/us/ 1994-campaign-republicans-more-black-candidates-find-places-republican -ballots.html?src=pm (accessed March 30, 2012).

Chapter 4

1. http://www.tshirthell.com/funny-shirts/learn-to-speak-native-american-or -get-the-fuck-out (accessed March 30, 2012).

2. Maldwyn Allen Jones, *American Immigration*, 2nd ed. (Chicago: University of Chicago Press, 1992), 10–11, 16–17, 19–21.

3. Ibid., 14–15, 23–26, 27–28; Ronald Takaki, *A Different Mirror: A History of Multicultural America* (Boston: Back Bay Books, 1993), 56–58. The literature on the slave trade and colonial slavery is vast, but the best books on the development of racism and slavery include Winthrop D. Jordan, *White Over Black: American Attitudes toward the Negro, 1550–1812* (Chapel Hill: University of North Carolina Press, 1968) and Edmund S. Morgan, *American Slavery, American Freedom: The Ordeal of Colonial Virginia* (New York and London: W. W. Norton and Co., 1975). For an overview of colonial slavery, see Ira Berlin, *Many Thousands Gone: The First Two Centuries of Slavery in North America* (Cambridge and London: Harvard University Press, 1998). For a study of ethnic diversity in colonial America, see Gary B. Nash, *Red, White & Black: The Peoples of Early North America*, 4th ed. (Upper Saddle River, NJ: Prentice Hall, 2000).

4. Jones, *American Immigration*, 17, 19, 24, 40.

5. Ibid., 41–43, 34–35, 38.

6. Takaki, *A Different Mirror*, 79–80.

7. Ibid., 82; Daniel J. Tichenor, *Dividing Lines: The Politics of Immigration Control in America* (Princeton, NJ and Oxford: Princeton University Press, 2002), 46; Jones, 64–65.

8. Jones, *American Immigration*, 72–75.

9. Ibid., 79, 81–82.

10. Takaki, *A Different Mirror*, 143–45; Alexander Keysser, *The Right to Vote: The Contested History of Democracy in the United States*, rev. ed. (New York: Basic

Books, 2009), 65; Eric Foner, *The Story of American Freedom* (New York and London: W.W. Norton & Co., 1998), 79.

11. Takaki, *A Different Mirror*, 149–50.

12. Ibid., 150–53.

13. Ibid., 154.

14. Jones, *American Immigration*, 134–35; Keyssar, *The Right to Vote*, 66–68; Tichenor, *Dividing Lines*, 57–58. For example, the Whig ticket of 1844 had Henry Clay paired with Theodore Frelinghuysen, a member of several anti-Catholic and nativist organizations. The narrow loss to Democrat James K. Polk led Whig leaders to sever ties with nativist groups and thus inhibit nativist legislation in Congress. Tichenor, *Dividing Lines*, 57–58.

15. Tichenor, *Dividing Lines*, 89–92; Takaki, *A Different Mirror*, 194–95, 200–1.

16. Tichenor, *Dividing Lines*, 93–97, 102–3, 107–8; Takaki, *A Different Mirror*, 206–7; Transcript of the Chinese Exclusion Act, http://www.ourdocuments.gov/doc.php?flash=true&doc=47&page=transcript (accessed April 22, 2012).

17. Ronald Takaki, *Strangers from a Different Shore: A History of Asian Americans* (Boston: Back Bay Books, 1998), 45, 201–3.

18. Tichenor, *Dividing Lines*, 68, 70, 79; *Henderson v. Mayor of City of New York*, 92 U.S. 259 (1875).

19. Tichenor, *Dividing Lines*, 71–73; Jones, 230.

20. Tichenor, *Dividing Lines*, 76–77; Jones, 222–23; Keyssar, 115–18, 123–28.

21. Tichenor, *Dividing Lines*, 139–46.

22. Takaki, *A Different Mirror*, 207; *United States v. Bhagat Singh Thind*, 261 U.S. 204 (1923), *United States v. Wong Kim Ark*, 169 U.S. 649 (1898). For a study of the *Bhagat Singh Thind* case, see Jennifer Snow, "The Civilization of White Men: The Race of the Hindu in *United States vs. Bhagat Singh Thind*," in *Race, Nation, and Religion in the Americas*, Henry Goldschmidt and Elizabeth McAlister, eds. (Oxford and New York: Oxford University Press, 2004), 259–80.

23. Phyllis Goldstein, *A Convenient Hatred: A History of Antisemitism* (Brookline, MA: Facing History and Ourselves Foundation, 2012), 270, 272; Transcript of Executive Order 9066, http://www.ourdocuments.gov/doc.php?flash=true&doc=74&page=transcript (accessed April 23, 2012); *Korematsu v. United States*, 323 U.S. 214 (1944). See Adam Fairclough, *Better Day Coming: Blacks and Equality, 1890–2000* (New York: Viking Penguin, 2001), 185–95, for an overview of African Americans and World War II. For a study of the interment of the Japanese and Japanese Americans (Nisei) during the war, see Takaki, *Strangers from a Distant Shore*, 379–405 and also Roger Daniels, *Prisoners without Trial: Japanese Americans in World War II* (New York: Hill and Wang, 1993).

24. Takaki, *Strangers from a Different Shore*, 376–78.

25. Ibid., 413. Of course, some scholars have also argued that the anticommunist hysteria of the Cold War damaged the civil rights movement. Fairclough, *Better Day Coming*, 211–18.

26. Tichenor, *Dividing Lines*, 209, 213–14.

27. Ibid., 215–16; Steven Gillon, *"That's Not What We Meant to Do,": Reform and Its Unintended Consequences in Twentieth-Century America* (New York: and London: W.W. Norton & Co, 2000) 173–75.

28. Gillon, *"That's Not What We Meant to Do,"* 176–77.

29. Tichenor, *Dividing Lines*, 216; Gillon, *"That's Not What We Meant to Do,"* 177–78.

30. Gillon, *"That's Not What We Meant to Do,"* 179; Tichenor, *Dividing Lines*, 223.

31. Gillon, *"That's Not What We Meant to Do,"* 181–82.

32. Lars Schoultz, *Beneath the United States: A History of U.S. Policy toward Latin America* (Cambridge and London: Harvard University Press, 1998), 14–18.

33. Ibid., 21–38.

34. Juan Mora-Torres, " 'Los de casa se van, los fuera no viene': The First Mexican Migrants, 1848–1900," in *Beyond La Frontera: The History of Mexico-U.S. Migration*, Mark Overmyer-Velazquez, ed. (New York and Oxford: Oxford University Press, 2011), 5–11, 13.

35. Gilbert G. Gonzalez, "Mexican Labor Migration, 1876–1924," *Beyond La Frontera: The History of Mexico-U.S. Migration*, Mark Overmyer-Velazquez, ed. (New York and Oxford: Oxford University Press, 2011), 31–33, 39.

36. Ibid., 39; Tichenor, *Dividing Lines*, 145–46.

37. Gonzalez, "Mexican Labor Migration,"46–48.

38. Fernando Saul Alanis Enciso, "The Repatriation of Mexicans from the United States and Mexican Nationalism, 1929–1940," *Beyond La Frontera: The History of Mexico-U.S. Migration*, Mark Overmyer-Velazquez, ed. (New York and Oxford: Oxford University Press, 2011), 51, 56–57.

39. Tichenor, *Dividing Lines*, 173–74; Michael Snodgrass, "The Bracero Program, 1942–1964," *Beyond La Frontera: The History of Mexico-U.S. Migration*, Mark Overmyer-Velazquez, ed. (New York and Oxford: Oxford University Press, 2011), 79–80.

40. Snodgrass, "The Bracero Program," 80, 91–92.

41. Tichenor, *Dividing Lines*, 224–29, 232–34, 236–37; Oscar J. Martinez, "Migration and the Border, 1965–1985," *Beyond La Frontera: The History of Mexico-U.S. Migration*, Mark Overmyer-Velazquez, ed. (New York and Oxford: Oxford University Press, 2011), 110–11.

42. Martinez, "Migration and the Border," 115–17.

43. Ibid., 120; Tichenor, *Dividing Lines*, 261–62.

44. Tichenor, *Dividing Lines*, 262–63, 265–66; *Ayuda, Inc. v. Meese*, 687 F. Supp. 650, 666–68 (D.D.C. 1988).

45. Tichenor, *Dividing Lines*, 269–74; Jones, 289–90.

46. Tichenor, *Dividing Lines*, 275–77.

47. Ibid., 277.

48. Ibid., 282–84.

49. For an example of a conservative endorsement of English as a national language, see Bernie Reeves, "Why English Is not the 'Official Language' of the United States," *American Thinker*, November 1, 2009, http://www.americanthinker.com/2009/11/why_english_is_not_the_officia.html (accessed May 9, 2012).

50. Matt S. Meier and Feliciano Ribera, *Mexican Americans/American Mexicans: From Conquistadors to Chicanos* (New York: Hill and Wang, 1990), 245–47; *Lau v. Nichols*, 414 U.S. 563 (1974). On Tancredo, see Carlos Illescas, "Foes Rip Bilingual-Ed Ban," *Denver Post*, April 14, 2000, http://extras.denverpost.com/news/election/pol0414.html (accessed 9 May 2012).

51. Leo R. Chavez, *The Latino Threat: Constructing Immigrants, Citizens, and the Nation* (Stanford, CA: Stanford University Press, 2008), 56–60.

52. Ibid., 60; Meier and Ribera, *Mexican Americans/American Mexicans*, 245–46.

53. Arlene Davila, *Latino Spin: Public Image and the Whitewashing of Race* (New York and London: New York University Press, 2008), 53; Tichenor, *Dividing Lines*, 285; Steven F. Lawson, *In Pursuit of Power: Southern Blacks and Electoral Politics, 1965–1982*, 258–59. 350n88; John A. Garcia, "The Voting Rights Act and Hispanic Political Participation in the Southwest," *Publius* 16, no. 4 (Autumn 1986), 49, 64, 66; Roman Hedges and Carl P. Carlucci, "Implementation of the Voting Rights Act: The Case of New York," *Western Political Science Quarterly* 40, no. 1 (March 1987), 119.

54. Garcia, "The Voting Rights Act and Hispanic Political Participation in the Southwest," 57; Mike Morris, "Hispanics Say Redrawn Precincts Unfair," *Houston Chronicle*, July 29, 2011, B2; Mike Morris, "Hispanics: New County Map Not Fair," *Houston Chronicle*, August 10, 2011, B1; Nolan Hicks, "2 N. Texas Democrats Fight Redistricting Plan," *Houston Chronicle*, August 4, 2011, B3.

55. Hope Yen, "Census: Births, Not New Immigrants, Push U.S. Latino Growth," *Houston Chronicle*, July 15, 2011, A7; Rick Casey, "A Suicidal Circular Firing Squad," *Houston Chronicle*, July 4, 2011, B3; Davila, 53.

56. Davila, *Latino Spin*, 46–48, 56, 60–61.

57. Ibid., 68; Chavez, *The Latino Threat*, 133; "Too Far Gone," *Economist*, March 3, 2011, http://www.economist.com/node/18284033 (accessed May 10, 2012). For more on the Tea Party, see Chapter 7.

58. Chavez, *The Latino Threat*, 152, 154–55, 157.

59. "Extreme Recall," *Economist*, June 4, 2011, 38; Amanda Lee Myers and Jacques Billeaud, "Arizona Lawmakers Say They Will Build Border Fence," November 24, 2011, http://news.yahoo.com/arizona-lawmakers-build-border-fence-140342049.html (accessed November 26, 2011).

60. "Extreme Recall," June 4, 2011; "A Hard Row to Hoe," *Economist*, June 18, 2011, 37; "Et in Alabama ego," *Economist*, July 23, 2011, 30; Harriet McLeod, "U.S. Challenges South Carolina Immigration Law," http://in.reuters.com/article/2011/11/

01/idINIndia-60231320111101 (accessed September 13, 2012); Jay Reeves, "Anti-Immigrant Law Stirs up Alabama Christians," *Houston Chronicle*, July 14, 2011, A2.

61. Jay Reeves, "Hispanic Students Vanish from Alabama Schools," September 30, 2011, http://news.yahoo.com/hispanic-students-vanish-alabama-schools-184555038.html (accessed October 3, 2011); Liz Goodwin, "American Kids Denied Food Stamps in Alabama under Immigration Law," February 7, 2012, http://news.yahoo.com/blogs/lookout/american-kids-denied-food-stamps-alabama-under-immmigration-143929070.html (accessed February 7, 2012); Phillip Rawls, "Ala. Loses Workers as Immigration Law Takes Effect," October 6, 2011, http://news.yahoo.com/ala-loses-workers-immigration-law-takes-effect (accessed October 6, 2011); "Caught in the Net," *Economist*, January 28, 2012, 28, 30; Phillip Rawls, "Ala. GOP Leaders Have 2nd Thoughts on Immigration," December 9, 2011, http://news.yahoo.com/ala-gop-leaders-2nd-thoughts-immigration-191341807.html (accessed December 9, 2011); Verna Gates, "Alabama Promises Revisions to Tough Immigration Law," December 10, 2011, http://www.reuters.com/article/2011/12/09/us-immigration-alabama-idUSTRE7B81 ZQ20111209 (accessed May 11, 2012).

62. Goodwin, "American Kids Denied Food Stamps in Alabama under Immigration Law," 7 February 2012; Joan Biskupic, "First Hispanic Supreme Court Justice Takes Prominent Role," April 25, 2012, http://news.yahoo.com/first-hispanic-supreme-court-justice-takes-prominent-role-004059717.html (accessed April 26, 2012); "Caught in the Net," 28.

63. Liz Goodwin, "Supreme Court Upholds Key Part of Arizona Anti-Immigration Law; Strikes Down Rest," June 25, 2012, http://news.yahoo.com/blogs/ticket/supreme-court-upholds-key-part-arizona-immigration-law-141927514.html (accessed June 25, 2012); Oliver Knox, "Both Sides Claim Victory after Supreme Court Rules on Arizona Immigration Law," http://news.yahoo.com/blogs/ticket/obama-hails-supreme-court-ruling-arizona-immigration-law-171927671.html (accessed June 25, 2012).

64. Liz Goodwin, "Newt Gingrich Mocks Romney for His 'Self Deport' Immigration Plan," January 25, 2012, http://news.yahoo.com/blogs/ticket/newt-gingrich-mocks-romney-self-deport-immigration-plan-165019307.html (accessed January 25, 2012).

65. Goodwin, "Newt Gingrich Mocks Romney for His 'Self Deport' Immigration Plan," January 25, 2012; Linda Feldmann, "Why Florida's Latino Republicans Tilt toward Mitt Romney," January 28, 2012, *Christian Science Monitor*, January 28, 2012, http://www.csmonitor.com/USA/Elections/President/2012/0128/Why-Florida-s-Latino-Republicans-tilt-toward-Mitt-Romney (accessed May 10, 2012); Liz Goodwin, "Marco Rubio Says Some Conservatives 'Harsh and Intolerable' on Immigration," January 27, 2012, http://news.yahoo.com/blogs/ticket/marco-rubio-says-conservatives-harsh-intolerable-immigration-194846662.html (accessed January 30, 2012).

66. Chavez, *The Latino Threat*, 88–90; Aliyah Shahid, "Michelle Bachmann, GOP Presidential Hopeful: I Would 'Not Do Anything' for Children of Illegal Immigrants," http://articles.nydailynews.com/2011-10-30/news/30340145 _1_michele-bachmann-children-of-illegal-immigrants-parents (accessed May 11, 2012). For Supreme Court precedents, see *U.S. v. Wong Kim Ark*, 169 U.S. 649 (1898).

67. "Crying Wolf," *Economist*, November 19, 2011, 31–32; Hope Yen, "New Asian Immigrants to U.S. Now Surpass Hispanics," June 19, 2012, http://news.yahoo.com/asian-immigrants-us-now-surpass-hispanics-041526805.html (accessed June 19, 2012).

68. "The Nativist Millstone," *Economist*, April 28, 2012, 31–32; Feldmann, "Why Florida's Latino Republicans Tilt toward Mitt Romney," January 28, 2012; Naureen Khan, "Could Immigration Law Turn Arizona Blue?" *National Journal*, April 23, 2012, http://news.yahoo.com/blogs/ticket/marco-rubio-says-conservatives-harsh -intolerable-immigration-194846662.html (accessed May 11, 2012).

69. Casey, "A Suicidal Circular Firing Squad," July 4, 2011; Gary Scharrar, "Texas Tea Party to Rick Perry: 'We Are Fed Up,' " September 19, 2011, http://blog.chron.com/rickperry/2011/09/texas-tea-party-to-rick-perry-we-are-fed-up/ (accessed May 11, 2012).

70. "Obama Celebrates Cinco de Mayo with Push for Dream Act, Immigration Reform," May 3, 2012, http://www.washingtonpost.com/politics/obama -celebrates-cinco-de-mayo-with-push-for-dream-act-immigration-reform/2012/ 05/03/gIQAIe6lzT_story.html (accessed May 11, 2012); Peter Slevin, "Deportations of Illegal Immigrants Increase under Obama Administration," *Washington Post*, July 26, 2010, http://www.washingtonpost.com/wp-dyn/content/article/ 2010/07/25/AR2010072501790.html (accessed May 11, 2012); Elise Foley, "DREAM Act Supporters Tell Obama to Quit Campaigning on DREAM Act," May 19, 2011, http://www.huffingtonpost.com/2011/05/19/dream-act-supporters -tell_n_864427.html (accessed May 11, 2012).

71. Julia Preston and John H. Cushman, Jr., "Obama to Permit Young Migrants to Remain in U.S.," *New York Times*, June 15, 2012, http://www.nytimes.com /2012/06/16/us/us-to-stop-deporting-some-illegal-immigrants.html?_r=1&nl =todaysheadlines&emc=edit_th_20120616 (accessed June 19, 2012).

72. Jennifer Preston, "Obama's Decision on Immigration Is Met with Joy, Anger, Skepticism," *New York Times*, June 15, 2012, http://thelede.blogs.nytimes.com/ 2012/06/15/online-reaction-to-obamas-immigration-decision-is-swift-and -polarized/?ref=us (accessed June 19, 2012).

73. Benjy Sarlin, "Poll: Latino Vote Devastated GOP Even Worse Than Exists Showed," November 7, 2012, http://news.yahoo.com/poll-latino-vote-devastated -gop-even-worse-exits-181922111—politics.html (accessed November 7, 2012); Liz Goodwin, "Sean Hannity, John Boehner say GOP should tackle immigration reform," November 9, 2012, http://news.yahoo.com/blogs/ticket/sean-hannity

-john-boehner-gop-tackle-immigration-reform-142212570—election.html
(accessed November 9, 2012); Liz Goodwin, "Latino groups to Obama: You owe
Latinos the election, now pass immigration reform," November 7, 2012, http://
news.yahoo.com/blogs/ticket/latino-groups-obama-owe-latinos-election-now
-pass-194113601—election.html (accessed November 7, 2012).

Chapter 5

1. Charles M. Payne, *I've Got the Light of Freedom: The Organizing Tradition
and the Mississippi Freedom Struggle* (Berkeley and Los Angeles: University of
California Press, 1995, 2007), 407–8.

2. Alexander Keyssar, *The Right to Vote: The Contested History of Democracy in
the United States* (Rev. ed. New York, Basic Books, 2009), 44–45.

3. Ibid., 73–74; David Herbert Donald, *Lincoln* (New York: Simon & Schuster,
1995). Lincoln endorsed this limited black suffrage in his final public address on
April 11, 1865, just days before his assassination. For more on Reconstruction
and black voting, see Chapter 2.

4. Keyssar, *The Right to Vote*, 82–83.

5. Ibid., 85–86. The cases were *U.S. v. Reese*, 92 U.S. 214 (1876) and *U.S. v.
Cruikshank*, 92 U.S. 542 (1876).

6. Keyssar, *The Right to Vote*, 86–93. For more on this, see Chapter 2.

7. Ibid., 103–4, 113, 115–28. For more on the effects of these changes on
immigrant voting, see Chapter 4.

8. Ibid., 182–83.

9. *Smith v. Allwright*, 321 U.S. 649 (1944); Keyssar, *The Right to Vote*, 199. For
the history of the anti–poll tax campaigns and a fuller treatment of *Smith v.
Allwright*, see Steven F. Lawson, *Black Ballots: Voting Rights in the South, 1944–1969*
(Lanham, MD: Lexington Books, 1999), Chapters 2 and 3, and Patricia
Sullivan, *Days of Hope: Race and Democracy in the New Deal Era* (Chapel Hill and
London, University of North Carolina Press, 1996), Chapter 4.

10. Keyssar, *The Right to Vote*, 208. See Lawson, *Black Ballots*, Chapter 7, for
extensive coverage of the bill's passage.

11. Keyssar, *The Right to Vote*, 208–10.

12. Ibid., 210–11; Lawson, *Black Ballots*, 329–30.

13. Keyssar, *The Right to Vote*, 211–13; Lawson, *In Pursuit of Power: Southern
Blacks and Electoral Politics, 1965–1982* (New York: Columbia University Press,
1985), 155–56, 252–53, 293.

14. Lawson, *In Pursuit of Power*, 288–89, 291–92.

15. Keyssar, *The Right to Vote*, 213–14.

16. Ibid., 213–15.

17. Frank R. Parker, *Black Votes Count: Political Empowerment in Mississippi after
1965* (Chapel Hill and London: University of North Carolina Press, 1990), 207–209.

18. *Northwest Austin Municipal Utility District No. 1 v. Holder*, 557 U.S. 193, 129 S.Ct. 2504 (2009).

19. Keyssar, *The Right to Vote*, 225–28, 229–30.

20. Chris Danielson, *After Freedom Summer: How Race Realigned Mississippi Politics, 1965–1986* (Gainesville, Fla.: University Press of Florida, 2011), 162–63; Keyssar, *The Right to Vote*, 253–55.

21. Keyssar, *The Right to Vote*, 254–57.

22. Parker, *Black Votes Count*, 49, 51, 63.

23. *Gomillion v. Lightfoot*, 364 U.S. 339 (1960); *Baker v. Carr*, 369 U.S. 186 (1962); *Reynolds v. Sims*, 377 U.S. 533 (1964); Richard C. Cortner, *The Apportionment Cases* (Knoxville: University of Tennessee Press, 1970), 125–25; Danielson, 112–13.

24. *Allen v. State Board of Elections*, 393 U.S. 544 (1969); Lawson, *In Pursuit of Power*, 160–61; Keyssar, *The Right to Vote*, 234–35.

25. *Whitcomb v. Chavis*, 403 U.S. 124 (1971); *White v. Regester*, 412 U.S. 755 (1973); *Zimmer v. McKeithan*, 467 F.2nd 1381 (1972); Lawson, *In Pursuit of Power*, 218–221; Keyssar, *The Right to Vote*, 235; Danielson, *After Freedom Summer*, 123.

26. *United Jewish Organizations of Williamsburg, Inc. v. Carey*, 430 U.S. 144 (1977); Keyssar, *The Right to Vote*, 236.

27. *City of Richmond v. United States*, 422 U.S. 358 (1975); *Beer v. United States*, 425 U.S. 130 (1976); Lawson, 213–17.

28. *City of Mobile v. Bolden*, 446 U.S. 55 (1980); Lawson, *In Pursuit of Power*, 276–80.

29. Steven Andrew Light, *"The Law Is Good": The Voting Rights Act, Redistricting, and Black Regime Politics* (Durham, NC: Carolina Academic Press, 2010), 77. For more on *Mobile* and the Voting Rights Act of 1982, see Chapter 1. For more on the effects of the results test on Mississippi, see Danielson, Chapters 7–9.

30. *Thornburg v. Gingles*, 478 U.S. 30 (1986); Keyssar, *The Right to Vote*, 238; Light, *"The Law Is Good,"* 78.

31. *Shaw v. Reno*, 509 U.S. 630 (1993); *Miller v. Johnson*, 515 U.S. 900; *Holder v. Hall*, 512 U.S. 874 (1994); Keyssar, *The Right to Vote*, 239–41.

32. *Bush v. Vera*, 517 U.S. 952 (1996); J. Morgan Kousser, *Colorblind Injustice: Minority Voting Rights and the Undoing of the Second Reconstruction* (Chapel Hill and London: University of North Carolina Press, 1999), 5–7, 70–72, 384–87. Parker died in 1997, which largely left commentary on the 1990s shift to other historians. Eric Pace, "Frank R. Parker, Authority On Civil Rights Law, Dies at 57," *New York Times*, July 14, 1997, http://www.nytimes.com/1997/07/14/us/frank-r-parker-authority-on-rights-law-dies-at-57.html (accessed July 9, 2012).

33. *Georgia v. Ashcroft*, 539 U.S. 461 (2003); Keyssar, *The Right to Vote*, 242–43.

34. "The Preclearance Problem," *Economist*, February 5, 2011, 45.

35. Abigail M. Thernstrom, *Whose Votes Count? Affirmative Action and Minority Voting Rights* (Cambridge, MA and London: Harvard University Press, 1987), 3–5, 25–27, 193, 234, 236–37, 243–44.

36. Parker, *Black Votes Count*, 193–96; Kousser, *Colorblind Injustice*, 58–65.

37. See, for example, "Democrats Sue over SC's US House Plan," http://www.carolinalive.com/news/story.aspx?id=685575#.T_tWg_WvPoQ (accessed July 9, 2012) and "Turf Wars," *Economist*, December 3, 2011, 43.

38. Lani Guinier, *The Tyranny of the Majority: Fundamental Fairness in Representative Democracy* (New York: Free Press, 1994), 14–16; Keyssar, *The Right to Vote*, 245–46.

39. "The Preclearance Problem," *Economist*, February 5, 2011, 45; Manning Marable, *Race, Reform and Rebellion: The Second Reconstruction and Beyond in Black America, 1945–2006*, 3rd ed. (Oxford, Miss.: University Press of Mississippi, 2007), 236; Keyssar, *The Right to Vote*, 258–59.

40. Keyssar, *The Right to Vote*, 260, 262; *Bush v. Gore*, 531 U.S. 98 (2000).

41. Keyssar, *The Right to Vote*, 261; Marable, *Race, Reform and Rebellion*, 236; Malcolm Brabant, "Bush's Brother to Face Vote Inquiry," January 5, 2001, http://news.bbc.co.uk/2/hi/americas/1102806.stm (accessed July 11, 2012).

42. Keyssar, *The Right to Vote*, 262–63, 266–67.

43. Ibid., 269–73.

44. Marable, *Race, Reform and Rebellion*, 246; Keyssar, *The Right to Vote*, 273, 278–79.

45. Keyssar, *The Right to Vote*, 283–85.

46. Keyssar, *The Right to Vote*, 285; "First, Show Your Face," *Economist*, September 17, 2011, 30; *Crawford v. Marion County Election Board*, 553 U.S. 181 (2008).

47. Mike Baker, "Tough ID Laws Could Block Thousands of 2012 Votes," July 8, 2012, http://news.yahoo.com/tough-id-laws-could-block-thousands-2012-votes-120503561.html (accessed July 10, 2012); Jeff Mayers, "Judge Temporarily Blocks Wisconsin Voter ID Law," March 7, 2012, http://www.reuters.com/article/2012/03/07/us-wisconsin-voterid-idUSTRE8251UH20120307 (accessed July 13, 2012).

48. "First, Show Your Face," *Economist*; "No Go Again," *Economist*, March 17, 2012, 38; Richard S. Dunham and Elizabeth Traynor, "Voter ID Law Fight Arriving in Court," *Houston Chronicle*, July 8, 2012, A20; Tom Humphrey, "Tennessee Democrats Use Chattanooga Photo ID Denial in Fundraising," October 10, 2011, http://timesfreepress.com/news/2011/oct/10/tennessee-democrats-use-chattanooga-photo-id-denia/ (accessed July 13, 2012).

49. "Holder v States," *Economist*, January 7, 2012, 25–26; Letter by U.S. Assistant Attorney General Thomas E. Perez to South Carolina Assistant Deputy Attorney General C. Havird Jones, Jr., U.S. Department of Justice, Civil Rights Division, December 23, 2011, 2, http://www.justice.gov/crt/about/vot/sec_5/ltr/l_122311.php (accessed 30 October 2012); "No Go Again," *Economist*, March 17, 2012, 38.

50. Dunham and Traynor, A20; Drew Singer, "Attorneys for Texas Say Study of Voter ID Law Flawed," July 13, 2012, http://news.yahoo.com/attorneys-texas

-study-voter-id-law-flawed-023149329.html (accessed July 13, 2012); Charlie Savage and Manny Fernandez, "Court Blocks Texas Voter ID Law, Citing Racial Impact," August 30, 2012, http://www.nytimes.com/2012/08/31/us/court-blocks -tough-voter-id-law-in-texas.html (accessed September 10, 2012).

51. Baker, "Tough ID Laws Could Block Thousands of 2012 Votes," July 8, 2012; Mike Baker, "Across Country, GOP Pushes Photo ID at the Polls," March 25, 2011, http://www.guardian.co.uk/world/feedarticle/9564977 (accessed July 13, 2012); "First, Show Your Face," *Economist*.

52. Baker, "Tough ID Laws Could Block Thousands of 2012 Votes," July 8, 2012, July 8, 2012; "Voter ID Law Set for Review by State Supreme Court," September 9, 2012, http://www.pennlive.com/midstate/index.ssf/2012/09/voter _id_law_set_for_review_by.html (accessed September 10, 2012); Charles Wilson, "Indian Election Chief Found Guilty of Voter Fraud," February 4, 2012, http:// news.yahoo.com/indiana-election-chief-found-guilty-voter-fraud-073551102.html (accessed July 12, 2012); Dunham and Traynor, July 8, 2012, A20; Ethan Bronner, "Judge Is Told to Examine Effect of Law on Voter ID," September 18, 2012, http:// www.nytimes.com/2012/09/19/us/pennsylvania-voter-id-effort-to-get-a-closer -look.html (accessed September 22, 2012); Ethan Bronner, "Voter ID Rules Fail Court Test Across Country," October 2, 2012, http://www.nytimes.com/2012/ 10/03/us/pennsylvania-judge-delays-implementation-of-voter-id-law.html? _r=0 (accessed October 30, 2012).

53. Baker, "Tough ID Laws Could Block Thousands of 2012 Votes," July 8, 2012, July 8, 2012.

54. "Tennessee: Court Upholds Voter Identification Law," October 25, 2012, http://www.nytimes.com/2012/10/26/us/tennessee-court-upholds-voter-identification -law.html?_r=0 (accessed October 25, 2012).

55. Heather Ann Thompson, "Why Mass Incarceration Matters: Rethinking Crisis, Decline, and Transformation in Postwar American History," *Journal of American History* 97, no. 3 (December 2010), 703; Marable, *Race, Reform and Rebellion*, 221.

56. Thompson, "Why Mass Incarceration Matters," 707–8; Julilly Kohler-Hausmann. " 'The Attila the Hun Law': New York's Rockefeller Drug Laws and the Making of the Punitive State," *Journal of Social History* 44, no. 1 (Fall 2010), 71–95.

57. Marable, *Race, Reform and Rebellion*, 222, 225; Michelle Alexander, *The New Jim Crow*, 52–55. For a study of the "moral panic" the media created over crack cocaine, see Erich Goode and Nachman Ben-Yehuda, *Moral Panics: The Social Construction of Deviance*, 2nd ed. West Sussex, U.K.: Wiley-Blackwell, 2009, 207–11.

58. Marable, *Race, Reform and Rebellion*, 177–78, 179–80, 203–4, 206, 247–48; Alexander, *The New Jim Crow*, 218.

59. Alexander, *The New Jim Crow*, 153–55; Keyssar, *The Right to Vote*, 274.

60. Alexander, *The New Jim Crow*, 155–56; Neil R. McMillen, *Dark Journey: Black Mississippians in the Age of Jim Crow* (Urbana and Chicago: University of Illinois Press, 1989), 43.

61. Keyssar, *The Right to Vote*, 273–75.

62. Ibid., 275–77.

63. Shawn Ghuman, "Florida, Iowa Target Voting Rights for Ex-Felons," July 11, 2012, http://www.usatoday.com/news/nation/story/2012-07-10/felon-voting-rights/56137692/1 (accessed July 14, 2012).

64. Ghuman, July 11, 2012; Kyle Muzenrieder, "Bill Clinton Calls Rick Scott's Felon Disfranchisement Rules Racist and Politically Motivated," July 6, 2011, http://blogs.miaminewtimes.com/riptide/2011/07/bill_clinton_calls_rick_scotts.php (accessed July 14, 2012); James Ridgeway, "The Mother of All Vote-Suppression Tactics?" July 5, 2012, http://www.motherjones.com/politics/2012/07/felon-disenfranchisement-florida-vote-obama (accessed July 14, 2012); Kevin Gray, "Judge to Lift Restrictions on Florida Voter Registration," August 29, 2012, http://www.reuters.com/article/2012/08/30/us-usa-voting-florida-idUSBRE87S1AK2012 0830(accessed September 22, 2012); "Gov. Rick Scott won't extend early voting through Sunday," November 2, 2012, http://www.abcactionnews.com/dpp/news/state/gov-rick-scott-wont-extend-early-voting-through-sunday (accessed November 7, 2012); Patricia Zengerle, "Voting Laws May Disenfranchisee 19 Million Hispanic U.S. Citizens: Study," September 23, 2012, http://news.yahoo.com/voting-laws-may-disenfranchise-10-million-hispanic-u-015903517.html (accessed September 24, 2012); "Counting voters, counting votes," *The Economist*, October 27, 2012, 34; Benjy Sarlin, "Poll: Latino Vote Devastated GOP Even Worse Than Exit Polls Showed," November 7, 2012,http://news.yahoo.com/poll-latino-vote-devastated-gop-even-worse-exits-181922111—politics.html (accessed November 7, 2012).

65. Marable, *Race, Reform and Rebellion*, 249; Chris Moody, "On Drug Reform, Chris Christie Shows His Gentler Side," July 9, 2012, http://news.yahoo.com/blogs/ticket/drug-reform-chris-christie-shows-gentler-side-174222543.html (accessed July 10, 2012). See Alexander, *The New Jim Crow*, especially Chapter 6.

Chapter 6

1. Toni Morrison, "Clinton as the First Black President," *New Yorker*, October 1998, http://ontology.buffalo.edu/smith/clinton/morrison.html (accessed July 14, 2012).

2. http://www.politico.com/blogs/michaelcalderone/0110/Matthews_I_forgot_he_was_black_tonight_for_an_hour.html (accessed July 19, 2012).

3. Jason Carroll, "Will Obama Suffer from the 'Bradley effect'?" October 13, 2008, http://articles.cnn.com/2008-10-13/politics/obama.bradley.effect_1_bradley-effect-bradley-campaign-exit-polls?_s=PM:POLITICS (accessed July 19, 2012).

4. Barack Obama, *Dreams from My Father: A Story of Race and Inheritance* (New York: Three Rivers Press, 1995, 2004 reprint), 3–6, 9–10.

5. Ibid., 24, 44–45, 60–61, 154; Barack Obama, *The Audacity of Hope: Thoughts on Reclaiming the American Dream* (New York: Three Rivers Press, 2006), 273–75.

6. Obama, *Dreams*, 104, 133, 135–36, 164–66, 184, 256, 197, 202, 256, 280–84.

7. Ibid., vii–viii, 289–90; Obama, *Audacity of Hope*, 1–3; David Remnick, "The Joshua Generation," *New Yorker*, November 17, 2008, http://www.newyorker.com/reporting/2008/11/17/081117fa_fact_remnick?currentPage=all (accessed August 3, 2012).

8. Remnick, "The Joshua Generation," November 17, 2008; Obama, *Audacity of Hope*, 234, 354.

9. Obama, *Audacity of Hope*, 62–63, 243, 256.

10. Ibid., 227–33, 236; Michael Tesler and David O. Sears, *Obama's Race: The 2008 Election and the Dream of a Post-Racial America* (Chicago and London: University of Chicago Press, 2010), 1–2.

11. Tesler and Sears, *Obama's Race*, 2–3.

12. "Obama Placed under Secret Service Protection," May 3, 2007, http://www.msnbc.msn.com/id/18474444/ns/politics-decision_08/t/obama-placed-under-secret-service-protection/#.UB1BP6N0joQ (accessed August 4, 2012); "Obama Placed," May 3, 2007, http://articles.cnn.com/2007–05–03/politics/obama.protection_1_advisory-board-chertoff-secret-service?_s=PM:POLITICS (accessed August 4, 2012); "Obama Chooses 'Renegade' as His Secret Service Codename (while Bush Gets to Keep 'Trailblazer')," November 13, 2008, http://www.dailymail.co.uk/news/article–1085316/Obama-chooses-Renegade-Secret-Service-code-Bush-gets-Trailblazer.html (accessed August 4, 2012).

13. Tesler and Sears, *Obama's Race*, 29–30. For more on the Bradley effect, see Chapter 3.

14. Ibid., 30–31; "Bill Clinton Says Race, Gender to Decide S.C. Vote," January 24, 2008, http://www.usatoday.com/news/politics/election2008/2008-01-24-sc-bill-clinton_N.htm (accessed August 6, 2012).

15. Tesler and Sears, *Obama's Race*, 30–31; Lietee Gidlow, "Taking the Long View of Election 2008," in *Obama, Clinton, Palin: Making History in Election 2008*, Liette Gidlow, ed. (Urbana and Chicago: University of Illinois Press, 2011), 4; Rebecca Sinderbrand, March 11, 2008, "Ferraro; 'They're attacking me because I'm white," http://www.cnn.com/2008/POLITICS/03/11/ferraro.comments/index.html (accessed October 29, 2012).

16. Tesler and Sears, *Obama's Race*, 31–32; Brian Ross, "Obama's Pastor: God Damn America, U.S. to Blame for 9/11," March 13, 2008, http://abcnews.go.com/Blotter/DemocraticDebate/story?id=4443788&page=1#.UB_gI6N0joQ (accessed August 6, 2012).

17. Tiffany Ruby Patterson, "Barack Obama and the Politics of Anger," in *Obama, Clinton, Palin: Making History in Election 2008*, Liette Gidlow, ed. (Urbana and Chicago: University of Illinois Press, 2011), 29–30.

18. Ibid., 30–33; "Text of Obama's Speech: A More Perfect Union," March 18, 2008, http://blogs.wsj.com/washwire/2008/03/18/text-of-obamas-speech-a-more -perfect-union/ (accessed August 6, 2012); Gidlow, "Taking the Long View of Election 2008," 4; Tera W. Hunter, "The Forgotten Legacy of Shirley Chisholm," *Obama, Clinton, Palin: Making History in Election 2008*, Liette Gidlow, ed. (Urbana and Chicago: University of Illinois Press, 2011), 66–67.

19. Sean Wilentz, "Barack Obama and the Unmaking of the Democratic Party," May 23, 2008, http://www.huffingtonpost.com/sean-wilentz/barack-obama-and -the-unma_b_103353.html (accessed August 6, 2012); Tesler and Sears, *Obama's Race*, 86–87.

20. Hunter, "The Forgotten Legacy of Shirley Chisholm," 73.

21. Gidlow, "Taking the Long View of Election 2008," 4.

22. In the summer of 2012, researchers at Ancestry.com, the genealogical website, reported that Barack Obama *was* likely descended from one of the first reported African slaves in the English colonies, John Punch of Virginia. However, that ancestry was on his white mother's side, as Punch had children with a free white woman, and the mixed-race children of that union then became prominent landowners in the colony. Amy Bingham, "Obama, Romney Family Trees Hold Slaves, British Country Folk," July 30, 2012, http://abcnews.go.com/Politics/ OTUS/obama–romney–family–trees–hold–slaves–british–countryfolk/story? id=16889505#.UCEcIqN0joQ (accessed August 7, 2012).

23. Mitch Kachun, "Michelle Obama, the Media Circus, and America's Racial Obsession," in *Obama, Clinton, Palin: Making History in Election 2008*, Liette Gidlow, ed. (Urbana and Chicago: University of Illinois Press, 2011), 42–45, 47.

24. Tesler and Sears, *Obama's Race*, 137–39. For more on Obama and the Muslim and birth certificate conspiracies, see Chapter 7.

25. Ronald P. Formasio, "Populist Currents in the 2008 Presidential Campaign," in *Obama, Clinton, Palin: Making History in Election 2008*, Liette Gidlow, ed. (Urbana and Chicago: University of Illinois Press, 2011), 114–16.

26. Ibid., 116–18; Eduardo Bonilla-Silva, *Racism without Racists: Color-Blind Racism and Racial Inequality in Contemporary America*, 3rd ed. (Lanham, MD and Boulder, CO: Rowman & Littlefield, 2010), 224, 229.

27. David R. Sands and Andrea Billups, "Obama Term Expected To Be Post-Racial," 9 November 9, 2008, http://www.washingtontimes.com/news/2008/nov/ 09/obama-presidency-expected-to-be-post-racialpostracial/ (accessed 9 August 9, 2012); "Blacks Upbeat about Black Progress, Prospects," 12 January 12, 2010, http://pewresearch.org/pubs/1459/year-after-obama-election-black-public -opinion (accessed 9 August 9, 2010).

28. Toby Harnden, "Barack Obama's Support Falls among White Voters," http://www.telegraph.co.uk/news/worldnews/barackobama/5961624/Barack-Obamas-support-falls-among-white-voters.html (accessed October 29, 2012); Tracy Jan, "Gates Accepts White House Meeting Offer; http://www.boston.com/

news/local/breaking_news/2009/07/obama_calls_cam.html (accessed October 29, 2012). For more on the Tea Party, see Chapter 7.

29. Kevin Connelly, "U.S. Officials Stumble on the Firing of Shirley Sherrod," *BBC Online*, July 22, 2010, http://www.bbc.co.uk/news/world-us-canada-10722121 (accessed February 4, 2011).

30. Catherine Dodge and Alan Bjerga, "Vilsack Apologizes to Ousted USDA Official over Firing, Offers Post Back," July 21, 2010, http://www.bloomberg.com/news/2010-07-21/usda-employee-ousted-over-24-year-old-video-deserves-apology-gibbs-says.html (accessed August 10, 2012); Cindy Adams, "Glen Beck Says President Obama Hates White People and Is a Racist," July 29, 2009, http://www.examiner.com/article/glenn-beck-says-president-obama-hates-white-people-and-is-a-racist (accessed August 9, 2012); David Limbaugh, *Crimes against Liberty: An Indictment of President Barack Obama* (Washington, D.C.: Regnery Publishing, 2010), 31, 197–99, 324–27; Abigail Thernstrom, "The New Black Panther Case: A Conservative Dissent," July 6, 2010, http://www.nationalreview.com/articles/243408/new-black-panther-case-br-conservative-dissent-abigail-thernstrom (accessed August 10, 2012).

31. Jerome R. Corsi, *The Obama Nation: Leftist Politics and the Cult of Personality* (New York: Threshold Editions, 2008), 183; David Freddoso, *Gangster Government: Barack Obama and the New Washington Thugocracy* (Washington, D.C.: Regnery Publishing, 2011). See Chapter 7 of Corsi for the discussion of black liberation theology and Wright. Freddoso does give some coverage to the New Black Panther Party voter intimidation case. Freddoso, *Gangster Government*, 176–79.

32. Bonilla-Silva, *Racism without Racists*, 209–10.

33. For more on voter ID laws, see Chapter 5.

34. Rob Kampia, "Medical Marijuana Meets Hostility from Obama Administration," http://www.washingtonpost.com/opinions/medical-marijuana-meets-hostility-from-obama-administration/2012/05/04/gIQA80GK2T_story.html (accessed August 11, 2012); Eduardo Bonilla–Silva, 219; Deborah Dupre. "Davis: 'Most celebrated death row case,' 'Obama could intervene,' Troy's letter," September 16, 2011, http://www.examiner.com/article/davis-most-celebrated-death-row-case-obama-could-intervene-troy-s-letter (accessed August 11, 2011); Joy Freeman-Coulbary, "Obama silent on Troy Davis," September 21, 2011, http://www.washingtonpost.com/blogs/therootdc/post/obama-silent-on-troy-davis/2011/09/21/gIQAH9tIlK_blog.html (accessed August 11, 2011); Agence France-Presse, "Obama won't act in Troy Davis execution case," September 21, 2011, http://www.rawstory.com/rs/2011/09/21/obama-wont-act-in-troy-davis-execution-case/ (accessed August 11, 2011).

35. Nia Malika-Henderson, "As Joblessness Continues, Obama Faces Tough Challenge In Reengaging Black Voters," September 23, 2011, http://www.washingtonpost.com/politics/obama-faces-growing-discontent-among-black-voters/2011/09/23/

gIQA3vYurK_story_1.html (accessed August 11, 2012); Joshua Altman, "Rangel Says Black Community Can Be Angry and Still Support Obama," September 27, 2011, http://thehill.com/video/house/184193-rangel-says-that-black-community-is-not-shooting -elected-officials-in-anger (accessed August 11, 2011).

36. Matt DeLong, "Obama to Congressional Black Caucus: 'March with Me,' " September 25, 2011, http://www.washingtonpost.com/blogs/44/post/obama-to -congressional-black-caucus-march-with-me/2011/09/25/gIQAP4qGwK_blog.html (accessed August 11, 2011); "Remarks by the President at Congressional Black Caucus Foundation Annual Phoenix Awards Dinner," September 24, 2011, http://www .whitehouse.gov/the-press-office/2011/09/24/remarks-president-congressional -black-caucus-foundation-annual-phoenix-a (accessed August 11, 2012); "Maxine Waters: Obama's Speech to Congressional Black Caucus Was 'A Bit Curious,' " September 26, 2011, http://www.huffingtonpost.com/2011/09/26/ maxine-waters-barack-obama_n_980832.html (accessed August 11, 2011); Joseph Williams, "Barack Obama speech reopens rift with black critics," 29 September 29, 2011, http://www.politico.com/news/stories/0911/64680.html (accessed August 11, 2011).

37. For more on the creation of the New Deal coalition and the 1936 election, see William E. Leuchtenberg, *Franklin D. Roosevelt and the New Deal* (New York: Harper & Row, 1963), Chapter 8.

38. Manning Marable, *Race, Reform, Rebellion: The Second Reconstruction and Beyond in Black America, 1945–2006*, 3rd ed. (Oxford, Miss: University Press of Mississippi, 2007); 248; Jesse Washington, "Recession Beats Back Black Gains," *Houston Chronicle*, July 10, 2011, A8; Patrick Wall, "Wealth Gap Widens: Whites' Net Worth Is 20 Times That of Blacks," July 26, 2011, http://www.csmonitor.com/ USA/2011/0726/Wealth-gap-widens-Whites-net-worth-is-20-times-that-of -blacks (accessed October 29, 2012); "U.S. Voter Turnout Shaping up to Be Lower Than 2008," November 7, 2012, http://www.straitstimes.com/breaking -news/world/story/us-voter-turnout-shaping-be-lower-2008-20121107 (accessed November 7, 2012); Thomas Beaumont, "U.S. Election: With Robust Minority, Youth Turnout, 2012 Voters Tilt for Obama Like in 2008," November 7, 2012, http://www.thestar.com/news/world/uselection/article/1283984—u-s-election -with-robust-minority-youth-turnout-2012-voters-tilt-for-obama-like-in-2008 (accessed November 7, 2012).

Chapter 7

1. David Weigel, " 'N-Word' Sign Dogs Would-Be Tea Party Leader," January 4, 2010, http://washingtonindependent.com/73036/n-word-sign-dogs-would-be-tea -party-leader (accessed August 23, 2010).

2. Kate Zernike, *Boiling Mad: Inside Tea Party America* (New York: Henry Holt and Co., 2010), 13; Theda Skocpol and Vanessa Williamson, *The Tea Party and*

the Making of Republican Conservatism (Oxford and New York: Oxford University Press, 2012), 7.

3. Zernike, *Boiling Mad*, 13–14, 16–19; Skocpol and Williamson, *The Tea Party and the Making of Republican Conservatism*, 8–9, 130–31.

4. Skocpol and Williamson, *The Tea Party and the Making of Republican Conservatism*, 35–36; Joshua Green, "The Tea Party's Brain," November 2010, http:// www.theatlantic.com/magazine/archive/2010/11/the-tea-partys-brain/308280/ (accessed August 25, 2012); Juan Williams, "The Surprising Rise of Rep. Ron Paul," May 10, 2011, http://www.foxnews.com/opinion/2011/05/10/juan -williams-surprising-rise-rep-ron-paul/ (accessed August 25, 2012).

5. Skocpol and Williams, *The Tea Party and the Making of Republican Conservatism*, 9–10, 106–8, 112.

6. Ibid., 34–40; "The Tea Party and Religion," February 23, 2011, http://www .pewforum.org/Politics-and-Elections/Tea-Party-and-Religion.aspx (accessed August 25, 2012). The literature on the rightward shift in U.S. politics is vast and growing, but for an overview of various influences and issues, see Bruce J. Schulman and Julian E. Zelizer, eds., *Rightward Bound: Making America Conservative in the 1970s* (Cambridge and London: Harvard University Press, 2008).

7. This anti-intellectualism is detailed in Richard Hofstadter, *Anti-Intellectualism in American Life* (New York: Vintage Books, 1963). For a history of Wallace, see Dan Carter, *The Politics of Rage: George Wallace, The Origins of the New Conservatism, and the Transformation of American Politics* (Baton Rouge: Louisiana State University Press, 1995). For more on Boston and the anti–busing backlash, see chapter one.

8. Skocpol and Williamson, *The Tea Party and the Making of Republican Conservatism*, 23–26, 36; "The Tea Party and Religion."

9. "The Tea Party and Religion."

10. Skocpol and Williamson, *The Tea Party and the Making of Republican Conservatism*, 68–69; Zernike, *Boiling Mad*, 51, 138–39.

11. Scott Rasmussen and Douglas Schoen, *Mad as Hell: How the Tea Party Movement is Fundamentally Remaking Our Two-Party System* (New York: HarperCollins Publishers, 2010), 194–95; Skocpol and Williamson, *The Tea Party and the Making of Republican Conservatism*, 69–70.

12. Susan Page and Jackie Kucinich, April 28, 2011, "Obama releases long-form birth certificate," http://www.usatoday.com/news/washington/2011-04-27-obama -birth-certificate_n.htm?csp=34news (accessed September 1, 2012).

13. Ben Smith and Byron Tau, "Birtherism: Where It All Began," April 22, 2011, http://www.politico.com/news/stories/0411/53563.html (accessed September 1, 2012); Jeffrey Cass, "Birthers, Tea Partier, and Islamophobes: Obama and the Problem of American Orientalism" (paper presented at the annual meeting for the Popular Culture Association/American Culture Association, San Antonio, Texas, April 20–23, 2012); "Tea Party Member Who Sent Racist Email Depicting

Obama and Parents as Chimps Cannot Be Fired—And Refuses to Resign," April 19, 2011, http://www.dailymail.co.uk/news/article-1378380/Official -apologizes-Obama-chimpanzee-email-Tea-party-member-fired.html?ito=feeds -newsxml (accessed September 1, 2012).

14. Smith and Tau, April 22, 2011; "Mitt Romney's Birther Joke: Did He Cross the Line?" August 24, 2012, http://theweek.com/article/index/232415/mitt -romneys-birther-joke-did-he-cross-the-line (accessed September 1, 2012); Cass, "Birthers, Tea Partier, and Islamophobes."

15. Bob Bernick, Jr., August 10, 2009, http://www.deseretnews.com/article/ 705321969/13-of-Utahns-question-Obama-birthplace.html (accessed September 1, 2012); "58 Percent of GOP Not Sure/Doubt Obama Born in US," July 31, 2009, http://www.politico.com/blogs/glennthrush/0709/58_of_GOP_not_suredont _beleive_Obama_born_in_US.html (accessed September 1, 2012).

16. Cass, "Birthers, Tea Partier, and Islamophobes."

17. Trip Gabriel, "Ryan Says Obama Policies Threaten 'Judeo-Christian' Values," November 5, 2012, http://thecaucus.blogs.nytimes.com/2012/11/05/ ryan-says-obama-policies-threaten-judeo-christian-values/ (accessed November 7, 2012); Kate Phillips, "House Admonishes Wilson on Outburst," September 15, 2009, http://thecaucus.blogs.nytimes.com/2009/09/15/blogging-the-house-action -on-wilson/ (accessed September 2, 2012); "Brewer, Obama Exchange Tense Words over Book, Border at Airport," January 25, 2012, http://www.azcentral.com/news/ politics/articles/2012/01/25/20120125brewer-obama-exchange-tense-words -immigration.html (accessed September 2, 2012).

18. "Carter: Obama a target for racism," September 16, 2009, http:// www.aljazeera.com/news/americas/2009/09/2009916172057802997.html (accessed September 2, 2012).

19. "Rep. West: Ellison "Antithesis" of Country's Founding Principles," January 24, 2011, http://www.startribune.com/politics/blogs/114507899.html (accessed September 3, 2012); Tim Murphy, "Allen West's Rise from the Florida Fever Swamps," *Mother Jones*, July/August 2012, http://www.motherjones.com/politics/ 2012/08/allen-west-tea-party-congressman (accessed September 3, 2012); Cullen Dirner, "Tim Scott Will Not Join Congressional Black Caucus: 'My Campaign Was Never About Race,'" December 1, 2010, http://abcnews.go.com/blogs/ politics/2010/12/tim-scott-will-not-join-congressional-black-caucus-my-campaign -was-never-about-race/ (accessed September 3, 2012).

20. For more on this, see Chapter 3 of Eduardo Bonilla-Silva, *Racism without Racists: Color-Blind Racism and Racial Inequality In Contemporary America*, 3rd ed. (Lanham, MD and Boulder, CO: Bowman & Littlefield, 2010).

21. Skocpol and Williamson, *The Tea Party and the Making of Republican Conservatism*, 4; Doug Mataconis, "Richard Lugar: Tea Party Cost GOP Senate Control In 2010," December 29, 2011, http://www.outsidethebeltway.com/richard -lugar-tea-party-cost-gop-senate-control-in-2010/ (accessed September 3, 2012).

22. Stephanie Hallett, "Abortion at Risk: Where Does Your State Stand?" February 1, 2011, http://msmagazine.com/blog/blog/2011/02/01/abortion-at-risk-where-does-your-state-stand/ (accessed September 3, 2012); Doug Mataconis, "Maine Governor Skips MLK Events, Tells NAACP 'Kiss My Butt,'" January 15, 2011, http://www.outsidethebeltway.com/maine-governor-skips-mlk-day-events-tells-naacp-kiss-my-butt/ (accessed September 3, 2012); Richard Locker, "Tea Parties Issue Demands to Tennessee Legislators," January 13, 2011, http://www.commercialappeal.com/news/2011/jan/13/tea-parties-cite-legislative-demands/ (accessed September 3, 2012). See Chapter 5 for more on voter ID laws.

23. Philip Elliott, "Likely GOP Contenders Plot Tea Party Strategies," April 14, 2011, http://www.msnbc.msn.com/id/42607502/ns/politics-decision_2012/t/likely-gop-contenders-plot-tea-party-strategies/#.UET2TJHHZQA (accessed September 3, 2012); Amanda Carey, "FreedomWorks Not Crazy About Romney, Other 2012 Candidates," June 1, 2011, http://dailycaller.com/2011/06/01/freedomworks-not-crazy-about-romney-other-2012-candidates/ (accessed September 3, 2012).

24. Margery A. Beck, "Bachmann Criticizes Black Farmer Settlement," July 19, 2011, http://news.yahoo.com/bachmann-criticizes-black-farmer-settlement-225727223.html (accessed September 3, 2012). For more on the development of coded racial rhetoric on welfare, see Chapter 1.

25. Huma Khan, "What Did Rick Santorum Say? Welfare Comments Scrutinized," January 3, 2012, http://abcnews.go.com/blogs/politics/2012/01/what-did-rick-santorum-say-welfare-comments-scrutinized/ (accessed September 3, 2012); Suzanne Gamboa, "Gingrich to Black People: Paychecks, Not Food Aid," January 6, 2012, http://news.yahoo.com/gingrich-black-people-paychecks-not-food-aid-234405279.html (accessed September 3, 2012); Dan Carter, *From George Wallace to New Gingrich: Race in the Conservative Counterrevolution* (Baton Rouge: Louisiana State University Press), 122.

26. Robert Costa, "Gingrich: Obama's 'Kenyan, Anticolonial' Worldview," September 1, 2011, http://www.nationalreview.com/corner/246302/gingrich-obama-s-kenyan-anti-colonial-worldview-robert-costa (accessed September 3, 2012); Adam Hochschild, "What Gingrich Didn't Learn in Congo," December 4, 2011, http://www.nytimes.com/2011/12/05/opinion/what-gingrich-didnt-learn-in-congo.html (accessed September 3, 2012).

27. Dinesh D'Souza, *The Roots of Obama's Rage* (Washington, D.C.: Regnery Publishing, 2010), 13–15, 59–61, 84–85. For a historiographical overview, see Alden T. Vaughan, "The Origins Debate: Slavery and Racism in Seventeenth-Century Virginia," *Virginia Magazine of History and Biography* 97, no. 3 (July 1989), 311–54. While the debate over what came first, enslavement or anti-black racism, is the core of the debate among historians, even scholars who see racism developing out of slavery, like Edmund Morgan, see it in place by the eighteenth century.

28. Alex Murashko, "'2026: Obama's America' Co-Producer Wants AP to Apologize for Fact Check Story," September 4, 2012, http://www.christianpost.com/news/2016obamas-america-co-producer-wants-ap-to-apologize-for-fact-check-story-81029/ (accessed September 4, 2012); Ethan Sacks, "'2016: Obama's America' Shocks Film Industry after Becoming a Box Office Success Despite Having Virtually No Promotional Budget," September 3, 2012, http://www.nydailynews.com/entertainment/tv-movies/2016-obama-america-shocks-film-industry-a-box-office-success-virtually-promotional-budget-article-1.1150536 (accessed September 4, 2012); Beth Fouhy, " '2016 Obama's America' Fact-Check," August 28, 2012, http://www.huffingtonpost.com/2012/08/28/2016-obama-america-fact-check_n_1835710.html?ref=topposts (accessed September 4, 2012).

29. Sarah Wood, "Mitt Romney: I Can Relate to Black People, My Ancestors Once Owned Slaves," March 13, 2012, http://www.freewoodpost.com/2012/03/13/mitt-romney-i-can-relate-to-black-people-my-ancestors-once-owned-slaves/ (accessed September 6, 2012); MacKenzie Weinger, "Poll: 0 Percent of Blacks for Mitt Romney," August 22, 2012, http://www.politico.com/news/stories/0812/80015.html (accessed September 6, 2012); Jim Rutenberg and Ashley Parker, "Romney Stands Behind Remarks Caught on Video," *New York Times*, September 19, 2012, A1; Lara Seligman, "John Sununu Comments Spark Controversy," October 26, 2012, http://news.yahoo.com/john-sununu-comments-spark-controversy-075958000—politics.html (accessed October 30, 2012).

30. Lexington, "Ron Paul's Big Moment," *Economist*, December 31, 2011, 22; Ron Paul, "The Trouble with the '64 Civil Rights Act," June 4, 2004, http://www.lewrockwell.com/paul/paul188.html (accessed September 5, 2012); Matt Loffman, "Rand Paul Seeks to Clarify Stance on Civil Rights Act of 1964," May 20, 2010, http://abcnews.go.com/blogs/politics/2010/05/rand-paul-clarify-stance-civil-rights-act-1964/ (accessed September 5, 2012); Ujala Sehgal, "Ron Paul Would Have Opposed the Civil Rights Act of 1964," May 14, 2011, http://www.theatlanticwire.com/politics/2011/05/ron-paul-would-have-opposed-civil-rights-act-1964/37726/ (accessed September 5, 2012).

31. Lexington, "Ron Paul's Big Moment," December 31, 2011; Huma Khan, "Gingrich Attacks Ron Paul on Controversial Newsletters," December 23, 2011, http://abcnews.go.com/blogs/politics/2011/12/gingrich-attacks-ron-paul-on-controversial-newsletters/ (accessed September 5, 2012); Alicia M. Cohn, "Huntsman Campaign Hits Ron Paul with 'Twilight Zone' Video," January 1, 2012, http://thehill.com/video/campaign/201897-huntsman-campaign-hits-ron-paul-with-twlight-zone-scare-video (accessed September 6, 2012); "Huntsman: Paul Supporters' China Ad 'Stupid,' " January 6, 2012, http://boston.cbslocal.com/2012/01/06/huntsman-paul-supporters-china-ad-stupid/ (accessed September 6, 2012); Casey Gane-McCalla, "Ron Paul Supporter: 'Assassinate N-Word Obama and Monkey Children,' " December 19, 2011, http://newsone.com/1730175/jules-manson-ron-paul-obama-assassinate/ (accessed September 6, 2012).

32. "Paul Keeps Donation from White Supremacist," December 19, 2007, http://www.msnbc.msn.com/id/22331091/ns/politics-decision_08/t/paul-keeps-donation-white-supremacist/#.UEjtI5HHZQA (accessed September 6, 2012).

33. Jake Sherman, "Andre Carson: Tea Party Wants Blacks 'Hanging an aTree,'" August 31, 2011, http://www.politico.com/news/stories/0811/62396.html (accessed September 6, 2012); Nia-Malika Henderson, "Maxine Waters to Tea Party: Go to Hell," August 22, 2011, http://www.washingtonpost.com/politics/maxine-waters-to-tea-party-go-to-hell/2011/08/22/gIQAjgEeWJ_story.html (accessed September 6, 2012); "NAACP Delegates Vote to Repudiate Racist Elements within the Tea Party," July 13, 2010, http://www.naacp.org/blog/entry/naacp-delegates-vote-to-repudiate-racist-elements-within-the-tea-pary/ (accessed September 6, 2012); Brandi Fowler, "Morgan Freeman Calls Out Tea Party as 'Racist,'" September 24, 2011, http://www.eonline.com/news/265849/morgan-freeman-calls-out-tea-party-as-racist (accessed September 6, 2012); Tim Graham, "Actor Samuel L. Jackson: Tea Party Racism 'Pretty Obvious,'" October 5, 2011, http://newsbusters.org/blogs/tim-graham/2011/10/05/actor-samuel-l-jackson-tea-party-racism-pretty-obvious (accessed September 6, 2012); Jake Tapper, "VP Biden Says Republicans Are 'Going to Put Y'all Back in Chains,'" August 14, 2012, http://abcnews.go.com/blogs/politics/2012/08/vp-biden-says-republicans-are-going-to-put-yall-back-in-chains/ (accessed September 6, 2012); Arlette Saenz, "Biden Clarifies 'Chains' Remark, Romney Calls Statement 'Outrageous,'" August 14, 2012, http://abcnews.go.com/blogs/politics/2012/08/political-punch-biden-clarifies-chains-remark-romney-calls-statement-outrageous/ (accessed September 6, 2012).

34. Herman Cain, *This Is Herman Cain! My Journey to the White House* (New York and London: Threshold Editions, 2011), 12–13, 15, 32–33, 36; "Rising Cain," *Economist*, October 15, 2011, 35.

35. "Rising Cain," *Economist*, 35–36.

36. Cain, *This Is Herman Cain!*, 35–36, 188; Tiffany Gabbay, "Herman Cain: Obama Has 'Never Been a Part of the Black Experience in America,'" October 11, 2011, http://www.theblaze.com/stories/herman-cain-obama-has-%E2%80%98never-been-a-part-of-the-black-experience-in-america%E2%80%99/ (accessed September 9, 2012).

37. Gabbay, "Herman Cain: Obama Has 'Never Been a Part of the Black Experience in America,'" October 11, 2011; Catalina Camia, "GOP's Herman Cain: Obama 'Not a Strong Black Man,'" June 30, 2011, http://content.usatoday.com/communities/onpolitics/post/2011/06/herman-cain-barack-obama-black-man-/1#.UEzX6JHHb4g (accessed September 9, 2012); "Cain: Perry Insensitive over Name of Hunting Camp," October 2, 2011, http://www.usatoday.com/news/politics/story/2011-10-02/perry-cain-hunting-camp-name/50634568/1 (accessed September 9, 2012).

38. "White House Hopeful Herman Cain Gets Immediate Secret Service Protection after Receiving Death Threats," November 18, 2011, http://www.dailymail.co.uk/

news/article-2063085/Herman-Cain-gets-Secret-Service-Protection-receiving-death
-threats.html (accessed September 9, 2012); "Cain Suspends Presidential bid,"
December 3, 2011, http://www.cnn.com/2011/12/03/election/2012/cain-campaign/
index.html (accessed September 9, 2012); Michelle Goldberg, "The Right's Absurd
Cain Race Card," November 1, 2011, http://www.thedailybeast.com/articles/2011/11/
01/the-right-s-absurd-herman-cain-race-card.html (accessed September 9, 2012).

39. James Colaico, *Martin Luther King, Jr.: Apostle of Militant Nonviolence*
(New York: St. Martin's Press, 1993), 189, 192, 197; Cain, *This Is Herman Cain!*,
180–81; Mark Vansetti, "Herman Cain: Legal Immigration, Not Amnesty," October 13, 2011, http://news.yahoo.com/herman-cain-legal-immigration-not
-amnesty-235700234.html (accessed September 9, 2012).

40. Luke Johnson, "Herman Cain Says He Was Relieved when Doctor Who
Treated Him Was a Christian," November 21, 2011, http://www.huffingtonpost.com
/2011/11/21/herman-cain-holy-land-experience_n_1105725.html (accessed September 9, 2012); Devin Gordon, Chris Heath, and Alan Richman, "A Pizza Party with
Herman Cain," *GQ*, December 2011, http://www.gq.com/news-politics/politics/
201111/herman-cain-interview-alan-richman-chris-heath-devin-gordon?printa-
ble=true&printable=true (accessed September 9, 2012); "Herman Cain: Americans
Have the Right to Ban Mosques in Their Communities," September 16, 2011, http://
www.huffingtonpost.com/2011/07/17/herman-cain-fox-mosques_n_900939.html
(accessed September 9, 2012).

41. John Parkinson, "What Happened to the Tea Party?" November 7, 2012,
http://news.yahoo.com/blogs/abc-blogs/happened-tea-party-122103241—abc-
news-politics.html (accessed November 7, 2012); Matthew L. Wald, "Democrat
Wins Race for Senate in Indiana," November 6, 2012, http://www.nytimes.com/
2012/11/07/us/politics/indiana-senate-race.html (accessed November 7, 2012);
Jordain Carney, "Akin Never Recovered From 'Legitimate Rape' Comment,"
National Journal, November 7, 2012, http://news.yahoo.com/akin-never
-recovered-legitimate-rape-074206653—politics.html (accessed November 7, 2012).

Epilogue

1. *Citizens United v. Federal Election Commission*, 558 U.S. 50 (2010).

2. Brett LoGiurato, "Barack Obama Never Had a Problem with White Voters,"
November 8, 2012, http://www.businessinsider.com/obama-white-vote-exit-polls-
election-ohio-wisconsin-iowa-2012-11 (accessed November 9, 2012); Chris Cillizza
and Jon Cohen, "President Obama and the White Vote? No Problem," November 8,
2012, http://www.washingtonpost.com/blogs/the-fix/wp/2012/11/08/president-
obama-and-the-white-vote-no-problem/ (accessed November 9, 2012).

3. Amanda Terkel, "Karl Rove: Obama Won 'By Suppressing the Vote,'"
November 8, 2012, http://www.huffingtonpost.com/2012/11/08/karl-rove-obama
-suppressing-vote_n_2094459.html (accessed November 9, 2012); Michael Hirsh,

"Mitt Romney Had Every Chance to Win—But He Blew It," November 9, 2012, http://news.yahoo.com/mitt-romney-had-every-chance-win-blew-150005282—politics.html; _ylt=A2KJjbyAM51QPT4AyirQtDMD (accessed November 9, 2012).

4. Thomas Beaumont, "U.S. Election: With Robust Minority, Youth Turnout, 2012 Voters Tilt for Obama Like in 2008," November 7, 2012, http://www.thestar.com/news/world/uselection/article/1283984—u-s-election-with-robust-minority-youth-turnout-2012-voters-tilt-for-obama-like-in-2008 (accessed November 7, 2012).

5. The three states in which same-sex marriage was legalized by voters were Maine, Maryland, and Washington, and Minnesota voters rejected adding a ban on same-sex marriage to the state constitution. Gizelle Lugo, "Same Sex Marriage Ballot Initiatives: Voters in Strong Backing for Equality," November 7, 2012, http://www.guardian.co.uk/world/2012/nov/07/same-sex-marriage-ballot-initiatives (accessed November 7, 2012).

6. George Frederickson, *Racism: A Short History* (Princeton, NJ: Princeton University Press, 2002), 9.

Bibliography

Books

Alexander, Michelle. *The New Jim Crow: Mass Incarceration in an Age of Color-blindness*. New York: The New Press, 2010.

Ambrose, Stephen E. *Eisenhower: Soldier and President*. New York: Simon & Schuster, 1990.

Asch, Chris Myers. *The Senator and the Sharecropper: The Freedom Struggles of James O. Eastland and Fannie Lou Hamer*. New York: The New Press, 2008.

Ayers, Edward L. *The Promise of the New South: Life after Reconstruction*. New York and Oxford: Oxford University Press, 1992.

Bass, Jack and W. Scott Poole. *The Palmetto State: The Making of Modern South Carolina*. Columbia: University of South Carolina Press, 2009.

Black, Earl and Merle Black. *Politics and Society in the South*. Cambridge, MA and London: Harvard University Press, 1987.

Black, Earl and Merle Black. *The Rise of Southern Republicans*. Cambridge, MA and London: Harvard University Press, 2002.

Bonilla-Silva, Eduardo. *Racism without Racists: Color-Blind Racism and Racial Inequality in Contemporary America*,3rd ed. Lanham, MD and Boulder, CO: Bowman & Littlefield, 2010.

Brady, John. *Bad Boy: The Life and Politics of Lee Atwater*. Reading, MA: Addison Wesley, 1997.

Branch, Taylor. *At Canaan's Edge: America in the King Years 1965–68*. New York: Simon & Schuster, 2006.

Branch, Taylor. *Parting the Waters: America in the King Years, 1954–1963*. New York: Simon & Schuster, 1988.

Branch, Taylor. *Pillar of Fire: America in the King Years, 1963–65*. New York: Simon & Schuster, 1998.

Brands, H. W. *The Devil We Knew: Americans and the Cold War*. New York and Oxford: Oxford University Press, 1993.

Breitman, George, ed. *Malcolm X Speaks: Selected Speeches and Statements*. New York: Grove Press, 1990.

Brooke, Edward W. *Bridging the Divide: My Life*. New Brunswick, NJ and London: Rutgers University Press, 2007.

Brundage, W. Fitzhugh. *Lynching in the New South: Georgia and Virginia, 1880–1930*. Urbana and Chicago: University of Illinois Press, 1993.

Bryant, Nick. *The Bystander: John F. Kennedy and the Struggle for Black Equality*. New York: Basic Books, 2006.

Cain, Herman. *This Is Herman Cain! My Journey to the White House*. New York and London: Threshold Editions, 2011.

Carson, Clayborne. *In Struggle: SNCC and the Black Awakening of the 1960s*. Cambridge, MA and London: Harvard University Press, 1995.

Carter, Dan T. *From George Wallace to Newt Gingrich: Race in the Conservative Counterrevolution, 1963–1994*. Baton Rouge: Louisiana State University Press, 1996.

Carter, Dan T. *The Politics of Rage: George Wallace, The Origins of the New Conservatism, and the Transformation of American Politics*. Baton Rouge and London: Louisiana State University Press, 1995.

Carter, Dan T. *Scottsboro: A Tragedy of the American South*. Baton Rouge: Louisiana University Press, 1979.

Chalmers, David M. *Hooded Americanism: The History of the Ku Klux Klan*, 3rd ed. Dunrhamn, NC: Duke University Press, 1987.

Chavez, Leo R. *The Latino Threat: Constructing Immigrants, Citizens, and the Nation*. Stanford, CA: Stanford University Press, 2008.

Colaico, James A. *Martin Luther King, Jr.: Apostle of Militant Nonviolence*. New York: St. Martin's Press, 1993.

Corsi, Jerome R. *The Obama Nation: Leftist Politics and the Cult of Personality*. New York: Threshold Editions, 2008.

Cortner, Richard C. *The Apportionment Cases*. Knoxville: University of Tennessee Press, 1970.

Coski, John M. *The Confederate Battle Flag: America's Most Embattled Emblem*. Cambridge and London: Harvard University Press, 2005.

Courtwright, David T. *No Right Turn: Conservative Politics in a Liberal America*. Cambridge: Harvard University Press, 2010.

Crespino, Joseph. *In Search of Another Country: Mississippi and the Conservative Counterrevolution*. Princeton and Oxford: Princeton University Press, 2007.

Cutler, John Henry. *Ed Brooke: Biography of a Senator*. Indianapolis and New York: Bobbs-Merrill Company, 1972.

Dallek, Robert. *Flawed Giant: Lyndon Johnson and his Times, 1961–1973*. New York and Oxford: Oxford University Press, 1998.

Dallek, Robert. *Lone Star Rising: Lyndon Johnson and his Times, 1908–1960*. New York and Oxford: Oxford University Press, 1991.

Daniels, Roger. *Prisoners without Trial: Japanese Americans in World War II*. New York: Hill and Wang, 1993.

Danielson, Chris. *After Freedom Summer: How Race Realigned Mississippi Politics, 1965–1986*. Gainesville, FL: University Press of Florida, 2011.

Davila, Arlene. *Latino Spin: Public Image and the Whitewashing of Race*. New York and London: New York University Press, 2008.

Donald, David Herbert. *Lincoln*. New York: Simon & Schuster, 1995.

D'Souza, Dinesh. *The End of Racism: Principles for a Multiracial Society*. New York: Free Press, 1995.

D'Souza, Dinesh. *The Roots of Obama's Rage*. Washington, D.C.: Regnery Publishing, 2010.

Edds, Margaret. *Claiming the Dream: The Victorious Campaign of Douglas Wilder in Virginia*. Chapel Hill, NC: Algonquian Books of Chapel Hill, 1990.

Fairclough, Adam. *Better Day Coming: Blacks and Equality, 1890–2000*. New York: Viking Penguin, 2001.

Fergus, Devin. *Liberalism, Black Power, and the Making of American Politics, 1965–1980*. Athens and London: University of Georgia Press, 2009.

Foner, Eric. *Reconstruction: America's Unfinished Revolution, 1863–1877*. New York and London: W. W. Norton & Co., 1988.

Foner, Eric. *The Story of American Freedom*. New York and London: W. W. Norton & Co., 1998.

Fraser, Steven. *The Bell Curve Wars: Race, Intelligence, and the Future of America*. New York: Basic Books, 1995.

Freddoso, David. *Gangster Government: Barack Obama and the New Washington Thugocracy*. Washington, D.C.: Regnery Publishing, 2011.

Frederickson, George. *Racism: A Short History*. Princeton, NJ: Princeton University Press, 2002.

Germond, Jack and Jules Whitcover. *Whose Broad Stripes and Bright Stars? The Trivial Pursuit of the Presidency 1988*. New York: Warner Books, 1989.

Gillon, Steve M. *"That's Not What We Meant to Do": Reform and Its Unintended Consequences in Twentieth-Century America*. New York and London: W. W. Norton & Co., 2000), 142–45.

Goldstein, Phyllis. *A Convenient Hatred: A History of Antisemitism*. Brookline, MA: Facing History and Ourselves Foundation, 2012.

Goode, Erich and Nachman Ben-Yehuda. *Moral Panics: The Social Construction of Deviance*, 2nd ed. West Sussex, UK: Wiley-Blackwell, 2009.

Gordon-Reed, Annette. *The Hemingses of Monticello: An American Family*. New York and London: W. W. Norton & Co., 2008.

Guinier, Lani. *The Tyranny of the Majority: Fundamental Fairness in Representative Democracy*. New York: Free Press, 1994.

Herrnstein, Richard J. and Charles Murray. *The Bell Curve: Intelligence and Class Structure in American Life*. New York: Free Press, 1994.

Hofstadter, Richard. *Anti-Intellectualism in American Life*. New York: Vintage Books, 1963.

Holt, Thomas. *Black Over White: Negro Political Leadership in South Carolina during Reconstruction*. Urbana and Chicago: University of Illinois Press, 1977.

Jacoby, Russell and Naomi Glauberman, eds. *The Bell Curve Debate: History, Documents, Opinions*. New York: Three Rivers Press, 1995.

Jeffries, J. L. *Virginia's Native Son: The Election and Administration of Governor L. Douglas Wilder*. West Lafayette, IN: Perdue University Press, 2000.

Jones, Maldwyn Allen. *American Immigration*, 2nd ed. Chicago: University of Chicago Press, 1992.

Jordan, Winthrop D. *White Over Black: American Attitudes toward the Negro, 1550–1812*. Chapel Hill: University of North Carolina Press, 1968.

Kalman, Laura. *Right Star Rising: A New Politics, 1974–1980*. New York and London: W. W. Norton & Co., 2010.

Kelley, Robin D. G. *Race Rebels: Culture, Politics, and the Black Working Class*. New York: Free Press, 1996.

Key, V. O. *Southern Politics in State and Nation*. New York: Alfred A. Knopf, 1949.

Keyssar, Alexander. *The Right to Vote: The Contested History of Democracy in the United States*, rev. ed. New York: Basic Books, 2009.

Kousser, J. Morgan. *Coloblind Injustice: Minority Voting Rights and the Undoing of the Second Reconstruction*. Chapel Hill and London: University of North Carolina Press, 1999.

Kruse, Kevin M. *White Flight: Atlanta and the Making of Modern Conservatism*. Princeton, NJ: Princeton University Press, 2005.

Lawson, Steven F. *Black Ballots: Voting Rights in the South, 1944–1969*. Lanham, MD: Lexington Books, 1999.

Lawson, Steven F. *In Pursuit of Power: Southern Blacks and Electoral Politics, 1965–1982*. New York: Columbia University Press, 1985.

Lawson, Steven F. *Running for Freedom: Civil Rights and Black Politics Since 1941*. New York: McGraw Hill, 1997.

Leuchtenberg, William E. *Franklin Roosevelt and the New Deal, 1932–1940*. New York: Harper & Row, 1963.

Light, Steven Andrew. *"The Law Is Good": The Voting Rights Act, Redistricting, and Black Regime Politics*. Durham, NC: Carolina Academic Press, 2010.

Limbaugh, David. *Crimes Against Liberty: An Indictment of President Barack Obama*. Washington, D.C.: Regnery Publishing, 2010.

Link, Arthur S. *Woodrow Wilson and the Progressive Era, 1910–1917*. New York: Harper & Row, 1954.

Marable, Manning. *Race, Reform and Rebellion: The Second Reconstruction and Beyond in Black America, 1945–2006*, 3rd ed. Oxford: University Press of Mississippi, 2007.

Martin, Bradford. *The Other Eighties: A Secret History of America in the Age of Reagan*. New York: Hill and Wang, 2011.

Mayer, Jeremy D. *Running on Race: Racial Politics in Presidential Campaigns, 1960–2000*. New York: Random House, 2002.

Matusow, Allen J. *The Unraveling of America: A History of Liberalism in the 1960s*. New York: Harper & Row, 1984.

McCullough, David. *Truman*. New York: Simon & Schuster, 1992.

McGuire, Danielle L. *At the Dark End of the Street: Black Women, Rape, and Resistance: A New History of the Civil Rights Movement from Rosa Parks to the Rise of Black Power*. New York: Alfred A. Knopf, 2011.

McMillen, Neil. *Dark Journey: Black Mississippians in the Age of Jim Crow*. Urbana and Chicago: University of Illinois Press, 1989.

McPherson, James. *Battle Cry of Freedom: The Civil War Era*. New York and Oxford: Oxford University Press, 1988.

Meier, Matt S. and Feliciano Ribera. *Mexican Americans/American Mexicans: From Conquistadores to Chicanos*. New York: Hill and Wang, 1990.

Morgan, Edmund S. *American Slavery, American Freedom: The Ordeal of Colonial Virginia*. New York and London: W. W. Norton & Co., 1975.

Morris, Edmund. *Theodore Rex*. New York: Modern Library, 2001.

Mounger, William D. and Joseph L. Maxwell III. *Admidst the Fray: My Life in Politics, Culture and Mississippi*. Brandon, MS: Quail Ridge Press, 2006.

Murray, Charles. *Losing Ground: American Social Policy, 1950–1980*. New York: Basic Books, 1984.

Murray, Robert K. *The Harding Era: Warren G. Harding and His Administration*. Minneapolis: University of Minnesota Press, 1969.

Nash, Gary B. *Red, White & Black: The Peoples of Early America*. Princeton and Oxford: Princeton University Press, 2002.

Oakes, James. *The Ruling Race: A History of American Slaveholders*. New York and London, W. W. Norton & Co., 1988.

Obama, Barack. *The Audacity of Hope: Thoughts on Reclaiming the American Dream*. New York: Three Rivers Press, 2006.

Obama, Barack. *Dreams from My Father: A Story of Race and Inheritance*. New York: Three Rivers Press, 1995, 2004.

Parker, Frank R. *Black Votes Count: Political Empowerment in Mississippi after 1965*. Chapel Hill and London: University of North Carolina Press, 1990.

Parsons, Lynn H. *The Birth of Modern Politics: Andrew Jackson, John Quincy Adams, and the Election of 1828*. New York and Oxford: Oxford University Press, 2009.

Patterson, James T. *America's Struggle Against Poverty, 1900–1994*. Cambridge, MA and London: Harvard University Press, 1994.

Patterson, James T. *Grand Expectations: The United States, 1945–1974*. New York: Oxford University Press, 1996.

Patterson, James T. *Restless Giant: The United States from Watergate to Bush v. Gore*. New York and Oxford: Oxford University Press, 2005.

Payne, Charles M. *I've Got the Light of Freedom: The Organizing Tradition and the Mississippi Freedom Struggle.* Berkeley and Los Angeles: University of California Press, 1995, 2007.

Perman, Michael. *Struggle for Mastery: Disfranchisement in the South, 1888–1908.* Chapel Hill and London: University of North Carolina Press, 2001.

Pettigrew, Thomas F. and Denis Alston. *Tom Bradley's Campaigns for Governor: The Dilemma of Race and Political Strategies.* Washington, D.C.: Joint Center for Political Studies, 1988.

Quadagno, Jill. *The Color of Welfare: How Racism Undermined the War on Poverty.* New York and Oxford: Oxford University Press, 1994.

Rasmussen, Scott and Douglas Schoen. *Mad as Hell: How the Tea Party Movement Is Fundamentally Remaking Our Two-Party System.* New York: HarperCollins Publishers, 2010.

Salvatore, Nick. *Eugene V. Debs: Citizen and Socialist.* Urbana and Chicago: University of Illinois Press, 1982.

Sandbrook, Dominic. *Mad as Hell: The Crisis of the 1970s and the Rise of the Populist Right.* New York: Alfred A. Knopf, 2011.

Schoultz, Lars. *Beneath the United States: A History of U.S. Policy toward Latin America.* Cambridge, MA and London: Harvard University Press, 2011.

Schulman, Bruce J. and Julian E. Zelizer. *Rightward Bound: Making America Conservative in the 1970s.* Cambridge, MA and London: Harvard University Press, 2008.

Skocpol, Theda and Vanessa Williamson. *The Tea Party and the Making of Republican Conservatism.* Oxford and New York: Oxford University Press, 2012.

Sonenshein, Raphael J. *Politics in Black and White: Race and Power in Los Angeles.* Princeton, NJ: Princeton University Press, 1993.

Sullivan, Patricia. *Days of Hope: Race and Democracy in the New Deal Era.* Chapel Hill and London: University of North Carolina Press, 1996.

Takaki, Ronald. *A Different Mirror: A History of Multicultural America.* Boston: Back Bay Books, 1993.

Takaki, Ronald. *Strangers from a Different Shore: A History of Asian Americans.* Boston: Back Bay Books, 1998.

Tesler, Michael and David O. Sears. *Obama's Race: The 2008 Election and the Dream of a Post-Racial America.* Chicago and London: University of Chicago Press, 2010.

Thernstrom, Abigail M. *Whose Votes Count? Affirmative Action and Minority Voting Rights.* Cambridge, MA and London: Harvard University Press, 1987.

Wallenstein, Peter. *Tell the Court I Love My Wife: Race, Marriage, and the Law: An American History.* New York: Palgrave Macmillan, 2002.

Watson, Harry L. *Liberty and Power: The Politics of Jacksonian America.* New York: Hill and Wang, 1990.

Wilkinson III, J. Harvie. *From Brown to Bakke: The Supreme Court and School Integration, 1954–1978.* New York and Oxford: Oxford University Press, 1979.

Wilentz, Sean. *The Age of Reagan: A History, 1974–2008*. New York: HarperCollins Publishers, 2008.

Wilson, William Julius. *The Declining Significance of Race: Blacks and Changing American Institutions*. Chicago and London: University of Chicago Press, 1978.

Wolters, Raymond. *The Burden of Brown: Thirty Years of School Desegregation*. Knoxville: University of Tennessee Press, 1984.

Wolters, Raymond. *Right Turn: William Bradford Reynolds, the Reagan Administration, and Black Civil Rights*. Piscataway, NJ: Transaction Publishers, 1996.

Woodward, C. Vann. *Tom Watson: Agrarian Rebel*. New York and Oxford: Oxford University Press, 1963.

Zernike, Kate. *Boiling Mad: Inside Tea Party America*. New York: Henry Holt and Co., 2010.

Articles and Chapters

Becker, John F. and Eugene E. Heaton, Jr. "The Election of Senator Edward W. Brooke." *Public Opinion Quarterly* Vol. 31, No. 3 (Autumn 1967). 346–58.

Bejarano, Christina. "What Goes Around, Comes Around: Race, Blowback, and the Louisiana Elections of 2002 and 2003." *Political Research Quarterly* Vol. 60, No. 2 (June 2007): 328–37.

Citrin, Jack, Donald Philip Green, and David O. Sears. "White Reactions to Black Candidates: When Does Race Matter?" *Public Opinion Quarterly* Vol. 54, No. 1 (Spring 1990): 74–96.

Deslippe, Dennis A. " 'Do Whites Have Rights?': White Detroit Policemen and 'Reverse Discrimination' Protests in the 1970s." *Journal of American History* Vol. 91, No. 3 (December 2004). 932–60.

Eagles, Charles W. "Towards New Histories of the Civil Rights Era." *Journal of Southern History* Vol. 66, No. 4 (November 2000): 815–48.

Edds, Margaret and Thomas R. Morris. "Virginia: Republicans Surge in the Competitive Dominion." In *Southern Politics in the 1990s*, Alexander P. Lamis, ed., pp. 136–64. Baton Rouge: Louisiana State University Press, 1999.

Enciso, Fernando Saul Alanis. "The Repatriation of Mexicans from the United States and Mexican Nationalism, 1929–1940." In *Beyond La Frontera: The History of Mexico-U.S. Migration*, Mark Overmyer-Velazquez, ed., pp. 51–78. New York and Oxford: Oxford University Press, 2011.

Finkel, Steven E., Thomas M. Guterbock, and Marian J. Borg. "Race-of-Interviewer Effects in a Preelection Poll: Virginia 1989." *Public Opinion Quarterly* Vol. 55, No. 3 (Autumn 1991): 313–30.

Formasio, Ronald P. "Populist Currents in the 2008 Presidential Campaign." In *Obama, Clinton, Palin: Making History in Election 2008*, Lietee Gidlow, ed., pp. 105–22. Urbana and Chicago: University of Illinois Press, 2011.

Garcia, John A. "The Voting Rights Act and Hispanic Political Participation in the Southwest." *Publius* Vol. 16, No. 4 (Autumn 1986): 49–66.

Gidlow, Liete. "Taking the Long View of Election 2008." In *Obama, Clinton, Palin: Making History in Election 2008*, Lietee Gidlow, ed., pp. 1–15. Urbana and Chicago: University of Illinois Press, 2011.

Gonzalez, Gilbert G. "Mexican Labor Migration, 1876–1924." In *Beyond La Frontera: The History of Mexico-U.S. Migration*, Mark Overmyer-Velazquez, ed., pp. 28–50. New York and Oxford: Oxford University Press, 2011.

Hedges, Roman and Carl P. Carlucci. "Implementation of the Voting Rights Act: The Case of New York." *Western Political Quarterly* Vol. 40, No. 1 (March 1987): 107–20.

Hunter, Tera W. "The Forgotten Legacy of Shirley Chisholm." In *Obama, Clinton, Palin: Making History in Election 2008*, Lietee Gidlow, ed., pp. 66–85. Urbana and Chicago: University of Illinois Press, 2011.

Jeffries, Judson L. "Press Coverage of Black Statewide Candidates: The Case of L. Douglas Wilder of Virginia." *Journal of Black Studies* Vol. 32, No. 6 (July 2002): 673–97.

Kachun, Mitch. "Michelle Obama, the Media Circus, and America's Racial Obsession." In *Obama, Clinton, Palin: Making History in Election 2008*, Lietee Gidlow, ed., pp. 39–49. Urbana and Chicago: University of Illinois Press, 2011.

Kohler-Hausmann, Julilly. " 'The Attila the Hun Law': New York's Rockefeller Drug Laws and the Making of the Punitive State." *Journal of Social History* Vol. 44, No. 1(Fall 2010): 71–95.

Lamis, Alexander P. "The Two-Party South: From the 1960s to the 1990s." In *Southern Politics in the 1990s*, Alexander P. Lamis, ed., pp. 1–49. Baton Rouge: Louisiana State University Press, 1999.

Martinez, Oscar J. "Migration and the Border, 1965–1985." In *Beyond La Frontera: The History of Mexico-U.S. Migration*, Mark Overmyer-Velazquez, ed., pp. 103–21. New York and Oxford: Oxford University Press, 2011.

Mora-Torres, Juan. " 'Los de casa se van, los fuera no viene' The First Mexican Migrants, 1848–1900." In *Beyond La Frontera: The History of Mexico-U.S. Migration*, Mark Overmyer-Velazquez, ed., pp. 3–27. New York and Oxford: Oxford University Press, 2011.

Oakes, James. "Natural Rights, Citizenship Rights, States' Rights, and Black Rights: Another Look at Lincoln and Race." In *Our Lincoln: New Perspectives on Lincoln and his World*, Eric Foner, ed., pp. 109–34. New York and London: W. W. Norton & Co., 2008.

Patterson, Tiffany Ruby. "Barack Obama and the Politics of Anger." In *Obama, Clinton, Palin: Making History in Election 2008*, Lietee Gidlow, ed., pp. 26–38. Urbana and Chicago: University of Illinois Press, 2011.

Rozell, Mark. J. "Local vs. National Press Assessments of Virginia's 1989 Gubernatorial Campaign." *Polity* Vol. 34, No. 1 (Autumn 1991): 69–89.

Schexnider, Alvin J. "The Politics of Pragmatism: An Analysis of the 1989 Gubernatorial Election." *PS: Political Science and Politics* Vol. 23, No. 2 (June 1990): 154–56.

Sinha, Manisha. "Allies for Emancipation?: Lincoln and Black Abolitionists." In *Our Lincoln: New Perspectives on Lincoln and his World*, Eric Foner, ed., pp. 167–96. New York and London: W. W. Norton & Co., 2008.

Snodgrass, Michael. "The Bracero Program, 1942–1964." In *Beyond La Frontera: The History of Mexico-U.S. Migration*, Mark Overmyer-Velazquez, ed., pp. 79–102. New York and Oxford: Oxford University Press, 2011.

Snow, Jennifer. "The Civilization of White Men: The Race of the Hindu in *United States vs. Bhagat Singh Thind*." In *Race, Nation, and Religion in the Americas*, Henry Goldschmidt and Elizabeth McAlister, eds., pp. 259–80. Oxford and New York: Oxford University Press, 2004.

Thompson, Heather Ann. "Why Mass Incarceration Matters: Rethinking Crisis, Decline, and Transformation in Postwar American History." *Journal of American History* Vol. 97, No. 3 (December 2010): 703–34.

Traugott, Michael W. and Vincent Price. "Exit Polls in the 1989 Virginia Gubernatorial Race: Where Did They Go Wrong?" *Public Opinion Quarterly* Vol. 56, No. 2 (Summer 1992): 245–53.

Vaughan, Alden T. "The Origins Debate: Slavery and Racism in Seventeenth-Century Virginia." *Virginia Magazine of History and Biography* Vol. 97, No. 3 (July 1989), 311–54.

Winn, Mylon. "The Election of Norman Rice as Mayor of Seattle." *PS: Political Science and Politics* Vol. 23, No. 2 (June 1990), 158–59.

Conference Papers

Jeffrey Cass. "Birthers, Tea Partiers, and Islamophobes: Obama and the Problem of American Orientalism." Paper presented at the annual meeting for the Popular Culture Association/American Culture Association, San Antonio, Texas, April 20–23, 2012.

Legal Cases

Allen v. State Board of Elections. 393 U.S. 544 (1969).
Ayuda, Inc. v. Meese. 687 F. Supp. 650, 666–68 (D.D.C. 1988).
Baker v. Carr. 369 U.S. 186 (1962).
Beer v. United States. 425 U.S. 130 (1976).
Bob Jones University v. United States. 461 U.S. 574 (1983).
Brown v. Board of Education. 347 U.S. 483 (1954).
Bush v. Gore. 531 U.S. 98 (2000)
Bush v. Vera. 517 U.S. 952 (1996).
City of Mobile v. Bolden. 446 U.S. 55 (1980).

City of Richmond v. United States. 422 U.S. 358 (1975).

Citizens United v. Federal Election Commission. 558 U.S. 50 (2010).

Crawford v. Marion County Election Board. 553 U.S. 181 (2008).

DeFunis v. Odegaard. 416 U.S. 312 (1974).

Dred Scot v. Sandford, 60 U.S. 393 (1857).

Gideon v. Wainwright. 372 U.S. 335 (1963).

Georgia v. Ashcroft. 539 U.S. 461 (2003).

Green v. County School Board of New Kent County. 391 U.S. 430 (1968).

Griggs v. Duke Power Co. 401 U.S. 424 (1971).

Grove City College v. Bell. 465 U.S. 555 (1984).

Goldberg v. Kelly. 397 U.S. 254 (1970).

Gomillion v. Lightfoot. 364 U.S. 339 (1960).

Henderson v. Mayor of City of New York. 92 U.S. 259 (1875).

Holder v. Hall. 512 U.S. 874.

Korematsu v. United States. 323 U.S. 214 (1944).

Lau v. Nichols. 4141 U.S. 563 (1974).

Miller v. Johnson. 515 U.S. 900.

Milliken v. Bradley. 418 U.S. 717 (1974).

Miranda v. Arizona. 384 U.S. 436 (1966).

Northwest Austin Municipal Utility District No. 1 v. Holder. 557 U.S. 193, 129 S.Ct 2504 (2009).

Plessy v. Ferguson. 163 U.S. 537 (1896).

Regents of the University of California v. Bakke. 438 U.S. 265 (1978).

Reynolds v. Sims. 377 U.S. 533 (1964).

Roe v. Wade. 410 U.S. 113 (1973).

Shapiro v. Thompson. 394 U.S. 618 (1969).

Shaw v. Reno. 509 U.S. 630 (1993).

Smith v. Allwright. 321 U.S. 649 (1944).

Swann v. Charlotte-Mecklenburg Board of Education. 402 U.S. 1 (1971).

Thornburg v. Gingles. 487 U.S. 30 (1986).

United Jewish Organizations of Williamsburg, Inc. v. Carey. 430 U.S. 144 (1977).

United States v. Bhagat Singh Thind. 261 U.S. 204 (1923).

United States v. Cruikshank. 92 U.S. 542 (1876)

United States v. Reese. 92 U.S. 214 (1876).

United States v. Wong Kim Ark. 169 U.S. 649 (1898).

United Steelworkers v. Weber. 443 U.S. 193 (1979).

Webster v. Reproductive Health Services. 492 U.S. 490 (1989).

Whitcomb v. Chavis. 403 U.S. 124 (1971).

White v. Regester. 412 U.S. 755 (1973).

Williams v. Mississippi. 170 U.S. 213 (1898).

Zimmer v. McKeithan. 467 F.2nd 1381 (1972).

Government Documents

Chinese Exclusion Act (1882), at http://www.ourdocuments.gov
Civil Rights Act of 1964, at http://www.ourdocuments.gov
Executive Order 9066 (1942), at http://www.ourdocuments.gov

Online Publications

Keeter, Scott and Nilanthi Samaranauyake. "Can You Trust What Polls Say about Obama's Electoral Prospects?" Pew Research Center Publications, February 7, 2007, accessed March 30, 2012. http://pewresearch.org/pubs/408/can-you -trust-what-polls-say-about-obamas-electoral-prospects

Moyers, Bill. "Second Thoughts: Reflections on the Great Society." *New Perspectives Quarterly* Vol. 4, No. 1 (Winter 1987), accessed September 11, 2012. http://www.digitalnpq.org/archive/1987_winter/second.html

"The Tea Party and Religion." Pew Research Center Publications, February 23, 2011, accessed August 25, 2012. http://www.pewforum.org/Politics-and -Elections/Tea-Party-and-Religion.aspx

Video Recordings

Boogie Man. Directed by Stefan Forbes. InterPositive Media, 2008.

Index

About the Author

CHRIS DANIELSON is currently an Associate Professor of History at Montana Tech of the University of Montana. His most recent major work is *After Freedom Summer: How Race Realigned Mississippi Politics, 1965–1986*, part of the new Perspectives on the History of the South series with the University Press of Florida. Danielson holds a PhD in American History from the University of Mississippi and has previously taught at the University of Otago in New Zealand.